EDUCATING ABLE LEARNERS

EDUCATING ABLE LEARNERS

Programs and Promising Practices

By June Cox, Neil Daniel, and Bruce O. Boston

A National Study Conducted by the Sid W. Richardson Foundation

UNIVERSITY OF TEXAS PRESS ◆ AUSTIN

Fourth paperback printing, 1988

Requests for permission to reproduce material
from this work should be sent to:
   Permissions
   University of Texas Press
   Box 7819
   Austin, Texas 78713-7819

LIBRARY OF CONGRESS
CATALOGING IN PUBLICATION DATA
Cox, June, 1919–
   Educating able learners.
   "A national study conducted by the Sid W. Richardson
Foundation."
   Bibliography: p.
   Includes index.
   1. Gifted children—Education—United States.
I. Daniel, Neil, 1932–   . II. Boston, Bruce O.
III. Title.
LC3993.9.C68 1985   371.95'0973   85-7405
ISBN 0-292-70386-4
ISBN 0-292-70387-2 (pbk.)

To the memory of Sid W. Richardson

whose generosity made this study and report possible

Contents

Illustrations

Foreword

Education is today's commitment to tomorrow. It is the wager we make that our children will have a future. That being so, our nation and its schools must accept the complex responsibility of meeting young minds at appropriate levels, challenging them, stimulating them, sharpening them. Are minds all alike, to be treated alike? Are horizons all the same? We think not.

It has been relatively easy for our nation to reach consensus on the need for special programs for students with learning disabilities, physical handicaps, and language differences. There has been a tendency, however, to overlook the special needs of the able learner. Often in the past, educators have assumed that bright students could prosper within the framework of the normal academic program. This point of view either ignored the need of these students for challenges commensurate with their abilities or assumed that they would be self-starters who would find individual ways to reach beyond basic requirements. Some parents have questioned the basic principle of providing special opportunities for groups of able learners, asking, "Why your child and not mine?"

As the directors of the Sid W. Richardson Foundation and I considered how the foundation might respond to this educational environment, we began to focus on able learners. We believed that these students, in all too many cases, do not develop the initiative necessary to challenge their abilities. There are too many indications that able learners fail to live up to their potential, find boredom rather than challenge, and drop out rather than achieve. We also suspected, however, that there was too little information available about the kinds of educational opportunities available to able learners nationally and about the effectiveness of those programs that did exist. And so the Richardson Study was conceived.

My earlier career as a teacher and administrator in two New England independent schools gave me some background in the education of able students, and I recognized their need for special programs and special challenges. As the Richardson Foundation considered a study of programs for able learners, many questions arose in my mind. Would we identify an organization in the field of education to carry on our study, or would we construct and manage it as an in-house project? Would it be limited to those students generally recognized as "gifted and talented," or would we deal with a somewhat larger group of able learners? How would we amass and evaluate information about existing programs across the nation? And how could we best assure that the project would stay on course?

The answer to many of these questions involved June Cox. She had been an advocate and participant in the movement for more and better educational provisions for this special population in Illinois, where she had coordinated demonstration centers for gifted and talented students throughout the state. Later she had come to Arlington, Texas, as director of the Gifted Students Institute. Together with many educators across the country, she had spent many years working on the idea of an ability continuum. Increasingly she had begun to suspect that many programming efforts had too little impact on the total educational program of able learners. Like us, she was eager to explore the national scene and find out what really was going on.

I had come to know June Cox a year earlier when the foundation provided a grant supporting the activities of the Gifted Students Institute. Therefore, I quite naturally turned to her for advice and counsel as we continued discussions of our proposed study. When we reached the decision that we would proceed on an in-house basis, Cox was the logical choice as the project's director.

In a series of meetings we developed a basic strategy. The foundation would conduct a four-year project that would move through three stages: a study of educational programs for able students, the preparation of a report outlining existing programs, and the development of recommendations for comprehensive programs that would better address the needs of able learners throughout their educational careers.

At the outset we decided that the study should focus on three major questions: What programs for able learners exist and where are they located? Of the existing models, which are most effective and offer the best chance for adaptation in many school environments? Can new ground be broken in the field and can we provide recommendations to assist all types of schools in serving able learners?

In thinking about the process that we might follow, I was convinced that June Cox would benefit from continuing support in the form of an advisory committee that would assist in initial planning and would then meet on a regular basis to review progress, challenge findings, and suggest future steps. We also agreed that many other educators should be asked to meetings of the committee to present papers on existing programs. Other guests would include teachers, program coordinators, researchers, school superintendents, school board members, and other interested parties who could learn something about the study and provide a variety of viewpoints on the basic question of educational opportunity for able learners.

Because the foundation intended to disseminate the results of the study widely, we decided to produce a series of articles describing many types of programs. Arrangement was made with *G/C/T* magazine to publish the articles. This process assured an early awareness of the study by all of those interested in education for the gifted and talented and produced some helpful feedback. In a different form, these articles have now become a part of the final report. In turn, our hope is that the report will become the basis for specific programs that our foundation and others can support.

As our discussions progressed, Cox and I discovered that we shared a deep concern about current programs for the gifted and talented. We suspected that the large majority of them were fragmented, often addressing one or two grade levels only, with little effort being made to extend such opportunity through all grades. Programs might well be focused on one subject area only, with little attempt to expand into other parts of the curriculum. Others might involve only a few hours a week, with activities having little or no relation to other parts of the curriculum. We both wanted to explore programming possibilities that would address the needs of able learners in all parts of the curriculum and throughout their educational careers.

The reader will note that I have used "gifted" and "talented" when referring to existing programs. But the terms created some difficulty. First, although the terms are common in education circles, they do not mean the same thing to all educators. Second, our own concern was for a broader student population than the 3–5 percent who are normally thought of as "gifted" and "talented." Therefore, the foundation agreed to emphasize programs for "able learners," a group substantially larger. We wanted to encourage curricula and educational activities that would let students learn as much and as fast as they could, wherever their major interests lay. A big order indeed, but one that we believed was attainable.

More than four years have passed—years of extensive travel, intensive study of programs, and careful evaluation and description of these programs. Gradually, sometimes painfully, the recommendations for the future emerged. They deal with a variety of ways that schools of varying sizes in urban, suburban, and rural areas can provide appropriate educational opportunities for able learners. By addressing the needs of able learners, we hope we have also spoken to the needs of all students.

I want to express my sincere appreciation to committee members Richard Benjamin, Jacob Getzels, Marvin Gold, Robert Sawyer, and Dorothy Sisk for their contribution to the study. Robert Sawyer found it necessary to withdraw from the project early on because of other professional commitments. The others, however, with the assistance of adjunct members Laura Allard, Charles Patterson, and Ann Shaw, guided the study through to completion. Their knowledge, energy, and concern were invaluable to us.

Our thanks, too, to Alexinia Baldwin, Eleanor Hall, Frances Karnes, and Harry Passow for their assistance in developing the questionnaire. Thanks are also due to William R. Nash, Leonard J. Lucito, Harry Passow, Joseph Renzulli, Irving Sato, and Joyce VanTassel-Baska for helping evaluate the study in progress.

Finally, we want to thank the many teachers and administrators who welcomed us into their schools and who came to Fort Worth to present papers and discuss their educational programs with us. By sharing their ideas, all of these educators contributed to the conclusions we drew. In any study such as this, however, conclusions are not reached by majority vote; the foundation assumes full responsibility for the content of this report.

It might be said that we have now done our job. The report is in your hands, and it is the reader—whether a school board member, administrator, teacher, parent, legislator, or generally interested citizen—who must create the reality that will touch large numbers of able students. But not alone. The directors and staff of the foundation, the director of the study, the advisory committee, the hundreds of others who have participated in this effort are determined that the report will not be relegated to a long shelf life and little use, but that it will serve as a stimulus for a continuing discussion of the needs of able learners and for programs that best meet those needs. The foundation will fund model programs in Texas (we are thus limited by our charter) and will continue to encourage other donors in this effort to do justice to our best young minds. This drumbeat, once sounded, must not die away until comprehensive programs are the rule, not the exception, across our land.

VALLEAU WILKIE, JR.
Executive Vice-President
Sid W. Richardson Foundation

EDUCATING ABLE LEARNERS

Introduction

At the beginning of this study, the Richardson Foundation was acutely aware that most of what we know about programming for able learners clustered around a few key themes. From the onset of the renewed interest in gifted and talented education in the late sixties and early seventies, most of the reporting on programming has focused on how to set up a program for gifted and talented learners. Naturally, as teachers, program coordinators, and specialists gained more experience and as research and practice offered more insight into the way these children learn, new approaches were tried. But basically programming was displayed along three continua: (1) an elementary/secondary continuum, which recognized that programming had to be, to some extent, age specific; (2) a typological continuum derived from readily identifiable kinds of giftedness, namely, those pointed to in the report of Commissioner of Education Sidney P. Marland to the Congress in 1972—general intellectual ability, specific academic aptitude, creative or productive thinking, leadership ability, visual and performing arts, and psychomotor ability; and (3) a continuum of teaching strategies based on specific ideas about the way the mind is structured (e.g., the ideas of Guilford and Piaget), on learning taxonomies (e.g., the ideas of Benjamin Bloom), and on strategies for encouraging creativity (e.g., ideas derived from the research of Torrance, Khatena, Taylor, and others). Thus, age level, kind of giftedness, and instructional strategy have become three essential ingredients of a "program" for the gifted.

As teachers and program personnel experimented, as programs prolif-erated, and as sophistication developed, programming approaches ex-panded more rapidly than they could be monitored or assessed. As reports on individual successful programming experiments abounded, a sense of the whole began to disappear.

In part, the need for some new sense of the whole is what lies behind this report. After more than a decade of articles and workshops on how to develop programs for able learners, the foundation has tried to get a more accurate picture of what is actually happening nationally in programming for these youngsters. The foundation's survey is, so far as we know, the most complete examination of current programming for able learners yet attempted. In "What's Happening," we summarize the findings of our questionnaire in lay terms in the hope of making the current scene com-prehensible to a general audience.

Even as the Richardson Study was in progress, the country was pulled to attention by others concerned for the educational welfare of the nation. The recent spate of reports on the state and quality of American educa-tion, ranging from the clarion call of *A Nation at Risk* to the sedate prose of John I. Goodlad's *A Place Called School*, are an important background to our study.*

Significantly, none of these reports sees the education of gifted and tal-ented or highly able students as a high priority. Nor does any of them see the neglect of their education as a calamity. None devotes significant space to highly able students and the pedagogical concerns they raise. The most extensive discussion of the special needs of these students is offered in a subsection of *High School*, where "the gifted student" is discussed directly (pp. 236–238) and then indirectly in sections entitled "Accelerating Stu-dents" (pp. 255–260) and "Enriching Classrooms and Teachers" (pp. 260–264). *A Nation at Risk* has more to recommend about highly able students, but still only in passing; it includes them in commentary on recommenda-tions about "special populations." Others may contain a specific mention

---

*The reports discussed here are: *A Nation at Risk* (Washington, D.C.: National Commis-sion on Excellence in Education, 1983); Mortimer Adler, *The Paideia Proposal* (New York: Macmillan, 1982); *Action for Excellence* (Denver: Task Force on Education for Economic Growth, Education Commission of the States, 1983); *Making the Grade* (New York: Twentieth-Century Fund, 1983); *Academic Preparation for College* (New York: College En-trance Examination Board, 1983); John I. Goodlad, *A Place Called School* (New York: McGraw-Hill, 1984); Ernest L. Boyer, *High School* (New York: Harper & Row, 1983).

or recommendation as part of an overall strategy to better educate "under-served" students.

It is important not to fault these reports for their lack of serious attention to the able student population. Without exception, they are concerned with much broader issues: how the schools are serving the needs of the society as a whole; the dynamic tension between equality and quality of education in a democratic society; the correlation between the quality of education and the success of the nation; and the nature, function, and goals of education itself. That able students do not appear prominently should neither surprise nor anger those with a special concern for educating them. We should be grateful that their needs are at least recognized.

One thing is surprising, however. Given the magnitude of the central concerns of these reports, the size of the canvas on which they have painted their portraits of American schooling, and the case they make, it is strange that the writers and task forces have not been more opportunistic. Reading through the reports, we find an unwitting failure to make plain the connection between the need for academic excellence in our schools and the contribution toward that excellence to be made through special provisions for those who have the greatest potential.

The absence of a specific focus on able learners in the other national reports on American education underscores the role and significance of the Richardson Study. In addition to conducting a survey of programming options for able learners, we have sought the cooperation of many practicing professionals in the field of education for the gifted, both active researchers and those working with able youngsters in the schools. In the pages that follow we present an overview of our four-year study. This section details how the study was conducted, which programs were visited, and whose expertise and opinions were sought.

Our introduction concludes with a close look at the educational backgrounds of an unusual group of able learners, the MacArthur Fellows. The MacArthur Fellows Program has brought national attention to a dazzling cluster of creative and talented individuals. We have sought the cooperation of those individuals by soliciting their reflections on home life and school life and other elements of their education that made a difference to them. We believe that the perspectives they offer on their own development corroborate many of the findings of this report and serve as a natural introduction to it. A broad sampling of the opinions of this extraordinary group of achievers about their own schooling is offered here for the first time.

After the introductory portion of the report, we present the main findings of our study in three parts, structured to respond to the three questions posed by the foundation's chief executive, Valleau Wilkie, Jr. The first part, "What's Happening," examines what programs for able learners exist and where they are located. The next part, "What Works Best," makes some judgments to explain which models are most effective and offer the best chance for adaptation in many school environments. In the third part, "What Next," the report seeks to suggest a direction for action as an answer to the questions of whether new ground can be broken and whether we can provide recommendations to assist all types of schools in serving able learners.

DESIGNING THE STUDY

> Nothing, of course, ever begins at the time you think it did.
> —Lillian Hellman, *An Unfinished Woman*

From Conference to Committee

Lillian Hellman's words are a reminder that origins are always hard to trace. The difficulty lies, in part, in the fuzzy boundaries that mark off the first glimmerings of an idea from the beginning of actual work, and the beginning of the work from its completion. There was, of course, a time when no one had even conceived of anything called the Richardson Study. But the general idea of such a study had simmered on the back burner of the Richardson Foundation's awareness for some time before June Cox was invited to take charge of a series of goals and objectives.

Once the decision had been made to proceed with a full study, Valleau Wilkie, Jr., executive vice-president of the Richardson Foundation, and Cox, the study director, began in earnest by sponsoring an exploratory, invitational conference at the Dallas/Fort Worth International Airport on March 26–27, 1981. This meeting marked the official start of the study. Thirty leaders in the field of gifted and talented education from around the country were invited to examine practices in the field of gifted education and to challenge the status quo. (Appendix A provides a participant list.) A balance between practitioners and theorists was achieved by inviting a large group of teachers and administrators as well as academics.

Concurrently a series of visits to public and private schools across the country was undertaken by the study director in California, North Caro-

lina, Massachusetts, and Texas. Because they bridged the March conference, these visits served both to focus its concerns and to pose questions
for the other visits.

In California Cox visited individuals and programs in San Diego, where
special classes for the gifted have been conducted for thirty years, as well as
the Rancho Santa Fe and Rhodes schools. In Los Angeles she visited the
Structure of the Intellect (SOI) Institute, directed by Mary Meeker, and
the Mirman School for the Gifted. At UCLA she interviewed Dean John I.
Goodlad of the Graduate School of Education. In North Carolina Cox
joined a Southern Association of Colleges and Schools study of Mars Hill
College, focusing her attention on the college's Center for the Gifted and
Talented. She also visited the Winston-Salem public schools and the state's
two special schools for the gifted and talented: the North Carolina School
of the Arts and the North Carolina School of Mathematics and Science. In
Massachusetts Cox visited and interviewed officials at Phillips Academy,
one of the nation's top private educational institutions. In Texas visits were
made to Killeen, Longview, and Temple as well as to the Cistercian School
in Irving. Cox also interviewed several local coordinators for gifted and
talented programs throughout the state.

Those who gathered in March, 1981, heard two major speakers, each of
whom took seriously the charge to challenge the status quo. John Ehle, a
novelist from North Carolina, had worked closely with both Governor
Terry Sanford and Governor James Hunt to establish the state's two residential schools for gifted and talented youngsters. His presentation focused
on a rationale for residential schools and on strategies for securing funding
for tuition-free schools for these able learners.

But it was the conference's second speaker, President John Silber of Boston University, who challenged the group most directly. Presaging the "rising tide of educational reports" that would come in 1983, Silber pointed to
a "counterfeit notion of democracy as an egalitarian participatory society"
in which "everyone is equal not only in opportunity but in achievement."
He saw a connection between this "counterfeit notion of democracy" and
the decline in educational achievement in the past century.

His solution surprised many of the participants: "What is needed in this
society is not, in my judgment, separate programs for the gifted. It is rather
to bring the standard of the educational program up to a reasonably demanding level from which the gifted ones can take off on their own . . ."

Although challenged by Silber to question the status quo, conference participants remained convinced that special provisions for the gifted and talented have a continuing importance, in part because making these provisions was more feasible than reforming the entire American educational system! In the end, none were sure that the "right problem" had, in fact, been discovered. There was, however, a sense of gratitude that the foundation's study would look at a number of issues impinging on programming and would document what gifted programs were doing around the country.

In all, it was an interesting but not wholly satisfying beginning. Yet, writing about the opening conference later, Cox remained hopeful in her outlook:

> If the conference didn't give me the sense of direction I sought, it did provide a national perspective of gifted education from some of its best-known and active advocates. . . . It foretold many intense sessions with my committee when we worked through the superficial and kept the study on course. The study continues somewhat unevenly as we search for excellence in programs designated for the gifted and in others which appear to provide well for the able learner but are not so labeled. The dream is launched, but what a comfort to know I have time to find my own way. (Cox, 1982, p. 3)

Perhaps the most positive result to emerge from the first study conference was the appointment of the advisory committee. J. W. Getzels, distinguished professor of education and behavioral sciences at the University of Chicago; Marvin Gold, editor and publisher of *G/C/T*; Robert Sawyer, director of the Talent Identification Program at Duke University; and Dorothy Sisk, professor of education at the University of South Florida, were selected because of their national stature in the field (Sawyer later had to resign because of scheduling problems). Richard Benjamin, then assistant superintendent of the Fort Worth schools, now superintendent of the Ann Arbor public schools in Michigan, was selected to provide input from outside the specialized field of gifted and talented education. In addition, three Texas educators were selected as adjunct members: Ann Shaw, the director of gifted and talented education for the Texas Education Agency; Charles Patterson, then president of the Texas Association for the Gifted and Talented and an assistant superintendent in Killeen, Texas; and Laura Allard, then associate director of the Gifted Students Institute in Arlington, Texas.

Data Gathering

The initial pulse-taking by June Cox and the discussions of the conference provided the backdrop for a concern that has had a significant impact on the direction of the study. The lack of a clear focus in the kickoff conference and the diversity encountered in the initial site visits indicated that a report serving merely as a directory of best programs or even best practices would not make an important contribution. Fragmentation was widespread; what was needed was not to document it further, but to find a way to move ahead in programming for able learners. A related problem that surfaced from both the visits and the conference was the lack of widespread opportunity for even the brightest, most mature students to progress at a pace that matches their ability. This lack of what Silber had termed "flexible advancement" penalized both slow and rapid learners.

To gather the most representative information, a questionnaire was prepared and circulated nationally. Not only did it appear in several national publications in the field; it was sent to some 16,000 public and parochial school districts throughout the country. Although this first instrument was essentially a checklist, it provided the information required to follow up with a much more comprehensive instrument designed to give a clear picture of the status of gifted and talented programming across the country.* This second questionnaire was sent to 4,000 respondents to the initial request for information.

While this more specific information was being gathered, the gifted and talented consultants of the state education agencies were contacted. Each was provided with a list of the schools that had responded from that state, with a request for information on outstanding programs that had not responded. A request also went to each state association for the gifted and talented for similar information, asking that they publish the list of respondents from their state together with a request for more participants in the study.

Approximately 40 percent of the 4,000 who had responded to the original request provided extensive information about their identification and programming practices. These respondents make up the baseline group for

---

*The foundation was assisted by Frances Karnes of Southern Mississippi University; Alexinia Baldwin of the State University of New York at Albany; Eleanor Hall of Auburn University; and A. Harry Passow of Teachers College, Columbia University, in developing the questionnaire. A copy of the questionnaire is found in Appendix C.

a major portion of the study. Data from the survey are reported and discussed in the next section of our report, "What's Happening."

From this group, schools were selected for site visits. The visits served three major purposes: (1) they offered an opportunity to gather information first hand on a particular programming type; (2) they served as a check on the data that were being gathered through the questionnaire; and (3) they enabled the study director to begin formulating a national picture of the programming efforts for the gifted and talented.

Concurrent with the site-visit selection, the foundation sponsored a series of meetings or miniconferences in Fort Worth, each focusing on a different program option or practice. Consultants with experience in each type of programming for able learners were invited for one- or two-day brainstorming sessions with the committee. These actively involved teachers and administrators discussed specific programs, issues, programming ideas, theoretical approaches, and practical recommendations for others wishing to develop similar programs.

The site visits and the intensive meetings together resulted in thirteen articles published in *G/C/T* magazine in 1982–1985. Each article looks at a specific programming type or issue related to gifted and talented education, summarizes advantages and drawbacks, and tries to arrive at some conclusions. These program options are summarized in "What Works Best."

The articles cover the following topics and program models:

▶ "Continuous Progress and Nongraded Schools," *G/C/T*, no. 25 (Nov./Dec. 1982): 15–21. The article focuses primarily on elementary schools, pointing out that although "continuous progress" and "nongraded schools" are often used synonymously, they are not necessarily the same thing. What they have in common is that both allow students to move ahead as they achieve mastery. On hand to discuss continuous progress and nongraded schools at a conference in Fort Worth, Texas, June 6–8, 1982, were Margaret Wang from the Learning Research and Development Center at the University of Pittsburgh; Kathy Hargrove from the Plano, Texas, Independent School District; Paul Heckman, representing the UCLA Elementary Laboratory School; and Betty Yarborough, former project director of the Chesapeake Demonstration School.

▶ "Advanced Placement: An Exemplary Honors Model," *G/C/T*, no. 25 (Jan./Feb. 1983): 47–51. This report grew out of an intensive two-day conference in which six participants met with the committee in Fort Worth to discuss this approach to meeting the needs of able learners. Participating were Jewell Bindrup, director of gifted/talented programs for the Utah State Department of Education; Steven Brown, director of academic enrichment programs for Madison Elementary School District in Phoenix, Arizona; Robert Crawford, director of college counseling at Phillips Academy, Andover, Massachusetts; Dennis Day, a teacher at Highland Park High School, Dallas; Marie Laine, a teacher at O. D. Wyatt High School, Fort Worth; and Irwin Spear, professor of biological sciences at the University of Texas at Austin. The article looks at the national Advanced Placement program offered through the College Entrance Examination Board as an "honors" program. College policies, teacher selection and training, student selection, grading, Junior Advanced Placement (e.g., junior high school students being placed in high school classes), and motivation are discussed.

▶ "The International Baccalaureate" and "Concurrent Enrollment: School and College" (dual article), *G/C/T*, no. 27 (Mar./Apr. 1983): 24–30. The IB program is examined as another form of the honors option for able learners; concurrent enrollment in high school and college is examined as a form of accelerated programming for high-ability students. The basis for the dual article was a two-day conference held with the committee in Fort Worth on December 15–16, 1982. Representing the IB program were H. Gilbert Nicol, executive director of the International Baccalaureate North America; Mary McElroy, instructional supervisor for English of the Houston Independent School District; and Betty Herbert, Houston's instructional supervisor for mathematics. Addressing concurrent enrollment were Sanford Cohn, then assistant professor and director of the Project for the Study of Academic Precocity at Arizona State University; Terry O'Banion, vice-chancellor for educational affairs for the Dallas County Community College District; and Gail Riley, secondary consultant for gifted education for the Hurst-Euless-Bedford Independent School District.

▶ "Specialized Schools for High Ability Students," *G/C/T*, no. 28 (May/June 1983): 2–9. Representatives from three specialized schools met with the committee in Fort Worth on February 13–14, 1983, to talk about this relatively uncommon programming option for able learners. On hand were Norma Lowder, principal of the Houston School for the Performing and Visual Arts; Samuel Stone, director of development for the North Carolina School of the Arts; and Ward Ghory, assistant principal of the Walnut Hills High School in Cincinnati. Also discussed in the article are the North

Carolina School of Science and Mathematics and Cincinnati's School for Creative and Performing Arts.

▶ "The Role of the Mentor," *G/C/T*, no. 29 (Sept./Oct. 1983): 54–61. The committee met with six educators who presented models and concepts related to programming described as mentorships, internships, or assistantships. Assisting the committee were Bruce O. Boston, a Fairfax, Virginia, education writer; Donald Davis, chairman of the Executive High School Internship Association of Springfield, Illinois; Martha Fulbright, program director from Weslaco, Texas; Joan Shelley, program director from Carrollton, Texas; and Mike Stuart, program director from Dallas, Texas. William Nash, professor of education at Texas A&M University, presented a career education model based on mentorship ideas.

▶ "Identification: Special Problems and Populations," *G/C/T*, no. 30 (Nov./Dec. 1983): 54–61. To explore the identification problems associated with special populations, the committee met in Fort Worth on May 29–31, 1983, with Ernest Bernal, president of Creative Educational Enterprises, Austin, Texas; Mary Frasier, associate professor of educational psychology at the University of Georgia; Phillip Powell, assistant professor of educational psychology at the University of Texas at Austin; C. K. Rekdal, gifted/talented specialist at the Medina Resource Center, Bellevue, Washington; Bess Tittle, founder of the Creative Learning Center, Dallas; and de Saussure Trevino, coordinator of gifted and talented programs, McAllen, Texas. Problems addressed were those associated with ethnic and cultural minorities, the gifted female in mathematics, and the very young.

▶ "Programming for Excellence in the Summer," *G/C/T*, no. 31 (Jan./Feb. 1984): 54–57. The article is based on site visits by June Cox to intensive and highly focused summer programs for able learners at the National Music Camp at Interlochen, Michigan; the National High School Institute at Northwestern University; two talent search programs, one at Northwestern and the other at Duke University; and Governor's Schools in Arkansas, North Carolina, South Carolina, and Virginia.

▶ "Comprehensive Programs for Able Learners," *G/C/T*, no. 32 (Mar./Apr. 1984): 47–53; and "Comprehensive Programs: The Role of the State Agency and Other Partners in Education," *G/C/T*, no. 33 (May/June 1984): 57–60. The first article examines the efforts and approaches of five different school districts to put together comprehensive (i.e., across the grade levels and disciplines) programs for able learners. The second article, based on the same conference, discusses the role of state agencies, the need for state legislation of special provisions for able learners, and cooperation with universities and other institutions concerned with education. The committee met in Fort Worth on September 12–14, 1983, with Nancy McClaran, director of resources and coordinator of language arts and second languages in the Marshall Independent School District, Marshall, Texas; Gayle Mineweaser, coordinator of the Southfield Senior High School Gifted Program, Southfield, Michigan; and Elizabeth Wendell, district coordinator of special education programs in Albuquerque, New Mexico. Other participants were Paul Plowman, consultant for gifted and talented programs in California; William Vassar, consultant for gifted and talented programs in Connecticut; and Ann Shaw, director of gifted and talented education at the Texas Education Agency (also an adjunct member of the committee).

One article in the series deals with part-time special classes, "The Pull-Out Model," *G/C/T*, no. 34 (Sept./Oct. 1984): 55–61, the subject of several site visits, but not the topic of a miniconference. There were also articles discussing these topics: the educational experiences of the MacArthur Fellows ("The MacArthur Fellows Look Back," *G/C/T*, no. 35 [Nov./Dec. 1984]: 16–25); the data gleaned from the national survey ("Richardson Study Q's and A's," *G/C/T*, no. 36 [Jan./Feb. 1985]: 2–9); and the implications and recommendations arising from the four-year study ("The Richardson Study Concludes," *G/C/T*, no. 37 [Mar./Apr. 1985]: 33–36). These articles were published in *G/C/T* essentially as they appear here.

Evaluation

Toward the conclusion of the site visits and miniconferences a set of articles written on the various program types was sent to a team of readers who offered their reactions and critiques. The readers were invited to join the committee and foundation staff for a two-day conference, October 27–28, 1983, at the Mandalay Four Seasons in Irving, Texas.

This interim evaluation process drew on the talents and expertise of Joyce VanTassel-Baska, director of the Midwest Talent Search at Northwestern University; Irving Sato, director of the National/State Leadership Training Institute on the Gifted and Talented; Joseph S. Renzulli of the University of Connecticut; A. Harry Passow of Teachers College, Columbia University; William R. Nash of Texas A&M University; and Leonard J. Lucito of Georgia State University.

A final evaluation conference, cosponsored by the Richardson Foundation and the Wye Institute, was called together by the Aspen Institute. Among those convened at the Aspen Institute and the Wye Plantation, Queenstown, Maryland, November 27–29, 1984, were the study committee as well as eighteen persons who had not been involved with the study and who were invited to review the report and critique a late draft. They were foundation executives, school officials, association personnel, education journalists, a Senate legislative aide, an education lobbyist, and others. (See Appendix A for a list of participants.) All were interested in the education of able learners; several were professional advocates of better educational provisions for the gifted/talented.

Their comments were most encouraging. With the substance of the report and its argument for comprehensive programs, most had no quarrel. Many of their comments on the form and presentation of the report have been gratefully received and included in the final version. Chief among their concerns was that the report reflect the great urgency that surrounds the education of able students.

Two points of agreement surfaced during the discussion at Wye: (1) making special provisions for this group is clearly in the national interest because we must develop our best young minds in order to secure our nation's future, and (2) the report's stress on "elasticizing" and expanding the able population (by insisting on criteria of inclusion in programs rather than criteria for exclusion) was a correct bias.

The special thanks of the foundation are due to all those who gave so freely of their time and energy at all our conferences and seminars. Without their input, the product would have been significantly impoverished.

THE MACARTHUR FELLOWS LOOK BACK

Most parents want their children to be inquiring, original, self-directed. Good teachers try to nurture these qualities of mind in their students. Our study of promising practices for educating able learners has a related motive. Perhaps by learning something about the educational background, at home and at school, of adults who have curiosity and creativity in abundance, we can discover some of the conditions that encourage such characteristics.

The MacArthur Fellows Program provides an irresistible sample. The John D. and Catherine T. MacArthur Foundation, of Chicago, has identified over one hundred persons whose creative lives have shown the fertility we normally associate with able learners, especially the gifted and talented.

The range of their abilities is enormous. They are artists—writers, musicians, filmmakers. They observe human behavior—as historians, anthropologists, psychologists. They follow abstract scientific theory—in chemistry, biology, mathematics, astrophysics. Their fields vary from the well-known—education, philosophy, the law—to the offbeat—Mayan hieroglyphics, book design. Shelly Errington, an anthropologist and a specialist in Southeast Asian cultures, herself one of the recipients, points out that the MacArthur Foundation is funding persons doing something unusual, innovative, exploratory. She adds that while the foundation does not make it a condition of selection, a majority of the recipients cross disciplines in their work.

The MacArthur Fellows are hand-picked. About one hundred anonymous nominators or "talent scouts" search for individuals of extraordinary promise. A committee of fifteen meets monthly to review the nominations, and the foundation calls the selected artists and scholars to inform them they have been chosen to receive awards ranging from $24,000 to $60,000 annually for a period of five years. The MacArthur Fellows submit no applications. They draw up no special plans or projects. They are not expected to submit reports or publish results. They have qualified for the awards by uncommon abilities, demonstrated across a broad spectrum of creative pursuits.

The MacArthur Fellows Program is often described as a risk, a bold gamble. But the late Roderick MacArthur, son of John D. MacArthur, felt the program is not so much risky as optimistic. MacArthur believed that if one masterpiece is produced by a Fellow, if one scientific breakthrough results from the program, the investment will have been justified. And although they are not being rewarded for past acomplishments, the persons selected are known achievers whose careers already have given evidence of "originality, dedication to creative pursuits, and a capacity for self-direction." *

Our brief look at the MacArthur Fellows will not explain or analyze their creative achievements. We don't expect to uncover the origins of genius. We are examining the education of highly able learners. We have sought the cooperation of the MacArthur Fellows in looking back on their schooling and other educational influences they could identify. We want to

---

* *Statement of Priorities and Programs* (Chicago: John D. and Catherine MacArthur Foundation, 1982).

learn, if they can tell us, what channeled their unorthodox interests and prepared them for their achievements.

We sent each MacArthur Fellow a letter containing nine questions. We asked for simple information: (1) Did they attend public or private schools? (2) Were they accelerated at any level? (3) Were they recognized achievers before they left secondary school? We wanted to know (4) whether grades were important and whether their grades were generally high; (5) whether they did much homework; and (6) whether they participated in extracurricular activities. We also looked for evaluative responses. We asked them (7) whether some significant teacher or other adult took a special interest in helping them; (8) whether school mattered much to them one way or another; and (9) whether their parents were unusually supportive.

About half of the MacArthur Fellows took the time to respond, some at considerable length. (See Appendix B for a list of MacArthur Fellows who responded to our request for information.) The MacArthur Fellows are thoughtful and intelligent, of course. Many remember their school experience in detail and with keen insight. They speak of the extraordinary support of their parents. They give us vivid accounts of their youthful experiences, both painful and delightful. As a group they have an unusual sense of themselves, a high degree of what Howard Gardner, also a MacArthur Fellow, calls "intrapersonal intelligence" (Gardner, 1983).

The replies are often refreshingly candid and colorful. In reporting on them we have tried where possible to summarize the information they provided. Where the questions we asked evoked longer, more emotional responses—as for example, whether a significant teacher or other adult took a special interest—we have intentionally relied on the words of the Fellows themselves. We have made every effort not to distort the sense and tone of what they said.

Public and Private Schools

The school backgrounds of the MacArthur Fellows who responded are diverse. Most of them came through the American school system, some in public schools, some in private; a rather high proportion, about one-third, attended both. The responses suggest their parents were alert to their needs and sought out the best that was available within their means.

Acceleration

About one-third of the MacArthur Fellows were accelerated at some level of their schooling. Acceleration takes various forms, of course. Several of the Fellows—Alexander George, Richard Rorty, and Robert Penn Warren, for example—graduated from high school earlier than is usual. William Clark, Henry Gates, and others mention being placed in accelerated or "fast" classes. Archaeologist Ian Graham points out that in the English schools he attended "there was no question of being accelerated, as promotion from one class to another is always on the basis of performance."

Not all the MacArthur Fellows regard acceleration as a benefit. Mott Greene, whose work is in the history of geology, was troubled by the competition that he encountered when he was accelerated. "I entered the seventh grade in the year of Sputnik," he says, "and my school district . . . responded with two strategies—educational tracking based on standard tests (Iowa, etc.) and curricular acceleration." Greene was placed in the top track and received accelerated instruction in all his subjects. He goes on to comment: "I did not do well in this acceleration; rather, my grades were adequate, but I hated the pressure and the high level of competition. For example, in my math class, the seating was rearranged after every test, with the highest average in the right front, the lowest in the left rear. I remember students being verbally abused in my classes for giving wrong answers, and an enormous premium being placed on grades."

Grades

The pressure that Greene identifies is not a necessary feature of acceleration. It results from an unreasonable emphasis on grades. The question about grades brought rather mixed responses from the MacArthur Fellows. In very general terms they were precocious, achievement-oriented school children who made good grades. Neurobiologist Howard Gardner's statement is representative of the responses: "I used to regularly break the curves, which annoyed some peers and a few teachers as well! Until college, I was never really forced to stretch intellectually, and that was probably a pity."

David Felten, also a neurobiologist, says grades were important to him "possibly because of continuous encouragement from my parents and reinforcement from a few good teachers. . . . However, I was never driven to achieve high grades by external sources. I took personal pride and great enjoyment in learning from the very first."

Journalist Richard Critchfield, in contrast, reports that he "deliberately falsified answers to get *lower* grades." He goes on to say: "Grades were important to me, but I wanted to keep them low enough to win acceptance with the gang (we played football in the vacant lot, stole apples, threw snowballs at policemen, and so on). My brothers were horrified and said I'd never get to college. Just go to jail."

Recognized Achiever

A substantial number of the MacArthur Fellows, about two-thirds of those who replied, were recognized one way or another as achievers. Joel Cohen, whose work is in population biology, won state and national prizes for musical composition and for mathematics; he was a published poet before he left secondary school. Physicist Richard Muller was recognized as an achiever when he was accepted to the Bronx High School of Science, although he claims he was only an average student there. Stephen Berry, a chemist and advisor on natural resources, says, "I became a 'recognized achiever' when I became a finalist in the 1948 Westinghouse Science Talent Search. The Westinghouse award obviously made me visible."

Some of the Fellows carefully qualify their status as achievers. A specialist in the history of ancient science, Francesca Rochberg-Halton says: "Achieving in school per se didn't mean anything to me. I think I had an innate feeling that one was obligated to do at least the minimum work required so as not to create problems for oneself or others, but I never realized that what I considered to be the minimum was often far more than it was for others."

Some of the MacArthur Fellows were identified as gifted students and offered special educational opportunities as a result. Most who had such opportunities speak highly of them. Randall Forsberg, for example, founder and director of the Institute for Defense and Disarmament Studies in Brookline, Massachusetts, participated in the Columbia University science honors program in mathematics on Saturdays during her senior year. Elaine Pagels, now a professor of religion, was included in some special classes for the gifted. She says, "I would have been bored to death without the advanced classes." Robert Root-Bernstein, a biochemist interested in the history of science, speaks at some length of his special opportunity:

> Perhaps the most lasting aspect of my primary education was a summer session for bright students held at University Elementary School, UCLA, between my fifth and sixth grades. The session focused upon ancient Greek culture (imagine: six or eight weeks of nothing but Greek culture from 9:00 a.m. to 3:00 p.m.). We were encouraged to try everything from building wood models of Greek temples (though I also built a cabinet for my butterflies) to painting Greek warriors, reading Greek literature, and recreating a decathlon. I even had the temerity to rewrite the story of Jason and the Golden Fleece as a play, and to cast, direct, and act in it (oh, the poor parents who had to watch!). There was something exciting about all those bright kids in one place, everyone learning and sharing without undue competition (the class was not, as far as I recall, graded).

Homework

About homework most of the MacArthur Fellows were dutiful if not enthusiastic. David Felten reflects the position of a student for whom the public schools did not provide an appropriate challenge: "I always did the usual busywork, as required for jumping the appropriate hurdles, but took greatest pleasure in carrying out my own projects (such as the geometric basis for inability to trisect an arbitrary plane angle with straight edge and compass, tenth grade; and linear regression analysis of break-even points in product lines in business, eleventh grade). I viewed most homework as useless busywork, especially in high school. In fact, most of high school was a joke, aimed at memorization at best, and certainly not problem solving."

Extracurricular Activities

Participation in activities outside the curriculum appears to have been either escape or protective coloration for many of the Fellows. Anthropologist Lawrence Rosen writes, "By junior and senior year I cut classes often, played tennis whenever I could, but continued to work hard enough to get good grades." John Toews, an historian of ideas, reports, "I was very active in high school, partly to overcome the negative connotations of being an egghead." Richard Muller, a physicist, admits, "Extracurricular activities were the minimal ones required for acceptance into college."

Robert Root-Bernstein tells of an activity that was not part of the school program:

> Another important educational experience of my high school years was a year of Saturday mornings spent as a volunteer at the Los Angeles County Natural History Museum. I worked in the paleontology section, carefully removing prehistoric animal bones from blocks excavated from tar pits. This was exacting and time-consuming work requiring a great deal of patience, and greatly increased my interest in natural history. This extracurricular outlet for my science interests was particularly necessary, since my high school did not even participate in science fair competitions. I had done some experiments on the ecology of soil fungi in junior high school, but never had the chance to follow up these experiments or expand my horizons in high school.

Did School Matter?

Sylvia Law, a professor of law and codirector of the Arthur Garfield Civil Liberties Program, speaks for a number of Fellows when she writes, "I do not think that school mattered much one way or another in my life." In contrast, several of the MacArthur Fellows honor American schooling even though they were not significantly pressed before they entered college. Novelist William Gaddis, for example, responds, "You ask, 'Did school matter much one way or another?' and of course it did. For instance, the reading I did well out of college was more important than what I'd done in college but I should never have done it, or be doing it now, without all that had gone before."

Richard Critchfield, after telling of several stern and quirky teachers, one of whom repeatedly sent him to the principal's office, confesses, "P.S.—I loved growing up the way I did in North Dakota, all those days facing the walls of the principal's office and all, and would not change any of it."

The response of poet Robert Hass comments on the value system of his high school peers. It may speak not only for the MacArthur Fellows but for many superior students: "School mattered to me a lot, especially as the social center of my life. I always loved learning things because I was good at it, but it is not a simple thing to love learning in an American high school. Most of the students, who are bored by it, don't understand the enthusiasm and read it as a betrayal of the adolescent collective. In an ordinary school it is a difficult passage, I think."

Significant Teachers

The MacArthur Fellows write with feeling about significant teachers. Michael Lerner, who directs a treatment center for disturbed children, says, "This is a very productive question for me. There were a whole succession of teachers and other adults who took a special interest in helping me and to whom I owe lasting gratitude." As we report on the responses to this question and the question on whether their parents were unusually supportive, we have drawn at length from the MacArthur Fellows' own words. No summary would represent the voice and tone of the replies.

Many of the good teachers were strict and demanding. David Felten talks first of an outstanding teacher in the fifth and sixth grades who allowed him to go at his own pace, reading independently and exploring his own interests. She provided, he says, "enough structure to give good guidance." Felten speaks then of a teacher whose rigor he appreciated: "In eighth grade, a hard-nosed English and social studies teacher forced me to learn how to speak in front of a group. He was very demanding, and got a lot from his students by expecting a lot." After mentioning a tenth-grade chemistry teacher and an eleventh-grade biology teacher, Felten summarizes:

> All of these teachers fit a common pattern—they were gifted and articulate in their own right, were innovative and creative while very demanding of the top students, still giving guidance and teaching with a problem-solving approach (e.g., the MIT problem-solving approach vs. the medical school bulk-memorization approach). They stand out as teachers who went a bit in their own direction, often without approval from higher administration (in fact, the biology teacher was forced out for being "too nontraditional"; yet he personally was worth more than all the mindless drivel the rest of high school poured forth).

Gratitude for demanding and supportive teachers is a recurrent theme. Astrophysicist James Gunn speaks of a mathematics teacher who taught him calculus, linear algebra, and number theory "so well that the relevant courses in undergraduate school were in fact irrelevant." Mott Greene remembers:

> Two teachers here were enormously influential on my life and orientation. The first was Ernest Krag, from whom I learned world history and sociology, who goaded me not to rest easy on my abilities and who was probably very influential in my eventual decision to become a historian. The other was Dr. Bettison Shapiro, a biologist who lived near the school and gave profound instruction

in natural history, and who obtained for me a job as naturalist in the Bear Mountain State Park nearby in two succeeding summers. He also guided me in advanced biology and showed me what a cultured person could be, and that one needn't be a pompous tweed-hat highbrow to do it.

Richard Critchfield recalls Donald Treadgold, who taught Russian studies at the University of Washington, as an inspired teacher. He adds: "Perhaps the best teacher I ever had was George Barrett, now retired from the *New York Times*, who taught national and international correspondence at Columbia in 1956, a day-long seminar. At the end of the course, he told me, "You are going to be a writer; you have it in you." We are still friends, meeting whenever I am in New York. He gave me confidence."

The experience of Bela Julesz of Bell Laboratories, who was educated in Europe between the wars, sheds light on the importance of effective teachers. "I had many charismatic high school teachers," he says. Julesz also pinpoints a weakness in the reward system and recognition enjoyed by the American teaching profession. Speaking of his Hungarian schools, he explains: "Teachers, at least in better high schools, had a high social standing, and the government supported their position until a university professorship opened up. Many of my high school professors were authors of well-known books and were respected, while in the United States even university professors are not."

Acknowledging teachers not in the regular schools, Francesca Rochberg-Halton says that her training in motivation and sustained work "stemmed from my dedication to ballet and the support of those teachers." Robert Root-Bernstein also gives credit to an adult who was not a classroom teacher: "Another tremendously important source of learning was the local library, which was blessed with a fabulous children's librarian named Miss Dyer (sp.?). She treated each child individually in recommending books and had an excellent sense of what was appropriate. Through her, I was introduced first to the Dr. Doolittle series, then to Tolkien's *Hobbit* and *Lord of the Rings*, Juster's *The Phantom Tollbooth*, and T. H. White's *Once and Future King* (most of these before they became the classics they are now)."

Supportive Parents

If there is a single theme that threads through the responses and strings them together, it is the crucial role of home life and parental guidance in shaping these unusually creative minds. David Felten speaks of parental support as essential: "This factor is probably the ground-floor reason why a student achieves and persists with academic interests. My parents are not highly educated or economically well off, but they offered genuine support, concern, and love, and made it clear that academic achievement was worth the effort. They are wise beyond their educational level, and gave me unreserved support (and still do)."

Howard Gardner offers similar testimony to the positive influence of family, both parents and grandparents: "My family all came from Germany (part of the forced emigration in the 1930s). None of them had been to college, but they instilled in me a love of learning and knowledge as well as plenty of positive reinforcement for thinking, writing, pursuing knowledge."

As these remarks suggest, the educational background of the parents was less important than their interest in the education and development of the children. Sylvia Law points out, "Although my parents were not well educated, I believe that dinner-table conversation was far more significant in instilling both social values and concern for knowledge and facts." In one of the most striking tributes to parental influence, Joel Cohen writes:

> Both of my parents were crucial to my education. I asked to begin the study of piano at the age of six. When I began, my parents encouraged me to make a commitment to stay with the piano until I reached the nominal age of reason (thirteen, in Jewish tradition). This meant that in spite of fluctuations in my desire to play the piano, I stuck with it until I was good enough to see how much fun it is. For the first few years, my mother sat with me at the piano bench while I practiced every single day. . . . I wrote a two-page article about a picnic for the employees where my father worked. I showed it to my father. In several hours of sharp and rational criticism, he boiled it down to one paragraph, with no loss of information. The one paragraph was published. . . . It is clear to me that I am the beneficiary of an extraordinary investment of time and concern by both of my parents.

David Hawkins, whose work has included developing a new methodology for teaching science, speaks of the good fortune of being born into a literate household addicted to books. Francesca Rochberg-Halton says, "I was very close to my parents and they were unusually supportive. I read a lot at home because I saw them reading all the time, and I suppose that helped in school." Philosopher Richard Rorty also says he educated himself largely out of his parents' well-stocked library.

Novelist Robert Penn Warren speaks of a pervasive family influence that supplemented the public education he received:

My father and mother had literary tastes, and for an hour [every evening] my father read to the children, the first book being, I remember, a child's history of Greece (then Rome, etc.). But always poetry, and I learned to read from "Horatius at the Bridge" when my father refused to read it aloud the thousandth time. My summers were spent on my maternal grandfather's farm, a place where (by his taste) nobody came. He was fond of poetry and quoted a great deal, was full of history, and had me read history to him (including Breasted's *Egypt*, I remember, and *Napoleon and His Marshals*). He would draw battle plans in the dust with his stick and explain basic strategy. (He was a veteran of the Civil War and had been in various battles.) He and my father were important to me.

What stands out in these accounts is the parents' care for their children's education. Mott Greene describes his family life at some length. His father, "though a busy physician in general practice with nearly 2,000 patients, ran for and gained the presidency of the local PTA in an attempt to upgrade the standard of education." Greene's father left the navy, which he loved, to take a position on the faculty of Columbia University teaching anesthesiology in the medical school, so his children could attend Columbia free. "My parents assumed that of course we would go to graduate school and were unflinching and unfailing in their support, even when it seemed that I, in particular, would never cease to go to school." After pointing out that his parents regarded education as an investment in the future, Greene adds, "My mother, though not college educated, was the one who instilled a love of reading. She drove us to the public library every Saturday morning of our lives. I used to think that everyone went to the library on Saturday and church on Sunday. She was and is a voracious reader, and books are a favorite gift in our family."

Brad Leithauser tells a similar story of supportive, proud parents: "My own dual career (poet/lawyer) appears to be something of a synthesis of their own. My father is an attorney in Detroit, my mother is the author of two children's books and a composition teacher at the University of Michigan. When I was a child, incidentally, I was paid a penny per line for poems I memorized—the first money I received in a field that is proverbially penurious but which has proved quite lucrative so far for me. My mother reports that I wrote my first poem when I was eight years old."

Although supportive, the parents of the MacArthur Fellows appear not to have applied unreasonable pressure. Stephen Berry says his parents never pushed him: "But they were quite ready, perhaps exceptionally ready, to allow me to pursue my own interests. They let me have a basement laboratory and darkroom, and they let me stay up into the early morning hours. They let me choose my hobbies, my friends, my activities." In a phone interview Berry added that a supportive family is necessary but not sufficient. Many with supportive families, he suggested, don't grow up to lead intellectually creative lives.

Others also credit their parents for not driving them unreasonably. William Clark, at the Institute for Energy Analysis, Oak Ridge, Tennessee, says most of his school experiences were "only an incidental sideshow to the teaching, guidance, and general treatment I was given by my parents." His parents both had graduate degrees, and he grew up

> in a house full of books and journals and newspapers and a continuing discussion of the things in them as though they mattered. All of this was very low-key, and as far as I can tell the only pressures on me were self-imposed. But I can't remember a time at home when I and my two brothers weren't involved in discussions ranging from politics to town zoning to science, as people with opinions to be respected. And, though I can't remember a time when I wasn't pretty sure I was going to be a scientist, my tendency to spread my interest, research, and writing across traditional disciplines stems directly from the example set me at home. This, my home experience taught me, was the normal way for a responsible, educated person to conduct himself.

The sense of self-direction that grows from good example without overt pressure is an important motif in Robert Root-Bernstein's thoughtful response to our inquiry:

> The most important educational influences in my life were undoubtedly my parents. Their philosophy of education was to make available whatever "learning tools" one desired ("learning tools" to be interpreted as broadly as possible), *when one desired them.* For example, both my brother and I learned to play musical instruments, but only after we *asked* to do so. Obviously, we were exposed to music long before we became active in it. And that is an important point, I think. There are two forms of education: one is *passive*, in which one learns *about* things; and one is *active*, in which one participates. Passive should precede and induce the active by creating a desire for participation. Then the motivation to learn is from within rather than imposed from without, and so it remains even when one leaves the institutional settings of education. Certainly I've always learned more out of school than in.

Root-Bernstein goes on to say, "Another aspect of my parents' philosophy was 'do it yourself.' . . . Further, my parents always insisted that we do *our* best—not *the* best, but *our* best."

Implications

The happy result of our survey, and particularly of the discursive replies we received, is that in addition to responding directly to our questions, the MacArthur Fellows provided insights we couldn't anticipate. The responses allow us to draw some conclusions about elementary and secondary schooling and other educational influences. The first two generalizations have already been treated at some length and can be briefly restated.

Almost without exception the MacArthur Fellows pay tribute to their parents. While the educational level of the parents varied, and the level of financial backing as well, virtually all the parents let their children know the value of learning by personal example. The parents supported without pushing. Their homes had books, journals, newspapers. They took the children to the library. The parents themselves read, and they read to their children. Most important, they respected their children's ideas.

Crucial to the experience of the MacArthur Fellows to whom schooling was important was the support of good teachers. The responses of the Fellows provide a profile of good teachers. They are competent, caring, and charismatic. The best are gifted, articulate, and innovative. Many are demanding and get the best from their students by goading, prodding, and encouraging them to do their best. Significantly, the best teachers treat their students as capable individuals.

The responses of some of the Fellows educated in Europe—Julesz and Kolakowski, in particular—suggest the principal impediment to attracting, educating, and promoting excellent teachers is the absence of legitimate status attached to the profession. The problem is circular, of course. Only highly competent teachers will earn the society's respect, and only a profession that enjoys respect will attract men and women with the qualities the task demands. Appropriate adult influence is not limited to the school environment, of course. Mentors model and inspire superlative performance in a wide range of settings. By expecting and recognizing excellent work, such teachers give young scholars confidence.

Sometimes as important as good teachers was the opportunity to be with supportive and challenging peers. Richard Muller, who attended Bronx High School of Science for the tenth, eleventh, and twelfth grades, says he had "some excellent teachers, and some really terrible ones." He adds: "With the terrible teachers (who tried to discourage extra work I was doing in math, for example), the support of other students helped. In high school I think it helped to be surrounded by other academically interested students." Stephen Berry talks of the impact of winning the Westinghouse Talent Search in similar terms: "It did have an *enormous* influence on my own conception of what I wanted to do and what I could do. The experience of being with thirty-nine other eager, budding scientists, many of them years and years ahead of me in scientific and mathematical knowledge, was perhaps the most influential single thing I can recall from my school years."

Robert Root-Bernstein's recollection of his summer session at UCLA, grouped with other bright youngsters, has already been quoted. Adrian Wilson speaks of his experience at the Smith College Day School: "Grades were rarely given, but my achievement was stimulated by the brightness of my schoolmates, most of whom were the children of Smith College professors. In the eighth grade three of us were assigned to tutor each other in a separate room. We worked together through books of algebra, literature, composition, and history in half the time required for usual class study."

The opportunity to teach enhances student learning. James Gunn describes his high school science courses as a "mixed bag." There was a succession of temporary teachers, at least one of whom was quite incompetent. "The upshot," Gunn adds, "was that I taught the physics course, to my immense advantage and probably somewhat to the detriment of my classmates." Robert Root-Bernstein also appreciates his opportunity to teach at an early age: "In sixth grade, I was fortunate enough to have had the opportunity to teach as well as to learn. In one case, we learned how to draw horses by a simple method that I still recall. I was the best artist in the class, and so was appointed to go teach the second graders how to draw horses." In addition, Root-Bernstein served as a student dance instructor for the class, learning and teaching a new dance each week. "These experiences were important," he says, "for teaching me very early the skills of verbal exposition, and I think required me to realize that one must master a subject and be able to reduce it to its principles to be able to teach it well."

Touching on the matter of students teaching students, historian Shelomo Goitein tells us that even in a heterogeneous class a teacher can accommodate the variable learning rates of students by grouping and regrouping for instruction. He draws on his experience in a small school in Bavaria before World War I:

Our Jewish school contained eight grades, plus a Sunday school for grown-up girls, all in one room with one teacher. Still the results were excellent. How was this achieved? By group teaching. From a very tender age we were trained to have initiative, to occupy ourselves and also to teach others. Group teaching became second nature to me. Later in Israel, where so many classes were heterogeneous, I often was able to help a teacher by showing him how, by constantly grouping and regrouping, he could make his teaching far more effective and rewarding.*

A feature of the educational style favored by this group of scholars and artists is freedom, but with appropriate structure. The kind of structure preferred by the Fellows is implicit in their comments on effective teachers. They performed well when a high level of achievement was expected and when clear goals were articulated. Yet they preferred to participate in determining how to reach or go beyond those goals. The aim of education, they seem to say, is intellectual independence. John Sayles, writer and filmmaker, describes what mattered to him: "In general, I feel like what was most helpful about school when it worked was the existence of a structure but with the leeway to go beyond it if you had the inclination. I think both the structure and the freedom were equally important; the structure giving something to react to or from and the freedom being that there was some encouragement for original thinking as long as you didn't make too much trouble."

The fullest discussion of the value of freedom and structure is in the Fellows' description of their parents' influence. What stands out in those descriptions is that the parents provided both an example of inquiry and substantial exposure to the world of ideas. Robert Root-Bernstein's statement quoted earlier, in which he discusses the value of passive exposure preceding active learning, makes the point that students of a creative bent should select their own pursuits, but need a rich educational context to make their choices.

Paul Oskar Kristeller warns that "danger lies in the current cult of creativity and self-expression, which serves as a pretext for not teaching solid knowledge even to gifted students. Behind this is the false assumption that gifted persons produce everything out of nothing or out of themselves, without having learned anything. The fact is that a gifted person needs even more knowledge than others before he or she can hope to make a significant contribution to his or her field." Kristeller describes his own rigorous European education with its heavy emphasis on languages (Latin, Greek, French) and mathematical thinking: "I do not think it would be

---

*"Life Story of a Scholar." Excerpt submitted with Goitein's response.

possible in this country to have a comparable curriculum for a significant portion of the students. However, it would be desirable to have at least such options for those interested and talented."

Richard Critchfield may more truly represent those MacArthur Fellows educated in this country when he says, "Education is not something in the classroom but something that lasts all through life, in all its aspects, and never ends." He goes on to say, "I was a rebel when young because I wanted to learn everything, but not in the structured way (and stuffy way) knowledge was offered in school. In a real sense, I'd have to say I was self-educated, and very slowly and very painfully."

The striking generalization that bubbles up from the MacArthur Fellows' letters is that our school system, public and private, most often rewards patterns of behavior inappropriate for an independent thinker, researcher, or artist. Michael Ghiselin, research professor of biology at the University of Utah, says, "My overall reaction to my early education is that there is no important connection between what is demanded of a student and what is needed by a scholar." John Cairns, a molecular biologist educated in both Scotland and America, suggests that, particularly in science, a different set of skills is required than those which dominate our educational practice. He says we reward students for conformity, whereas nonconformity is required for success in the academic sciences. In a phone interview, Cairns continued: "Especially in molecular biology, we are asking people to be successful where others aren't. If others are succeeding in this area, there is no role for the scientist."

Speaking of the goal of education, William Gaddis makes essentially the same point: "So it seemed to me then and it seems even more to me now that the main purpose of education from the start must be to stimulate questions—even those to which we've got no answer—rather than answering them; and to open every vista, even those which are distasteful, rather than closing them for that reason, only to see them gape open in their most destructive features later."

Howard Gardner describes his public school education as "a holding action" and says the impact of the American school system is more negative than neutral. "It was actually a deterrent to serious thinking and well-motivated productivity." He adds, "Unless one has strong countervailing values (as have many immigrant groups, including contemporary Orientals), sparks of talent are likely to be extinguished well before adulthood."

In a revealing, sustained response describing his own career, Ian Graham says he resisted being taught anything, "and as a result [I] remain woefully ignorant of many subjects. But on the other hand, I have gained a certain ability to master subjects on my own, sometimes finding out later that my techniques or approaches are not quite the standard ones, and that may occasionally be advantageous." Graham goes on to speak of his work in "a neglected area of study":

> This kind of archaeological exploration has not been done by academic archaeologists or their students because it does not lend itself to forming the basis of doctoral dissertations; the work is not "problem oriented." Thus as an outsider I found the field wide open and lacking established working procedures. I had an enjoyable time, therefore, improvising techniques on my own. Of course, all this was long after I left school, in fact I was in my mid-thirties, but I owe it all to my failure to stick to the accepted course of studies. It's pretty certain that if I'd gone through graduate school in the ordinary way, I should then have got a job as instructor or professor, and proceeded on the usual academic and rather ossified course of teaching and research. Yes, of course someone has to do that, but I'm lucky to have escaped it through indolence when young. A most immoral moral!

The moral is not immoral, of course, but most helpful to those in search of appropriate instructional modes for very able learners. These and other comments from the MacArthur Fellows suggest that for our most capable students a shift in educational style is needed.

It is to provide a shift in educational style that the Richardson Study was undertaken. The inference of our look at the MacArthur Fellows is that the best of educational worlds should bring together supportive parents, imaginative teachers, and other good role models wherever they can be found—at home, at school, or in the community. If these personalities come together in a system that combines freedom with structure and rewards original thinking, even as it demands the best that every student can produce, then we can increase our chances of nurturing the inquiring, self-directed learners we all cherish. Some ways to accomplish this ambitious goal are the subject and substance of the rest of this report.

Current Programming

Approaches

THE RICHARDSON STUDY SURVEY

As a first step toward discovering what kinds of programs exist for able learners, we conducted a national survey of school districts. Highlights of that survey are presented here. The questions and answers we present in this section are not those of the survey questionnaire. They are simply a rhetorical device to simplify a volume of material that might otherwise be overwhelming.

Why Did the Foundation Choose to Do a Survey?
The overriding reason was the lack of hard data about what is going on in programming for able learners, particularly noticeable on the national scale. No national pulse-taking has been done since Sidney Marland was commissioner of education. His "Report to the Congress" (1972) is usually credited for launching the renewed interest in the education of the gifted and talented. Since then there has been abundant policy and funding activity at federal, state, and local levels, but little reporting on the specifics of programming nationwide. We felt it was time to gather as much data as we could between two covers and to get a reasonably clear picture. We felt that, once we had some idea of what was happening, we could make some useful recommendations.

What Kinds of Things Did the Survey Try to Find Out?
The survey, like the entire study, focused on programming. One of the things we knew from studying the literature was that there was plenty of cookbook information about how to provide programs for the gifted and

talented—i.e., how to set them up. There was also an abundance of data on curriculum, teaching models, and learning styles. But there was very little data on what kinds of programming options were being provided.

How Was the Survey Developed?

The survey passed through several stages. At first, we developed a crude survey instrument—a checklist, really—that was sent to every public and parochial school district in the country (over 16,000). The information gathered was used to develop a second, much more comprehensive questionnaire (with ninety-six questions) that was sent to the more than 4,000 respondents to the first questionnaire. The 1,572 responses to this second effort (400 schools and 1,172 school districts) were what we analyzed. (See Appendix C for a copy of the full questionnaire and Appendix D for a tabulation of responses to the survey.)

What Kinds of Programs Was the Foundation Interested In?

We did not look at the program's academic content (the arts, math, biology, creativity, etc.). Instead we tried to gather information on sixteen program types, not all of which are programs per se, but which constitute practices or approaches for dealing with this population. All of the program types, however, satisfied three basic criteria: (1) they pretty much covered the programming spectrum; (2) they represented clearly defined options, even though there is some overlap (for example, it is possible to have a Mentorship component in a Special School program, but they are clearly different programming styles); and (3) they were appropriate for able learners. The programming categories we looked at were:

1. Enrichment in the Regular Classroom
2. Part-Time Special Class
3. Full-Time Special Class
4. Independent Study
5. Itinerant Teacher
6. Mentorships
7. Resource Rooms
8. Special Schools
9. Early Entrance
10. Continuous Progress
11. Nongraded School
12. Moderate Acceleration
13. Radical Acceleration
14. College Board and Advanced Placement
15. Fast-Paced Courses
16. Concurrent or Dual Enrollment

How Reliable Are the Results?

The first thing to remember is that, beyond its everyday meaning of "dependable," "reliable" is a technical term in statistics. Let's deal with that issue first. In lay terms, the results of a study can be called "reliable" when the study, if done again in the same way, would yield the same results (within allowable margins). One of the major criteria for a study's reliability is whether the sample used for the study was random.

Was the Richardson Sample Random?

It was not. Although we sent questionnaires to every school district, the respondents were self-selecting. We made no attempt to shape the sample in a way that would make it an accurate reflection of the nation's schools. Therefore, our results can only be said to reflect what is going on in the 1,172 districts that responded. We warn readers against generalizing from our sample. This is not a statistically legitimate, overall description of what is happening nationally in programs for able learners.

Nevertheless, we believe that two factors argue in favor of the "dependability" of our data in the common, everyday sense of the term. First, all the nation's school districts were contacted, and roughly a quarter of the extended questionnaires were returned. Remember that not all of the nation's school districts have programs for able learners to begin with, but a large proportion of those that do have them responded. In short, our sample is big enough to be taken seriously. We believe that our results present a picture that is reasonably accurate. Second, the responses we received were representative of the nation on a geographic basis. Those who responded did so in proportion to the size of their regions and to the number of school districts in each region.

How Were the Questionnaires Processed?

Each returned questionnaire was given an identification number and put into a computerized data base. The coding, analysis, and reporting on the data were done by a team of researchers headed by Robert Demaree of Texas Christian University. Brenda Mitchell, an independent consultant, assisted the foundation in interpreting the data.

What Does the Sample Look Like as a Whole?

The following are some of the general characteristics of the responding districts:

▶ *Size*. Eighty percent of the responses were from communities with a population of less than 50,000; 4 percent were from communities of more than 200,000.

▶ *Public/parochial*. Ninety-six percent of the respondents were from public schools; 99 percent were from coeducational schools.

▶ *Socioeconomic*. A median (mid-point of the list of respondents) of 20 percent of the students in the schools responding were receiving a free or reduced-price lunch.

▶ *Teachers' education*. An average of 40 percent of the teachers working with able learners had master's degrees.

▶ *Philosophy*. A written philosophy and goals for working with able learners were reported by 72 percent of the districts.

▶ *Evaluation*. Sixty-nine percent of the districts reported that they had formal evaluation procedures for their programs.

▶ *Programming options*. Ninety-four percent of the districts. reported that they used at least one of the program options we asked about.

What Were the Most Frequently Chosen Program Options?

We found all sixteen program options we asked about. The most commonly offered program option was the Part-Time Special Class or "pull-out" model (in 72 percent of the districts reporting). A "pull-out" program generally removes students from the regular class setting and places them with other able learners in a different setting. Inasmuch as the "pull-out" model is one of the easiest programs to carry out, its prevalence was not surprising. In terms of frequency, the Part-Time Special Class was followed by Enrichment (63 percent), Independent Study (52 percent), and Resource Rooms (44 percent).

What Were the Least Frequently Chosen Program Options?

The least prevalent options were the Nongraded School (3 percent), the Special School (4 percent), and Fast-Paced Courses (7 percent). Figure 1 shows the frequency distribution.

Did Any of the Districts Offer More Than a Single Programming Option?

Yes. In fact, 90 percent of the districts reporting showed multiple program options. The median number of program options was four; 13 percent of the districts had more than nine programs and three used fifteen of the

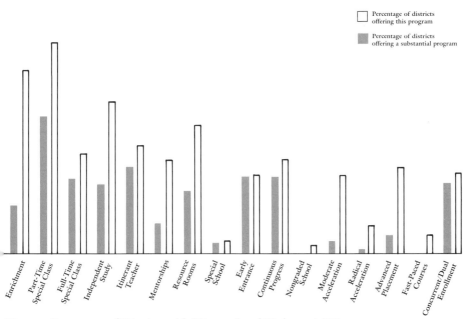

Figure 1. Percentage of Districts with "Present" and "Substantial" Programs

program options. Interestingly, a quarter of them offered both Part-Time Special Classes and Enrichment, which was the largest single combination.

How Do Districts Tend to Identify Students Eligible for Their Programs?
Only 3 percent of the districts reported no formal identification procedures. Teacher nomination was the most frequently used means of identification (91 percent), followed by achievement tests (90 percent), and I.Q. tests (82 percent). In both the everyday and statistical senses of the term, there is a "significant" drop (50 percent) to the next criterion—grades. (In statistics a "significant" result is usually one for which there is a 5 percent chance or less that the result could have come about randomly.) The least-used selection criteria were self-nomination and parent nomination; both appeared in 6 percent of the districts reporting.

*There Are Obviously a Lot of Programs around the Country. Was Any Attempt
Made to Determine Their Quality?*
Yes, but we avoided all distinctions having to do with the quality of the
educational product itself. We simply didn't feel we could offer that kind of
evaluation on the basis of the survey. We did divide the programs into two
groups, based essentially on the district's level of involvement. We thought
this was an indication of the level of the district's commitment to that type
of programming and that it probably indicated a strong program offering.
The first level was simply the "presence" of the program option. The other
was designated "substantial."

How Was the Distinction between "Present" and "Substantial" Made?
The criteria were minimal. The selection worked in a slightly different way
for each programming type, but in each case the respondent had to answer
all the questions we asked about a specific program type for the program to
be considered "substantial." If not all were answered, it fell into the "present" category. For example, in the case of the Enrichment type, we asked
four questions: one on the number of students participating, one on the
time allotted per week, one on the curricular materials, and one on the
content area. The first three questions presented forced options for lower
and higher levels, i.e., more students, longer time, and differentiated curriculum. Answers in the higher range got a "substantial" rating. To take another example, we asked six questions about College Board Advanced
Placement programs. "Substantial" programs were those that offered at
least three content areas, could report a specific number of students completing at least one course each year, and reported that 10 percent of those
students or more scored a 3 or above (a passing grade) on the Advanced
Placement test. (See Appendix E for the criteria used in selecting districts
with substantial programs.)

What Proportion of the Districts Had "Substantial" Programs?
Eighty-seven percent of the districts had at least one "substantial" program. Seventy-seven percent had between one and five such programs. No
substantial programs were found in 13 percent (N=153) of the districts.
Four districts had ten "substantial" programs in operation. The distribution
of "substantial" programs among the 1,172 districts is shown in Table 1.

Table 1. Distribution of "Substantial" Programs

Number of "Substantial" Programs Found	Number of Districts	Percentage of Districts
0	153	13.1
1	249	21.2
2	264	22.5
3	176	15.0
4	132	11.3
5	87	7.4
6	47	4.0
7	28	2.4
8	20	1.7
9	12	1.0
10	4	0.3
Total	1,172	99.9

After Applying the "Substantial" Criteria, Did the Frequency of Options Change?

Quite a bit! For example, the Part-Time Special Class ("pull-out" model) remained the most prevalent option, but whereas 72 percent of the districts reported having a program, only 47 percent of those programs were deemed "substantial" on the basis of the minimal criteria we applied (see Table 2). Similarly, only 16 percent of the Enrichment programs qualified as "substantial," although 63 percent of the districts said they had such a program.

What Other Changes Were Noted?

Several program types basically held their own, indicating that a high percentage were "substantial" by our criteria. The shaded and unshaded columns on Figure 1 show what percentage of districts offered a "substantial" program compared to the total percentage of districts that offered the type of program at all. Here are the percentages of the programs considered "substantial" for each of the higher-ranking program types:

Early Entrance	94%
Concurrent/Dual Enrollment	86%
Continuous Progress	82%

Itinerant Teacher	79%
Special Schools	75%
Full-Time Special Class	73%
Part-Time Special Class	65%

But there were many program types that didn't seem to hold up when we applied the criteria. For the following programs, less than half met the criteria for "substantial":

Resource Room	48%
Independent Study	44%
Mentorship	31%
Enrichment	25%
Advanced Placement	20%
Moderate Acceleration	16%
Radical Acceleration	9%

If we look at the different kinds of program offerings and their rank ordering before and after the criteria for "substantial" were applied, we get the data shown in Table 2.

What Kinds of Districts Tended to Offer "Substantial" Programs?
We noticed some trends, but they were not very surprising. For example, there is a definite correlation between the population of the school districts and the number of their "substantial" offerings. In districts with a population of 50,000 or more, there were more "substantial" programs across the board—all sixteen types—than in districts with less than 50,000. Similarly, for fourteen of the sixteen program types, the "substantial" offerings were greater in districts that had a per-pupil expenditure ratio of $2,500–4,500 than among those who spent less than this amount.

We did note some trends that we believe are significant. When we looked at districts with "substantial" programs and checked them against other criteria that we believe have a bearing on program quality, we found that the districts with "substantial" programs also tended to have supervisory staff for gifted/talented programs, a written philosophy and goals, and a special budget.

How Can the Drop between "Present" and "Substantial" Be Explained, Given That the Definition of "Substantial" Was So Minimal?

Table 2. **Distribution of Programs before and after "Substantial" Criteria Are Applied**

Program Type	Before: Rank (%) — All Programs	After: Rank (%) — "Substantial" Only
Part-time special class	1 (72)	1 (47)
Enrichment	2 (63)	9 (16)
Independent study	3 (52)	7 (23)
Resource room	4 (44)	8 (21)
Itinerant teacher	5 (37)	2 (29)
Full-time special class	6 (34)	5 (25)
Mentorship	7 (33)	10 (10)
Continuous progress	8 (32)	3 (26)
Advanced Placement	9 (30)	11 (6)
Moderate acceleration	11 (28)	12 (4)
Concurrent/dual enrollment	11 (28)	6 (24)
Early entrance	11 (28)	4 (26)
Radical acceleration	13 (11)	14 (0.9)
Fast-paced courses	14 (7)	*
Special schools	15 (4)	13 (3)
Nongraded schools	16 (3)	*
Total districts	1,172	1,019

* No criteria developed or applied.

We are not sure. One possible explanation is that the programs that held up were well defined and thought through, and that the people involved with them were sufficiently well informed to provide information about what they were doing. That the others could not provide even minimal information or meet these minimal criteria is, we believe, an indication of weakness and a cause for concern.

What Are Some Examples of This Weakness?
If we look at the Enrichment programs, we see that 58 percent of those reporting said that the students were involved in enrichment activities of some kind for fewer than three hours a week. That hardly constitutes a "program" of enrichment. Those activities involved "all of the class" in 26 percent of the cases, which means that there was no special effort among

that 26 percent to offer programs specifically geared to the needs of able learners. In the case of Moderate Acceleration, we decided that if more than 5 percent of the students spent more than ten but fewer than thirteen years to complete grades K–12, that would constitute a "substantial" program; in fact, only 4 percent of the programs qualified as "substantial" using that criterion. As we worked to define which programs had some substance, we got some insight from marginal notes on the questionnaires like "We should be doing that" or "That is a new idea to us."

At What Grade Levels Are the Programs Operating?
In some cases it is easy to tell, in others not so easy, since school level was not requested by programming type. For example, there are some program types that are clearly secondary-level programs, such as Advanced Placement and Concurrent/Dual Enrollment, which by definition bridge high school and college. With Acceleration (whether Moderate or Radical) it is not so easy.

Early Entrance programs seem to drop off as one goes up the grade ladder; 78 percent of the provisions for Early Entrance are at the kindergarten level, but only 15 percent and 16 percent are for middle and high school. More than a third of the respondents said "no" when asked whether they offered the possibility of entrance to college prior to graduation. Similarly, 80 percent of the Continuous Progress programs were at the elementary level, but this programming type dropped off sharply in middle school (53 percent) and high school (40 percent). It may be that the Continuous Progress model is not easily workable for those levels or that the high schools may adopt other programming options offering the same kind of flexibility, e.g., Advanced Placement.

But these figures may have some relation to the kinds of data we collected. The districts responding to the survey fell into two major groups: those that provided programming at only the elementary level and those that provided it across all grade levels. It was rare for a district to offer programs at middle and/or high school levels if it did not offer them at the elementary level as well.

Were There Any Noticeable Patterns in the Combinations of Offerings?
Overall we noted a total of fifteen different configurations or patterns among the sixteen different program types we asked about (see Appendix F). By far the largest was a pattern that offered Enrichment and the Part-

Time Special Class (291 districts or just under 25 percent), but it is notable that these programs were "substantial" in less than 50 percent of the districts. The two next most common patterns (10.3 percent and 9.5 percent of the districts, respectively) added the Full-Time Special Class and the Itinerant Teacher to this basic pattern.

In both of these cases the additions were "substantial" in more than half the districts, but again the criteria were not very rigorous. In the case of the Part-Time Special Class these criteria consisted simply of (1) occasional use of differentiated curricular material and (2) the coverage of a greater amount of material than in the regular class. In the case of the Itinerant Teacher, there had to be only regular coordination (as opposed to occasional coordination) between the itinerant teacher and the regular teacher of the able learners.

Can Any Significance Be Attached to Particular Groupings?
We think so. For instance, when we look at the occurrence of specific pairs of options we see that districts tend to develop their programs in areas where they are already involved. For example, the "pacing" options such as Concurrent/Dual Enrollment, Radical Acceleration, and Early Entrance tend to appear together in statistically significant ways (the correlation was at the .001 level, which means the odds of the result happening by chance alone are 1 in 1,000). It would be a good guess to say that new programs get developed not by striking out into unfamiliar territory but by building onto what people already know. Putting it differently, once a district's thinking changes about one pacing option, the district is more likely to be open-minded about other changes.

If we look at the fifteen patterns of programs, they appear to resemble the branches of a tree. We found, for example, that program options that manipulate resources tend to hold together in pattern groups. Thirteen of the program options appear in fifteen of the patterns, and some of the patterns are very common. For example, the Part-Time Special Class and the Enrichment types appeared in fourteen of fifteen patterns. These seem to be the most "combinable" of the program types. The next most common "combinable" was Independent Study, which appeared in nine of the fifteen patterns, again probably because it requires little extra on the part of the district to provide it.

Some program options are noticeable by their absence when we look for them in combination. Radical Acceleration appeared in only one of the fifteen patterns; it appeared in combination with seven other program types. This may be an indication that this demanding program type is attempted only by school districts that are really confident of their ability to work with very able learners. Advanced Placement courses were provided in only four of the fifteen configurations, again in patterns where there were from six to eight other options, but perhaps for a slightly different reason. Although it doesn't take any extra resources (beyond some administrative time) to run an AP course, it does take some pedagogical daring and the willingness of teachers to welcome advanced students into their classes. These are not always easy traits to come by.

One more thing is worth mentioning about the patterns of the programming options. Across all responses, the presence of Enrichment or Part-Time Special Class models did not appear to have any correlation with whether districts implemented a greater number of programming options. In other words, whereas it appears that these types are where people start with programming for able learners, it does not appear that their "substantial" quality either encourages or discourages districts in offering a varied programming diet.

What Relationships Were Found between "Substantial" Program Offerings and the General Information on Districts?

As noted above, there were clearly more "substantial" programs across all program options in districts with populations of more than 50,000. But two other options show especially large differences related to population. First, the Full-Time Special Class was present in 22 percent of the districts with less than 50,000, but in 40 percent of those with more than 50,000. In the case of Early Entrance, the difference was 23 percent versus 37 percent on the same population comparison.

What Difference Did the Affluence of the District Make?

The only check we did for affluence was to inquire about the number of students in the district who received a free or reduced-price lunch. For "substantial" program offerings, there was little difference in program offerings whether 0–10 percent of the students received such lunches or whether 31–91 percent or more received them. But more of the districts that showed a lower percentage of free lunches had "substantial" programs in Early Entrance, Continuous Progress, and Advanced Placement.

What Was Learned about the Cost of Various Programming Options?

First, we don't know which programming type is most expensive, although we can make some educated guesses about the relative costs of some programming types, given what we know about what goes on in such programs. For example, Enrichment and Independent Study programs are relatively inexpensive because they require only more intensive use of teaching personnel. The Full-Time Special Class has minimal extra costs because it usually just redistributes children among existing teachers and doesn't often require new ones. The real breakpoint on costs often lies between the Full-Time and the Part-Time class. A Part-Time class, because it pulls students from other classrooms, requires an additional teacher. Moreover, when Acceleration options and Resource Rooms require special curricular resources, a specially trained teacher, or additional administrative overhead, costs may escalate dramatically.

How Important Was a Written Philosophy?

Having a written philosophy was related to the number of "substantial" programs across all options. Seventy-two percent (N=847) of the districts said they had such a philosophy. This was one result that we found very encouraging, but we think the proportion should be even higher. Significantly, among Enrichment programs that were not "substantial" (84 percent), a majority indicated they had no written philosophy. A written philosophy was most strongly related to the number of "substantial" programs in the categories of Part-Time Special Class, Full-Time Special Class, and Resource Room. This may be explained by the fact that most programs for able learners are funded from outside the district, and written philosophies are usually requirements of public (and increasingly private sector) funding agencies.

Did Most of the Districts Evaluate Their Programs?

Yes. Evaluation was indicated as a regular procedure by 69 percent of the districts. In addition, we looked for whether districts had advisory groups for their programs and what the composition of these groups was. We found that three-quarters of the districts had such groups and that they included teachers (63 percent), administrators (61 percent), and parents (54 percent).

What Variables Were the Best and Worst Predictors of "Substantial" Programs?
The variable that emerged as the best predictor of a larger number of "substantial" programs was whether a district had a series of written goals for its educational efforts for able learners; this result was indicated in 72 percent of the districts. Conversely, the worst predictor was whether a given district had special requirements for teachers in the programs they offered. Although 33 percent required some in-service training, only 12 percent required state certification in gifted/talented education.

On the other hand, it is somewhat encouraging to note that in 35 percent of the districts, there is a full- or part-time coordinator for special programs or a director for gifted/talented programs. (See Appendix E for these variables.)

What Is Being Spent on Special Educational Provisions for Able Learners?
Special budgetary provisions are made for able learners in 73 percent of the districts. Sources for these dollars are state education agencies (64 percent), local funds (49 percent), federal funds (15 percent), and private/grants (8 percent). It should be noted that federal grants are counted in both the "federal" and "grants" categories (see Appendix D, item T).

There seemed to be no significant correlation between funding sources and the type of program offered, with the exception that the presence of private funds correlated positively with the presence of both Mentorship and Continuous Progress programs.

FRAGMENTATION: THE PULL-OUT MODEL

Among the observations that emerged from our survey of existing programs for able learners is that from a national perspective the efforts to improve education for our most capable students look fragmented and discontinuous. There is no national consensus, not even a common pattern or generally accepted approach to meeting the special needs of this population.

For a nation that prides itself on decentralized educational policy, perhaps the lack of a national program is inevitable, even desirable. So long as many individuals and many agencies are struggling toward improved approaches to sound education, our chances of discovering right solutions are better than if we were all constrained by national directives.

Less comforting is the realization that even in the separate locations—the districts, the individual schools—programming for the gifted or for superior students is likely to be hit-or-miss, more often characterized by zeal than informed by systematic planning. A school or district, feeling pressure from parents who want improved educational opportunities for their children or from teachers conscious of increased attention to excellence and the cultivation of excellent students, responds by seeking out programming options that are visible, adaptable, and easy to install.

Symptomatic of the patchwork approach to programming for able learners is the widespread use of the part-time special class, the "pull-out" program, which our survey shows is the nation's most prevalent practice for enriching the education of able learners. Of all the districts responding to the Richardson Study questionnaire, over 70 percent reported they have a pull-out program. In many districts part-time classes are the only provision for serving able learners.

The term "pull-out" describes an administrative arrangement that places gifted students in a heterogeneous classroom for most of their instruction and "pulls them out" to study with other bright youngsters in special classes in a different setting for a portion of the school week. The special classes may meet in the students' home school, or the students may be bused to another school or designated center. Time spent in pull-out classes varies from less than an hour a week to a full day per week.

Teachers and administrators committed to pull-out classes praise their strengths, and there are many. The arrangement is easily installed. A district can train a few eager, competent teachers who can develop their own curriculum and screen the students. The program can be put in place in short order. The special classes bring bright youngsters together for part of each week and leave them in heterogeneous classrooms most of the time. Pull-out programs are highly visible and easily evaluated.

The weaknesses of the approach, however, are a cause for concern. It is a part-time solution to a full-time problem. Able learners need a program that matches their abilities every hour of the school day, not just once or twice a week. More often than not, what happens in the pull-out program is divorced from what happens in the child's regular class. Thinking skills, one of the most popular areas of concentration in the special class, need to be incorporated in all of the child's classes: math, science, social studies, languages.

Pull-out arrangements, moreover, tend to be divisive. As one parent told us, "Nine times out of ten the teacher of the regular classroom does not like the program. It disrupts." This complaint has dogged the model from its inception despite earnest efforts to avoid it. Then there is the matter of cost effectiveness. A pull-out program often costs more than a full-time program. Full-time classes may simply require a reassignment of teachers; part-time classes generally require additional teachers.

While many believe that the pull-out program has served well, we think it is a model whose time has come—and gone. A serious drawback is the false sense of accomplishment it can provide a district; it is easy to establish such a program and believe that the needs of able learners are being met. But at best they are being met only part of the time. Moreover, the pull-out is not an easy first step that leads to more comprehensive programming. The data from our survey suggest that schools which begin with pull-out classes are likely to stay with that limited approach. As we become more sophisticated in devising educational arrangements for special learners, the need for pull-out programs—often the option of first trial or last resort—should diminish. In the next part of our report we present some of the options we have examined that offer strong promise for educating able learners and that have the ability to be adapted easily in a variety of educational contexts.

Some Promising Practices

Having presented a survey of programming for able learners around the country, we now examine in some detail practices we have found particularly successful in meeting the special learning needs of high-ability students. We have not felt it necessary to describe all the options we have examined. Instead we have made some value judgments. Because of the breadth of our survey we believe we are in a position to say, in effect, "These are programs that hold significant promise."

As we look at five specific and quite different ways of meeting the special needs of able learners, it is important to keep in mind that we are not endorsing these as the only options for educating able learners, or even the best options in all situations. How a school district can best serve its most capable students will depend on a number of conditions of size and resources that cannot be evaluated in the abstract. Nor are we suggesting that a school or district could select one they like among these options and consider that the single approach will provide a balanced and effective educational program for their best students. In a later section we present a case for developing a comprehensive approach to programming for superior students. The examples described here should be regarded only as elements to be incorporated in a total program.

The programs we will look at touch various points on the three continua we mentioned in our introduction: age, types of giftedness, and teaching strategies. Internships and mentor programs are most appropriate for students of secondary school age. Specialized schools, on the other hand, can serve students at various ages, even in some cases preschool children. Specialized schools often focus on and nurture a single type of intelligence, whereas education with an international perspective taps a wide range of abilities. And the programs described as internships and mentor programs, as well as some concentrated summer programs, provide teaching styles and educational strategies rather different from the regular classroom mode.

One value of our close look at five program types is that it provides a reasonably detailed account of how these options are practiced in real and diverse settings. Each, in fact, is illustrated in a variety of settings. So long as no one of these options is regarded as the best or only solution to the challenge of educating superior students, each can serve as a model for the school system that finds it appealing.

EDUCATION WITH AN INTERNATIONAL PERSPECTIVE

The twentieth century has witnessed a heightened need for international awareness based on developments tied for the most part, but not exclusively, to the technological revolution. Improved travel and communications systems have virtually eliminated distance as an element in international relations. Business contacts are frequently multinational, and even domestic industry depends on world commerce. Fluency in one or more foreign languages, therefore, has immediate practical value.

The political interdependence of nations is a fact of modern life, and the increasing cost of any failure in international understanding is brought home daily. Moreover, the increasing consciousness of ethnic and linguistic diversity in our own country gives the matter of intercultural awareness urgency even if we were not so dependent on international relations. We will deal with intercultural awareness from one perspective in the section on discovering and nurturing talent. Just as important as discovering talent among culturally diverse populations is cultivating sensitivity to ethnic and cultural differences.

The case, then, for providing able learners an international perspective is pragmatic. Knowledge of other countries and cultures offers a competitive edge to the individual as well as the best hope for understanding among peoples. An equally compelling argument can be made for the intrinsic value of a multilingual, intercultural, transnational education. The cultural receptivity it affords is an end in itself, of enormous value especially for the highly able learner (Daniel and Rayel, 1982).

The mastery of a foreign language, itself a worthy goal, offers important educational by-products. The more languages a person learns, the easier it is to acquire new ones. Increased sensitivity to language in general, to linguistic power, is an additional benefit. A student with more than one language has an expanded vocabulary even in the native language and a greater verbal agility and precision.

In an article on international high schools Dorothy Goodman and Glynis Scott point out that "with rare exceptions, the child's first language is actually enhanced by early exposure to a second" (Goodman and Scott, 1981, p. 155). Knowing more than one language opens the student's eyes to the symbolic nature of words. A student learns that there is no inevitable correspondence between word and idea and that in different languages the same or similar ideas often must be articulated in quite different ways. Such awareness of the nature of language is neither intuitive nor automatic. The person at home in two languages, therefore, has an educational advantage on several fronts. Indeed, some would say that the monolingual child is an underprivileged child (Goodman and Scott, 1981, p. 150).

In practice it is impossible to separate command of a foreign language from awareness of the customs, habits, and thought patterns of the second country. The two areas of intelligence are connected and mutually reinforcing. Language teachers have long capitalized on this disciplinary redundancy.

International awareness has two sides. The first is sensitivity to a foreign culture. Peoples of other cultures have different ways of celebrating holidays, of preparing meals, of conducting their daily lives. Dating customs, travel possibilities, and attitudes toward schoolwork vary from country to country. Even more important differences exist in attitudes toward government, authority, and the roles of institutions and traditions. Exposure to such differences can have an impact on sensitivity and tolerance.

The other side of international awareness is understanding the position and role of our country in the affairs of the world. The report of the President's Commission on Foreign Language and International Studies addresses this matter when it says, "Our schools graduate a large majority of students whose knowledge and vision stop at the American shoreline, whose approach to international affairs is provincial, and whose heads have been filled with astonishing misinformation" (*Strength through Wisdom*, 1979, p. 7).

It might be added that a solid education with an international perspective should make our students aware of international standards of education. American education, under fire in recent years, has suffered a particular loss of esteem when it has been compared with education in other highly developed nations—Japan, for example, and the nations of Western Europe (*A Nation at Risk*, 1983, p. 8). Schools, parents, and students considering the options presented in this chapter will discover that the minimum expectations of the international educational community, while not beyond the reach of able learners in this country, require the student to stretch beyond the normal expectations of an American high school.

There are many ways to acquire an international perspective in education. The most direct, of course, is travel abroad. A number of agencies like the American Field Service make living abroad for a summer, a semester, or a year attractive but not inexpensive. This is an option that students and their parents normally pursue on their own, without institutional support.

A corollary option is for a family to open its home to one or more students from abroad. The agencies that foster international exchange of students are as eager to find host families in this country as they are to find living arrangements in foreign countries. In addition, there are a number of summer programs, both in this country and abroad, that combine total immersion in a foreign language with exposure to peoples and cultures quite different from our own.

This study focuses on educational options in this country. For those districts and institutions and individuals seeking an international flavor and perspective in the schools instead of or in addition to independent, individual travel, we offer a look at American schools with an international perspective. We have selected as our examples an elementary school—the Denver International School—and the International Baccalaureate program in the Houston Independent School District. We close with a look at the United World College in Montezuma, New Mexico, because it brings together a truly international student body on a campus rooted in American soil.

Denver International School

Few language teachers would challenge the assertion that the best way to learn a foreign language is by immersion in the foreign linguistic milieu. Being exposed to a foreign language constantly and forced to depend on it for all communication is a marvelous incentive to learning. Both for acquiring the language and for absorbing a sympathetic attitude toward the adopted culture, the early years of schooling are better than later years

(Strassheim, 1981). The Denver International School, capitalizing on the immersion concept and on the ease with which young children learn language, brings together in a bilingual, bicultural setting native English-speaking and native French-speaking youngsters from the age of four through the eighth grade. The school includes children of other nationalities as well.

The Denver school, directed by Marcia and André Pasquer, is patterned after similar schools in Paris, Geneva, and London. French teachers are recruited from the French Department of National Education, the American staff from the Colorado Department of Education. Educators, parents, and friends work to make the school succeed because they share a commitment to bicultural education. The school avoids the labels "gifted" and "talented," but the students are screened by an educational consultant. In general they test above average, and they come from highly motivated, supportive families.

From the ages of four through seven, all students, whatever their native language, study and learn in French, except for one hour a day in English. During the two years of kindergarten and first grade, students learn primarily through songs, games, art, and dramatization. In the second grade students learn to write, first in French, then in English. They study mathematics in both languages. By the third grade students are comfortable with the French, and one half-day is devoted to the American curriculum. Through the fifth grade this pattern continues. The students study both French and English language skills. They study science and math in English; art, music, and physical education are taught in French.

"By the sixth grade," says Marcia Pasquer, "the students are fluent in French and ready to deepen their awareness of the two cultures." The academic program, accredited by both the French Department of National Education and the Colorado State Education Agency, incorporates all the elements the children would have in France while adhering to all the state's requirements. In French the students study world history and geography, biology, and literature, all on a level identical to that of a French *lycée*. The students also participate in a French conversation class designed to develop fluency and spontaneity. In English the students have U.S. history and social studies, American and English literature, and science. Mathematics is taught in both languages with two distinct approaches. As electives, the school offers beginning and intermediate Spanish. Students may also elect German beginning in the sixth grade.

While the school retains grade labels, classes frequently cross grades. For example, a single class might include several second and third graders and one fifth grader. Students move ahead as they achieve mastery, and an advanced, highly motivated fifth grader might go directly into seventh.

When we observed the school we were impressed with the small classes and individual attention. Young students whose native language was English practiced their French pronunciation quite uninhibitedly. Visiting fifth- and sixth-grade classes, we could scarcely distinguish native French speakers from English-speaking students. They moved between the languages with ease. During a class in which students were working with a computer, a girl who had recently arrived from France was having some difficulty following the instruction in English. Students would explain in French, then return to speaking English.

International Baccalaureate in Houston

The international school is one way to provide education with an international cast. It is a rather specialized option; the Denver International School might as easily be covered in our chapter on specialized schools. A means of achieving an international flavor in a rigorous curriculum that meets world standards, even within the familiar setting of an American high school, is provided by the International Baccalaureate.

The International Baccalaureate (IB), administered by the International Baccalaureate Office in Geneva, is designed to facilitate admission to colleges and universities throughout the world. In the United States students who satisfy the requirements of the IB diploma are often admitted to college with sophomore standing. The office in Geneva was established in 1965, and the first IB programs were offered in twenty schools in 1970. In this country the IB is partially or fully in place in dozens of schools in over half the states. The concept is exciting, and the number of schools adopting the IB grows every year.

The IB curriculum requires the mastery of at least two languages along with traditional courses of study, and it incorporates multicultural perspectives and internationally based standards of achievement. A pamphlet published in 1982 by the International Baccalaureate North America (IBNA) says, "The objectives to be achieved in each subject offered in the program are set forth in a syllabus that provides guidance without specifying the teaching methods to be used. Both the syllabuses and the examinations are prepared and administered under the direction of a multinational cadre of examiners. They are designed to emphasize the philosophy of teaching and thereby accommodate the diverse traditions adhered to in the 35 countries where more than 150 schools offer the program." *

In its two-year program for eleventh and twelfth graders, the IB reflects a widespread interest in getting back to general education. It responds to the need to restore challenge and motivation at the upper secondary level and offers an opportunity to achieve excellence. Each IB diploma candidate has nine academic requirements over the two years. Six are traditional courses. Three of these, considered higher-level, meet five times a week for a two-year period. Three subsidiary-level courses generally meet for about half that amount of time. Courses are selected from the following areas:

1. Language A (first language, generally that native to the student or the country in which the school is located; in North America this is almost always English), including a study of world literature in translation from at least two language areas.

2. Language B (second language, distinguished from Language A in not requiring the same depth and breadth of understanding of cultural and historical contexts of language), or a second language at the level of Language A. Latin may also be offered as a Language B.

3. Study of Man—one of the following options: history, geography, economics, philosophy, psychology, social anthropology, business studies.

4. Experimental Sciences—one of the following options: biology, chemistry, physics, physical science, scientific studies.

5. Mathematics.

6. One of the following: art, music, a classical language, a second Language B, an additional option under 3, 4, or 5, computer studies, special syllabuses developed by IB schools.

In addition to the six traditional courses, the diploma candidate takes a specially designed interdisciplinary course on the philosophy of learning, called Theory of Knowledge. According to Gilbert Nicol, executive director of IBNA, the Theory of Knowledge course epitomizes the IB program. The emphasis is on learning, but the course offers an umbrella of understanding that relates different modes of learning to one another. It asks that the student sit back and reflect; it helps the student understand that honest

---

* International Baccalaureate North America, "Restoring a Challenge to Secondary Education" (pamphlet distributed in 1982).

people can come to quite different conclusions based on sound learning. Each school is given great latitude in how it presents this course. Nicol says that the IB program requires only that it be taught for at least 100 hours over the two-year period. It may be offered as a regular subject in the school's curriculum. "It's being done in all ways in various schools throughout the participating countries."

IB students are also required to participate in some form of creative, aesthetic, or social service activity. Most schools in the United States already offer sufficient creative and aesthetic choices: music, art, dance, drama, creative writing, and the like. In addition, these schools must show how their extracurricular offerings satisfy the social service requirement of the IB. One of the goals of the IB is to educate students for compassion as well as competence. As a final requirement, each diploma candidate must submit an extended essay based on independent research—the equivalent of an undergraduate thesis.

Schools can qualify for participation in the IB program by applying to the Executive Committee of the International Baccalaureate Office in Geneva through the New York office of the International Baccalaureate North America. The IB organization charges fully participating schools a fee (in 1984, $4,640) and requires a credential fee for each student sitting for one or more examinations.

In a school that offers the IB, students may reach for the IB diploma or may earn a certificate in one or more specific courses, much as one might take an examination for Advanced Placement. Indeed, some courses at high schools offering both IB and Advanced Placement prepare students to be examined either way, depending on the interests and goals of the student. Nicol insists, however, that the IB and AP should not be compared. While both have the goal of higher-level instruction to prepare students for credit by examination, the IB is intended to be a curriculum, a comprehensive program that incorporates an emphasis on problem solving and the interrelation of knowledge, as well as the international emphasis involved in the mastery of a second language and in the transnational focus of its social studies courses.

Houston's Bellaire High School began offering the International Baccalaureate program in 1980. The IB program there represents well both the difficulties and the excitement of a program aimed at excellence, hoping to meet the tough standards of an international community. "It is a terrific public relations program," says Myrtle Nelson, who was assistant principal of Bellaire High School in Houston when the International Baccalaureate program was first established. The name itself, she points out, conjures up lofty ideas of excellence, of sophistication, of glamor. Parents envision an enriched and rigorous course even before they learn of its particulars. Nelson thinks the program merits the confidence the name inspires.

When the Houston district decided to introduce the program, Bellaire was a logical choice; it has a long tradition of academic excellence, and it was already a magnet school for foreign languages. Later eight other Houston schools began classes leading to the IB.

Like any good and novel program, the IB required selecting good teachers and investing in their development. The teachers had to design a curriculum that would meet the guidelines of the Texas Education Agency as well as satisfy the demands of the IB curriculum. As a starting place they selected faculty members with proven records of success in preparing students for college work. The school already had AP courses. With help from other schools around the country willing to share their curriculum ideas and with guidance from IBNA, they undertook to prepare themselves over the summer.

Betty Herbert, instructional supervisor for mathematics, explains that the math teachers began by taking previous IB mathematics examinations. They discovered that between 40 and 60 percent of the content on those examinations was material they normally covered. That meant another 40 to 60 percent had to be added to the curriculum—such topics as transformational geometry, logic set theory, vectors, statistics, and probability. "It is the teachers' role to show how these topics are related," Herbert says. "Sometimes they aren't related, and that needs to be pointed out, too."

Selection of students for IB classes is crucial. At Bellaire a committee of teachers, counselors, and administrators considers academic performance, attendance, conduct, extracurricular activities, motivation, and a written statement from the applicant. In general the IB program in Houston draws students from the ninetieth percentile and above.

As a consequence of instituting the IB program for the top two grades and in preparation for the work covered in that program, Houston found it useful to develop a pre-IB program that operates in the lower high-school grades and in eleven of Houston's middle schools. Beginning with the sixth grade, Houston offers in selected schools a curriculum that includes foreign language study and enriched courses across the board. The entrance requirements are slightly less stringent at the lower level; the program draws students from above the eightieth percentile. Mary McElroy, English specialist at the secondary level, points out that the only recruitment problem at this level is the result of success; parents are eager and the classes are overfull. "The time is right for a program of excellence," she says.

Both McElroy and Herbert, talking about getting ready to offer IB or pre-IB courses, stress the importance of the district's commitment. In simple terms the district's commitment means money. As they were preparing to expand into the middle school, one of the superintendents said to them, "Now submit a Plan A requiring money and a Plan B if money is not available." Their response was, "There is no Plan B. If we don't have the money, there is no plan."

As McElroy points out, they got the money—over $100,000 for materials for the four middle schools. The district's commitment was rewarded by an enthusiastic response all along the line. The curriculum supervisors wrote schools all over the country. They worked with universities; they read journals; they studied curriculum models of all sorts. The teachers willingly spent long hours after school and on weekends, responding to the promise that they could teach their subjects as they ought to be taught. Parents were invited to learn about the new program, and the crowds were large. When told of a high-quality program in which the parents would work hard, the teachers would work hard, and the students would really work hard, the parents responded, "Where do we sign up? When do you want us here?"

What the Houston story suggests, and what is recognized by the directors of the International Baccalaureate, is that adopting an IB program will inevitably have consequences for the whole system. Students, as well as their teachers and their parents, will become aware of the need for special preparation in the lower grades. At the same time, the school's adoption of even two or three subjects in a gradual expansion and preparation for the IB will have a wide influence on teaching in all the secondary grades. The IB also provides a comprehensive and cohesive framework for already existing honors courses.

One advantage of the International Baccalaureate is that it can be offered within the walls of an existing high school. It may constitute the principal curriculum, or the program can operate as a school within a school. The IB should be expected to have a positive impact on the level of regular offerings, wherever it is offered, but it does not require special facilities.

United World College

The IB also provides the central curriculum of a handful of schools, the United World Colleges, that take the concept of international education a step further. One is the Armand Hammer United World College of the American West (UWC). On a campus in the remote mountains near Montezuma, New Mexico, some 200 hand-picked students from nearly fifty countries undertake a two-year preparation for the International Baccalaureate.

The Armand Hammer College is the sixth United World College. The first of the schools, the United World College of the Atlantic, opened in South Wales. Others include the Lester B. Pearson College of the Pacific in British Columbia, the United World College of Southeast Asia in Singapore, the Waterford KaMhlaba School in Swaziland, and the United World College of the Adriatic in Italy. Because of the international texture of their student populations as well as their adoption of the IB curriculum, these colleges provide a rigorous and exciting program with a focus on international understanding and high academic achievement.

To meet the IB social service requirement at the United World College in New Mexico, some students do volunteer work at a nearby state psychiatric hospital or visit local schools to talk with students about their home countries. The school has a wilderness search and rescue program for which students prepare by learning rock climbing, evacuation techniques, navigation skills, and logistics.

The college enrolls approximately 100 students in each of the two grade levels, remaining small and selective so that the college can retain its community feeling. Each country has its own screening procedures, but generally the selection committees look for high-achieving students recommended by heads of their schools. They take note of a student's participation in extracurricular activities and motivation. The student with wide interests who is enthusiastic about an International Baccalaureate in a World College setting is more likely to adjust well and benefit from the program than a straight-A student who is lukewarm about being away from home and among students from many nations.

Students accepted to the World College clearly revel in the privilege of learning about other cultures by such exposure as well as in the challenge of the curriculum. As one boy at Montezuma put it, "I find myself discussing South American politics for two hours, and then I write—sometimes until four o'clock in the morning." Classes are small. In a biology class we visited, there were eight students, each from a different country.

Students from the United States have as much difficulty preparing for and adapting to the demands of the international school as students from other countries—sometimes more. Andrew Macklehose, dean of studies at the United World College in New Mexico, himself a Britisher, points out that although American students have the advantage of studying in their native language and are in general more used to class participation than students from other parts of the world, they still suffer from three disadvantages of the American school system.

First, they start to school later than many European students. In Britain, for example, children normally begin school at the age of four, and many of them attend preschools at the age of two or three. A second disadvantage for American students is the lower intensity of American schooling. Again citing England as an example, Macklehose says it is normal for European secondary students to encounter a solid fare of sciences, including three years of biology, three years of physics, and three years of chemistry. The third problem American students face stems from our lax foreign language requirements. Many European students are fluent in two or three languages. Many American students study no second language, and those who study a foreign language for two or three years in a secondary classroom setting cannot compete well with European students who have begun language study earlier and who have had frequent opportunities to interact with native speakers because of the proximity of other countries.

Admission standards are stiff at UWC; the work is demanding. The tuition is high—about $9,000 per year. Most students enter with financial assistance. The World Colleges make no claim that they are specifically for gifted students, but it would be difficult to imagine a more appropriate or more exciting program for the best students in this or any country. Living and studying together with students of all races from many nations must increase understanding and has important implications for the possibility of world peace. We visited UWC in Montezuma shortly after the death of Russian president Leonid Breshnev. We could sense that the American students responded personally and directly to the sadness of their friends Svetlana and Sergei over the loss of the national leader. Such immediate and human response is the key to understanding and perhaps the strongest argument for education with an international perspective.

Conclusion

We have examined the value of internationally oriented education from several viewpoints. The value to individual students of foreign language study and travel is scarcely open to question. Increased awareness makes for better educated persons and expanded opportunity. In addition, our very survival depends on intelligent leadership that understands other cultures and speaks their languages.

In truth, the finest education for able learners is that which is best for the individual and best for society. The late Elizabeth Drews called for education with "a new emphasis in order to meet the needs of the gifted for self-fulfillment and the equally great need of society for their insight and their service." Drews went on to say, "We must initiate programs of education where the gifts of the unusually talented will not only come to fruition but will also develop beyond the merely personal and selfish expression to an outreach in terms of others. The aims of these programs must be a synergic unity, where what is best for the self and what is best for society are the same" (Drews, 1976, p. 27).

We must improve our study of foreign languages if individuals and society are to benefit significantly. Two or three years of French or Spanish in high school are too little and much too late. Beginning at the kindergarten level, children should study in a second language, learning the second language as they learned their first—by singing, playing, counting. As we will suggest later, such programs can be open to all interested students. Those who demonstrate linguistic talent should be allowed to move ahead and perhaps be offered a third or fourth language during their elementary and secondary years.

The International Baccalaureate exemplifies secondary education with a world view. With its emphasis on rigorous, traditional learning, it prepares students to enroll in colleges throughout the world. One of the most exciting things about the International Baccalaureate is that it encourages a district to upgrade its offerings at earlier grade levels. The goal is an integrated program that may begin with foreign language study in kindergarten and maintain its international focus right through the twelfth grade.

The value of contact with students from other countries and of travel abroad must not be overlooked. Opportunities for travel during the summer and during the academic year are numerous and varied.

The kind of education we propose here is not a package one can purchase from a publisher or ask a consultant to install. It implies a philosophy that values other cultures and other languages. It entails sequential planning from the beginning grades all the way through college. Ideally the institutional programs will be enriched by contact with persons from other lands. The cost is perseverance and attention to opportunity. The rewards are great for the self and for society.

Recommendations

The recommendations presented here apply specifically to the International Baccalaureate program. Other recommendations are implicit in the chapter.

▶ Write to the International Baccalaureate North America, 680 Fifth Avenue, New York, New York 10019. Schools adopting the IB curriculum must affiliate with the International Baccalaureate Office, Geneva. IBNA will offer guidance in developing IB programs.

▶ Assign an administrator the responsibility for leadership and coordination on a part-time or full-time basis.

▶ Evaluate personnel and resources and begin with the areas where teacher strengths and present facilities combine to improve the chances of success.

▶ Consider local and state requirements as well as the International Baccalaureate guidelines when developing curriculum.

▶ Recognize the need for strengthening the curriculum in the elementary and middle schools as well as in the ninth and tenth grades. This pre-IB curriculum should include the study of foreign language at the elementary level, preferably beginning in kindergarten.

▶ Compensate teachers for curriculum development during the summer. This program, perhaps more than most, requires curriculum development at the local level.

▶ Plan extracurricular offerings that meet the IB requirement for social services. Determine community needs that students can meet in fulfilling these requirements.

▶ Allow students to enter the pre-IB program on the basis of interest. Those who prove able and interested should move on to the IB program.

▶ Develop a grading system for IB courses that will reflect the difficulty of the curriculum so as not to penalize students for accepting the challenge.

▶ Arrange for students to take the IB examinations. Monitoring the number of students who receive certificates and diplomas will indicate the program's effectiveness.

▶ Contact colleges and universities to learn their policies in awarding credit for IB courses and the IB diploma.

INTERNSHIPS AND MENTOR PROGRAMS

The relationship between Mentor and Telemachus preserves in myth one of the oldest instructional models we know. The goddess Athena assumes the form of Mentor and accompanies Telemachus in his search for Odysseus after the Trojan War. Athena's intervention can be seen as representing a divine spirit that enters the relationship of teacher and student under specially favored conditions. Mentor's name has come to signify a wise and trusted counselor providing guidance and individual instruction to a younger protégé. Socrates was mentor to Plato, Aristotle to Alexander the Great, Elijah to Elisha.

Most often in current usage the label refers to individual direction and role modeling outside the classroom and outside the home. It represents a mode of particularly effective education for able students whose needs are difficult to meet in the regular curriculum of our schools. Typically a student observes and assists an adult away from school on the site of some real-world occupation—a law office, civic center, or business. The student may be called an intern, an apprentice, or an assistant. The goal is usually some combination of practical experience, career education, and cooperation between the school and the other agency.

Some insist that true mentorship is a privileged relationship that should not be confused with other kinds of individualized and practical education. Mentorship can be distinguished from an experimental internship, from career education, and from community programs by presuming a shared, long-term commitment on the part of student and mentor to a particular tradition and by having as its goal the shaping of a student's life outlook.*

---

*B. O. Boston, "Beyond Awareness: Providing for the Gifted Child," in *Proceedings of the Fourth Annual Conference of the Northern Virginia Council for Gifted/Talented Education*, ed. J. H. Orloff (Falls Church, Va.: Northern Virginia Council for Gifted/Talented Education, 1979). Submitted to the Richardson Foundation, April, 1983.

Not everyone is so careful using the term *mentor*. Paul Torrance describes a mentor as "an older person in your [the protégé's] occupational field or educational experience who 'took you under his/her wing'" (Torrance, 1984). William Gray applies the label to future teachers in an educational psychology course, who are cooperating with elementary and secondary students on independent enrichment projects in the teacher-mentor's area of interest (Gray, 1982).

To keep the terms *mentor, intern, apprentice,* and *assistant* conceptually distinct, we assume that the relationship described by *intern, apprentice,* or *assistant* is functionally specific. That is, the association is confined to a specific learning task. An example is that of the teacher and the student in most college classes. The teacher's concern is properly confined to the subject matter of the class. Although the teacher and student may become friends as well—indeed, the teacher may become a mentor—the specific teacher-student relationship does not initially or necessarily extend to other activities.

The mentor relationship is functionally diffuse. It is not confined to particular tasks, projects, or situations, but spills over into other areas of the lives of both persons. Parenting is also functionally diffuse. In both mentoring and parenting the teaching and molding quite naturally reach a wide range of situations. In preparing this chapter we have been conscious of the special relationship that the term *mentor* implies. But we have used the labels as they are used in the programs we describe. It is clear that even those programs based on a functionally specific relationship hold the hope that a true mentorship will develop, a relationship that will extend beyond the limits of the formal arrangement.

Illinois Governmental Internship Program

In an office in Springfield, a young man from Downers Grove, Illinois, writes the statement of facts on an appellate brief. He does a first-class job; the document will require few corrections before being submitted to the Seventh Circuit of the United States Court of Appeals. David is not yet a lawyer, has not been to law school or even to college. He is a seventeen-year-old high school student taking a semester off during his senior year to participate in the Illinois Governmental Internship Program.

Greg Harris, an assistant U.S. attorney, is one of five lawyers who collectively sponsor David's exploration of a career in law. "I envy the students in

Student Intern at Neiman-Marcus Epicure Department

Student Intern in Dallas County District Attorney's Office

the program," says Harris, "and I wish it had been available when I was in school. I didn't write my first brief until I was out of law school." Sponsor and student agree that this on-the-job training cannot be duplicated in the classroom.

Like many other high-achieving students throughout the country, David had earned enough credits to graduate by the end of the first semester of his senior year. Still, he is taking geometry through independent study. Following an examination, he will receive credit in geometry, and he will also receive credit for his work experience, which will be recorded as an elective.

Harris praises David as a high academic achiever who is active in sports and other school organizations. He is most impressed, however, with David's unusual maturity. Maturity is essential for the students selected to work in an office that deals with confidential documents and with defendants sensitive about their constitutional rights. Yet neither David nor any intern who has preceded him has ever been a problem to the U.S. attorney's office.

Based in Springfield, the state capital, the program attracts able students from throughout Illinois. They are selected on the basis of their maturity, leadership, initiative, and special talents. The selection process includes four steps. Interested juniors apply to their local superintendents. The superintendents recommend those they believe are qualified to the Educational Service Region superintendents. A regional screening committee recommends up to five students (ten if the students are from very large regions) to a statewide selection committee. The statewide committee, composed of governmental officials and program staff, makes the final selection. The program is state-funded, and each region must be fairly represented to assure continued support.

Out-of-town students are housed with local families who receive reimbursement to cover food costs. Given the hearty appetites of most teenagers, though, the host families aren't making money. Motive? Caring and sharing.

This program enables seniors to explore career opportunities in government agencies and related organizations. Only a state capital has the unique resources to offer this specific program. Participating agencies include the Governor's Office, the Department of Conservation, the Department of Transportation, the State Board of Education, the Auditor General's Office, and the Attorney General's Office and legislative support staff.

Executive High School Internship Association

The Illinois Governmental Internship Program is affiliated with the national Executive High School Internship Association (EHSIA). The national program was founded in the early 1970s by Sharlene Hirsch. It began in the New York City schools with support from foundation grants. Hirsch expanded the program to high schools throughout the country. Each participating high school paid a fee to the national office. The combination of grants and substantial fees supported a full-time director and enabled the programs to flourish. Hirsch, herself a gifted child "grown up," identified strongly with the needs and frustrations of gifted secondary students. She devoted great energy to the program and traveled about the country sharing her interest and enthusiasm with local districts and their coordinators. Hirsch has since gone on to other interests; Donald Davis now coordinates the program on a more modest scale from his office in Springfield, Illinois.

The fee for participating schools is now low. Davis cites a number of advantages enjoyed by affiliated schools. They receive a monthly newsletter that keeps them posted about what the other affiliates are doing. Coordinators are invited to an annual conference for which no fee is charged. Copyright materials are available for nominal costs. Liability insurance is included as a part of the membership fee, and medical and accident insurance are available at low cost. Affiliating with the national association may enhance local credibility. Of these advantages to the schools, the most important is probably the communication network the association affords. Each participating school has the opportunity to benefit from the successes and failures of all the others.

Internships throughout the country typically follow the same general schedule. Students work with their individual sponsors during regular business hours Monday through Thursday. On Friday they come together with other interns for seminars. They keep a daily analytical log, and they present a project to their classmates at the end of the semester to demonstrate what they have learned.

Davis tells how the internship experience links the student's high school and college experience. Students are encouraged to select high-school course work that will prepare them for their internship. The internship in turn prepares them for college—they will understand the relevance of the curriculum to their future careers. This appreciation may well extend beyond their specialized course work to an appreciation of the basics. They will discover, for example, they can't expect to learn to write on the job. That they must learn in the classroom.

The encouragement of high-school course work related to the field of the internship is a recent development in EHSIA policy, designed to enhance the integration of the internship into the student's secondary education. In another recent policy shift, the association recommends that course credit for the internship relate directly to the experience. From the beginning of the program, students have received academic credit for the internship. A number of schools have allowed students to sign up for regular college preparatory classes and have given them credit for those classes while they participated in the internship even though there was no relation between the experience and the missed course work. Some schools, and perhaps all, note on the transcript that the credit was awarded on the basis of the internship. Even so, the practice of awarding credit for experience unrelated to courses raises a serious question in the minds of many. The association's policy shift should be welcome.

With these two improvements in place, districts may still need to address other areas of general concern. One surfaces when students participate earlier than the last semester of their senior year. Their experience of working in "the real world" with adults matures them beyond the level of their classmates. Some students report that they find it difficult to fit into the high school environment and social life when they return to their local schools.

The adjustment down from the excitement and pace of an internship may affect even the college experience of participants. Such was the case with Tom, a former Illinois intern who now works for the Intergovernmental Cooperation Commission. He recalls that he learned much from Representative Pete Peters about the grassroots aspects of legislation. He gained a more realistic understanding of politics than is available in many college classrooms. Tom learned about the intrigue of some legislation, what is said and what is unsaid.

Later Tom compared the excitement of real-world politics with college and found college dull. He became impatient with his professor's textbook approach. After three years Tom lost interest in college and went back to politics. Now he has returned to college part time. While still in the political arena he loves, he is taking course work to complete his bachelor's degree. "It was a mistake to drop out," he says.

Another concern—related to that expressed by some about specialized secondary schools—is that students may focus on a career interest before they have the experience to make such a decision wisely. Marshall Sanborn offers a way of responding to the concern. Most careers chosen by students of high ability require many years of preparation: college, graduate or professional school, and perhaps an adult internship. The young person who discovers a career path early may save precious time (Sanborn, 1974). Another response is that very able students, especially those with multiple talents, are more likely than others to change careers, perhaps several times during their lives. Their varied abilities allow them to adapt without serious dislocation.

Moreover, a high school internship need not necessarily determine the student's career choice. Kerry, a recent senior from Elmhurst, Illinois, cherishes her experience with Vic Wirth, a legislative liaison with the Department on Aging. She aspires to a career in criminal law, but she might opt for a degree in social services and work with children. Neither directly involves aging. Yet Wirth feels that Kerry's increased understanding will enable her to be an informed advocate and goodwill ambassador for the rapidly increasing aging population.

Kerry and other interns maintain that the experience is valuable even if they change their minds later. Students gain confidence from their concentrated examination of a career, which will be valuable to them whatever choices they make later. If they find the field isn't what they had envisioned, they will have saved themselves costly hours in college that can better be devoted to another area. Kerry so values the experience that she has no regrets about having to miss some Advanced Placement tests. Her experience is far more important to her than the credit. "He [Wirth] has taught me more than anyone ever has about decision making."

The agency, as well as the student, benefits from the program. "The interns bring fresh, young ideas to the agency," says Wirth. He talks admiringly about Kerry's written and oral communication skills. These skills, combined with her intelligence, enable her to function well in the governmental environment. Wirth obviously enjoyed a colleague's discomfiture when Kerry challenged him effectively on a bad bill.

Districts that might include handicapped students in an internship are encouraged to consult Hirsch's monograph, *Young, Gifted and Handicapped* (1979). The Mainstreaming Project conducted in 1977–1978 by eight school systems in the EHSIA network demonstrated dramatically that given proper support to compensate for physical disabilities, handicapped students could perform as effectively in their placements as nonhandicapped interns. Hirsch's comment on their growth is a moving testimony to the value of the experience: "Growth in self-confidence and self-esteem was marked in all instances. The interns became more poised and confident. Shyness was overcome. Posture and appearance improved. Students who formerly hovered in the background of any group made presentations before community organizations, fellow interns, agency staff, school classes, and even a national convention" (Hirsch, 1979, p. 7).

The Executive Assistant Program and the Creative and Performing Arts Program

Mike Stuart, coordinator of the Executive Assistant and the Creative and Performing Arts programs in Dallas, Texas, credits EHSIA and Sharlene Hirsch with helping him initiate the program. In the spring of 1973, Stuart spent five days with Hirsch in New York, observing interns at work with their sponsors. Sold on the success of the program, he wrote a proposal for a Dallas plan on the flight home.

The district already had a different kind of intern project, so administrators adopted the term "assistant" rather than "intern" to avoid confusion. Beginning with 25 students and 25 sponsors, the program opened in the fall of 1973. Ten years later approximately 150 students and 600 sponsors participate.

The Dallas Independent School District (DISD) began its plan as a part of the national organization but after three years decided to operate independently. Along the way, DISD added a second component, the Creative and Performing Arts Program, to encourage students seriously interested in the arts. Students may study in one of the generally recognized art areas—dance, instrumental music, voice, sculpture, and painting. Those who hear different drummers may elect one of the athletic arts (Stuart's term)—golf, tennis, gymnastics, ice skating, for example.

Students qualify for the Assistant Program by being in the upper 20 percent of their class and possessing excellent communication and computational skills. They must also demonstrate leadership and initiative. Add maturity, dependability, and creativity, and you have a good student profile.*

---

*M. Stuart, *The Executive Assistant Program and the Creative and Performing Arts Program.* Paper submitted to the Richardson Foundation, April, 1983.

The Arts Program seeks students who have already demonstrated their commitment to the arts, who are planning a professional career in the arts, and who have achieved an advanced level of proficiency in their chosen field. Faculty members generally judge the portfolios and auditions, but the staff sometimes turns to artists in the community to help evaluate a student's work.

Both programs follow the EHSIA pattern. Students work with executives or with artists four days a week and attend seminars on Friday for a full semester. The young artists attend academic classes half-days and pursue their art form under the tutelage of noted master teachers for the other half. Some assistants attend classes half-days, and others attend no classes, devoting full time to the work experience. Both groups keep daily logs and analyses of their activities, and they present projects to their classmates.

The DISD project enjoys an enviable relationship with the Dallas Chamber of Commerce. By housing the school program at its downtown office, the Chamber effectively communicates its support to prospective sponsors in the community.

Although assistants are not paid, their experiences may lead to paid, generally temporary, positions. For example, Reginald worked with Theocharis Georgiadis, a vice-president at Neiman-Marcus. He also worked with the buyer of kitchen utensils. Reginald participated in purchasing merchandise, processing it, and sending it to various Neiman-Marcus stores throughout the country. He had a hand in marketing merchandise through catalogs, newspapers, and mailers. Reginald learned how department heads were trained to understand the unique features of the merchandise. When Neiman-Marcus management decided to inaugurate a new department for electrical appliances, Georgiadis asked Reginald to propose procedures for setting up the department. This culminating activity required him to draw on his whole work experience and to study the steps required for the project, and Neiman-Marcus hired him for the summer. Georgiadis plans to keep in touch with Reginald through his college training. He hopes to bring him back to Neiman-Marcus as an executive trainee following his graduation.

Frequently the student maintains contact with the sponsor and goes back for consultation and later for employment. Stuart attributes this phenomenon to the special relationship that develops between assistants and sponsors. "Just time and again you see some wonderful things happening between the sponsor and the student," he says. "They become friends and colleagues."

Some assistants so value the experience that when they graduate and embark on their careers, they participate as sponsors. David Zumwalt at Compucon, Inc., served his high-school assistantship at Southwestern Bell. He contends that his present position would not have been available to him but for the Assistant Program. Once established at Compucon, he thanked the Chamber of Commerce for the help given him as a high-school student and signed on as a sponsor. "I am now," he said, "in a position to do for a young person what was done for me."

Texas A&M University's Career Education Model

William R. Nash and others at Texas A&M University developed a career educational model in the 1970s for gifted and talented students (Colson, Borman, and Nash, 1978). The designers noted the special need very able students have for career education. They frequently possess multiple abilities and therefore may face more complicated career and educational decisions than other students making the transition from secondary to higher education. Furthermore, students with high academic abilities, strong leadership skills, or special talents may be in a particularly favorable position to profit from an intensive relationship with one or more adults.

The model divides into three phases, each covering about one-third of a year. Selected seniors are released from school two hours a day to participate first in a guidance lab, then in a mentorship phase, and finally in an internship.

In the guidance lab students are introduced to multitalented adults who present and model a wide range of interests and occupational styles—a physician from Bryan, Texas, for example, who had a first career as a musician playing for a symphony orchestra. During this phase, attention focuses on self-investigation and career exploration. Problem solving is emphasized, and study of the future helps students envision future careers. High-school students, frequently unaware of where their individual talents lie and of what careers may be available to them in the future, find these studies useful.

Dwayne, for example, grew up in a university community and assumed he would enter the education arena as an adult. In the course of the guidance lab a counselor uncovered and capitalized on the boy's interest in electronics. Placed with the director of Texas A&M University's public television station for his mentorship experience, the young man stayed at the same site for his internship. His original interest in electronics grew into a love affair with television broadcasting. After high school he enrolled at Texas A&M and worked at the television station as a part-time sports reporter. Five years later he had graduated from college and was broadcasting the nightly sports news for a television station in Austin.

Like Dwayne, participating students are paired with university faculty members for the mentorship phase of the program. It is a coselection process, and students interview professors as prospective mentors. The staff helps them identify those who are highly productive. Frequently in the process a happy match of personalities results. They sometimes continue their relationship during and following the students' college years. "Basically," says Nash, "the student begins as an observer-aide; the personal involvement and commitment come later."

In the mentorship phase and in the internship phase following it, the goal is two-fold: (1) to give the student a close relationship with an adult whom the student can see as guide and role model and (2) to provide the student with a sense of both the lifestyle associated with the profession or occupation and the educational course that leads to it. A practicing physician or an attorney is in a favorable position to know exactly what it takes to get into medical or law school and is likely to have contacts that will be useful to the young friend.

Students work in the community a minimum of ten hours a week during their internship phase. The career interests they explore during this phase have been confirmed during the second phase of the program with their mentors. The internship advisors at the various sites help the interns gain a wide exposure to the various aspects of the field. During both the second and third phases, students meet in a seminar on the high school campus every other week to share their experiences and discuss what they have learned.

The staff screens students for the program during their junior year. They collect data on general intellectual ability, creative thinking, specific academic ability, and special talents. Although the staff establishes some guidelines, local experts conduct interviews and auditions. The students themselves help identify their special interests and talents. Sometimes the screening produces surprises. Two students had approximately equal but unspectacular scholastic test results—I.Q. scores, for example, around 120. The girl's grade average was 98; her teachers described her as a model student. The boy held an 84 academic average; he disliked school, and his teachers described him as a classroom nuisance. The girl scored in the average range on a creativity test; the boy scored in the ninety-ninth percentile. After interviewing the two students, a local bank president observed that the girl was bright, had a good vocabulary, and was neat and well organized. She would make an outstanding manager of one of their departments. The boy, who was not neat and orderly and did not like school, would probably not go to college. "But," the banker continued, "he has the most exceptional understanding of the dynamics of business of any seventeen-year-old I've ever encountered. He may be a millionaire by the time he is twenty-five!" On the basis of the banker's judgment, the young man ranked higher on the screening matrix than the young woman, and he was selected for the program. After high school he entered business directly, instead of going on to college, and set out in pursuit of his first million.

Sharon Colson describes the success of the Texas A&M University model in the *Gifted Child Quarterly* (Summer, 1980). She concludes that the career education program provides a depth of career information not available in other classes or programs, that the model provides an opportunity for self-evaluation not open to other students, and that useful information about career field entrance requirements is provided. Not surprisingly, Colson argues in favor of establishing a triadic career education model (the Texas A&M model) in high schools.

Weslaco Advanced Career Exploration

That the program at Texas A&M is a useful model for others is demonstrated by the success with which it has been adapted by the Weslaco Independent School District in South Texas. The different situation requires certain adaptations of the plan. Because there is no university in the city, the university mentorship phase is reduced to five field days when the students visit Pan American University, some thirty miles away. There the high-school students gain a sense of the intervening education required to prepare for the career they have chosen to study. The university mentors also consult with the students and help them gain access to university resources as they prepare their semester's project.

Because Martha Fulbright, director of the program at Weslaco, is a Future Problem Solving coach with considerable experience in futuristics, scenarios play an important role in phase one, the guidance lab. Students learn to visualize the future of the career field they have chosen to explore, and they place themselves in the future as adult professionals.

The principal focus of the Weslaco program, however, is on the community internship phase with professionals in a wide range of agriculture-related industry and research in the Rio Grande Valley, with business leaders, doctors, lawyers, and other professionals in a city of 20,000. One medical mentor, for example, a busy obstetrician, took his protégée everywhere legally and ethically allowable to experience the full range of his practice. He took the student on his calls after securing the patients' permission and approval from the hospital. He kept her informed of activities she could attend on her own. The doctor was determined that his ward would be the first woman physician from Weslaco, and he continued to sponsor her after the program was over, making contacts for her when she applied to universities. In this case the relationship that had begun as a form of career exploration developed into a true mentorship, involving a serious and extended commitment on both sides.

Another adaptation that distinguishes the Weslaco program from the Texas A&M model on which it is based is the semester's project that the students develop under the supervision of their community sponsors and often with the help of the university mentors. The projects are presented at a final ceremony to which are invited the students' families and friends, the school personnel, and the community and university mentors. Projects take many forms: a student-narrated slide show of veterinary procedures, electron microscope photography illustrating an experiment, a book of cartoons on meteorology created by a student whose interests included both drawing and the study of weather.

Although the Weslaco program lasts only one semester, it includes all the features of the Texas A&M model, and the impact is significant. Fulbright reports on responses to a questionnaire circulated at the end of the semester: "Mentors find that they enjoy their role and would not hesitate to participate as often as needed. Students generally desire to continue the relationship. Parents perceive an increased responsibility and sense of direction in their children." * She adds that the students and their mentors often maintain the relationship after the semester ends.

Carrollton – Farmers Branch Mentor Program

The Texas A&M model on which the Weslaco program was modeled also provided inspiration for one in Carrollton–Farmers Branch, a Dallas suburb. Joan Shelley, developer and director of the program, decided to adapt the model to suit her local situation after hearing Bill Nash present it at a conference.

Shelley designed the junior-high program as a career education project. She discovered soon enough that most junior-high students do not have career interests in focus. On a given day all the seventh graders might evidence interest in careers in science and history. Or all the eighth graders might express a strong interest in the theatre arts. Then in two weeks their interests would have changed. In addition, scheduling at the junior-high level proved to be a problem. Another problem surfaced to surprise Shelley. Finding a match of personalities between shy, self-conscious adolescents and adults who were talented but untrained for their role as mentors became a major stumbling block.* The unfamiliar off-campus setting added to the students' discomfort.

Although the program as originally designed didn't achieve unqualified success, Shelley found many talented people in the community eager to work with students. Some students developed exceptional projects with their off-campus mentors. One group, for example, working with an executive from the Warner Amex Cable Company, videotaped a clay animation episode in the home of one of the students using the Warner video equipment. The mentor advised that animation is not practical on TV tape because it requires high-speed film. The students ignored the advice and surprised the professionals with a successful "claymation."

Transportation problems and those mentioned earlier required a shift in the program. The business and professional people in the community, effective as they were, are no longer available to the junior-high students.

---

* M. Fulbright, *The Weslaco Mentorship Program*. Paper submitted to the Richardson Foundation, April, 1983.

* J. Shelley, *The Carrollton – Farmers Branch I.S.D. Mentor Program*. Paper submitted to the Richardson Foundation, April, 1983.

Someday an expansion to the high school will tap that resource.

Instead Shelley began matching the junior-high students with on-campus adults: principals, assistant principals, custodians, librarians, even a letter carrier who delivers to the school. Rather than focusing on career interests, students and adults engage in special-interest projects. The topics have included artificial intelligence, computer programming, science, science fiction, fashion designing, quilting, even camping. The program as it now operates might well be described as extracurricular enrichment except that it depends crucially on the child-adult relationship that can be deepened into a true mentorship. Shelley considers the concept a success. Now an elementary principal, she is offering even younger students a similar program.

Conclusion

The programs described here are related, but each is strikingly individual. The Executive Assistant Program in Dallas is quite different from others in the Executive High School Internship Association from which it branched off. The modifications of the Texas A&M model now operating in Weslaco and Carrollton–Farmers Branch have been adjusted to situations entirely unlike that of College Station. Because the regulating conditions and the opportunities vary from school to school, from community to community, adaptation is crucial.

But the programs have this in common: they all depend importantly on cooperation between diverse agencies. Except in the Carrollton–Farmers Branch program, students are placed with professional practitioners or with business leaders, with persons in decision-making positions in government, civic organizations, cultural institutions, and the like. The arrangements excite enthusiasm and generate energy on both sides of the desk, so to speak, in both partners to the agreement.

It has impressed us that the whole educational enterprise has much to gain from cooperative projects of this sort. When industry, government, and professional groups take an interest in our schools, they are likely to support the schools with their resources of time, talent, special knowledge, equipment, even money. Our schools desperately need such help. The agencies that cooperate have much to gain as well. The goodwill produced by such concern is considerable, and the long-range benefits from attracting capable students and cultivating their interest can hardly be denied.

Associated with these benefits is another that returns us to the Greek myth in which Athena takes the form of Mentor to oversee the instruction of Telemachus. Both Mentor and Telemachus are changed. Individual sponsors and perhaps whole agencies can be so affected. They may discover a new purpose as they assume a responsibility for the students with whom they work—future guardians and tenants of the tradition they embody. That responsibility may become a permanent mission.

Recommendations

Some of the recommendations presented here apply to both internships and mentor programs, but the emphasis is on internships because that kind of program generally requires more structure.

▶ Select a coordinator and other staff members with effective communication and interpersonal skills. The coordinator should be familiar with community resources and should have direct access to an administrator at a decision-making level.

▶ Vary the student selection procedure according to the age level of the students. For example, the ability to function independently may well be a key criterion for senior-high students. Selection may include a variety of measures, such as auditions for specific talents in addition to the usual achievement tests, grades, and recommendations. A less formal procedure may be used prior to the secondary level.

▶ Determine student interests and assess the resources in the community to meet their needs.

▶ Clearly define the role of the student and sponsor.

▶ Develop detailed plans for seeking outstanding sponsors in the community. They should be creative producers of acknowledged reputation with interest and skill in working with youth. Appropriate orientation is important. Avoid placing students with sponsors who will exploit them as "go-fers."

▶ Seek the best student-sponsor match possible.

▶ Prepare students for the internship with related courses prior to the work experience. Develop a clearly defined, defensible credit policy. If academic credit is to be given for the work experience, that experience should relate directly to the courses for which it is given.

▶ Plan appropriate orientation seminars for students. Acquaint them with the business and professional environments where they will work.

Emphasize the necessity of respecting the confidentiality of their student-sponsor relationship. The situation in some work places will be more sensitive than others.

▶ Incorporate seminars or other meetings at which students describe their experiences and exchange ideas related to them.

▶ Provide flexible scheduling so that students can leave the campus according to agreements established in advance.

▶ Keep lines of communication open among community, school personnel, and the student-sponsor teams. Hold periodic orientation sessions for the business and professional community. Make provisions for recognizing community participation in the program.

▶ Include college and career counseling as a part of the total counseling process.

▶ Affiliate with the Executive High School Internship Association or seek other means of exchanging ideas with districts having similar programs.

▶ Plan for an internal and an external program evaluation. Ask the sponsors to share with the program staff the responsibility for evaluating the students' work.

A SHARED COMMITMENT: SCHOOL AND COLLEGE

Of all the breaks in the continuum of American education from preschool through postgraduate education, none is more complete or more vexing than the gap between secondary school and college. Since the latter part of the nineteenth century, sustained professional attention to education has standardized education at both levels. Unfortunately, that same attention has produced autonomous systems that are widely separated from each other's concerns.

In recent years the school-college interruption has received thoughtful attention. The College Entrance Examination Board, the Carnegie Foundation, and the National Commission on Excellence in Education have led the public campaign to close the gap between school and college (*Academic Preparation for College*, 1983; Boyer, 1983; Maeroff, 1983; *A Nation at Risk*, 1983). These agencies and others have called for closer cooperation between the institutions that face each other across the gap. They have observed and chronicled with some optimism the significant, although sporadic, efforts to build the necessary bridge.

The case for a partnership that strengthens the bonding between our lower schools and higher education is so clear and so simple one wonders why it needs to be made at all. The students who come through the school system at the precollege level fill the classes of our colleges and universities. At one time only the brightest of high school graduates, or those from the wealthiest families, went on to higher education. Now approximately half of American high school graduates attend some kind of postsecondary educational institution (Maeroff, 1983, p. 7). School and college see the same students at different ages.

School and college also have the same curriculum, essentially, at different levels of depth and sophistication. Especially in the "basic" subjects— verbal skills, mathematical reasoning, understanding of human culture and the physical world—the content, teaching methods, and educational philosophies at the two levels are interdependent. Offerings and requirements at the high-school level determine what can be offered in college; conversely, what is expected of entering college freshmen establishes the goals of the secondary schools.

Our focus in this chapter is pragmatic. We are interested in the most able learners in our schools; therefore we have a particular concern for the transition between school and college. Because we have a commitment both to continuous progress and appropriate pacing, and to comprehensive, system-wide programs for able learners, we hope to encourage educators to take advantage of arrangements and options that enrich and accelerate the education of able learners. We agree with Ernest Boyer when he urges us to "overcome the tyranny of time" by allowing students to move at their own pace and make the transition from school to college more flexibly (Maeroff, 1983, p. viii). And we believe that well before they make the transition students should have an educational experience that offers steady and appropriate challenge. That means making the membrane between levels as permeable as possible, under controlled conditions.

Fortunately, ways to ease the transition are already in place. They simply need to be integrated into a comprehensive approach to providing opportunity to able learners. Advanced Placement courses, concurrent enrollment in school and college, and early entrance to college require only minor dislocation of either system; they can be managed with little administrative machinery. Despite some resistance on both sides of the boundary, it is relatively simple for a student who is adequately prepared and intellectually capable to move into college work well before the end of the high-school years.

Advanced Placement

The most formalized of the three provisions for able students to do college work at an early age is the Advanced Placement (AP) program. The national program is sponsored by the College Entrance Examination Board, an independent association of schools and colleges that has throughout this century sought to ease the transition of secondary students to post-secondary education.

In simple terms, the AP program is college-level work offered to secondary students to prepare them for AP examinations. On the basis of these examinations students may earn college credit at a wide range of colleges and universities. The College Board provides secondary schools with course descriptions in many disciplines: American history, art, biology, chemistry, English literature and composition, English language and composition, European history, French, German, Latin, mathematics, music, physics, and Spanish. The College Board added computer science to the AP offerings in the fall of 1983.

Each year in May, examinations for all courses except studio art and drawing are administered in over 5,000 schools in this country, plus others throughout the world. Because of the special nature of studio art and drawing, artists and teachers evaluate portfolios of students' work.

In each course the test scores (objective and essay) are combined and converted to a five-point scale: 1, no recommendation; 2, possibly qualified; 3, qualified; 4, well qualified; 5, extremely well qualified.

Although the examination scoring is uniform, college policies for accepting credits are not. Kirk, a seventeen-year-old senior in a southwestern private school, is taking AP history, biology, and calculus. He plans to take the AP examinations in those subjects and in English as well, even though his English course does not follow the AP course description. Aspiring to a career in medicine, he is counting on credit by examination to shorten his college stay by at least one year. His chances are good. Kirk is on the high honor roll even though he works twenty hours a week. He scored 32 on the ACT and has a combined score of 1380 on the SAT. A National Merit semi-finalist, he will probably make finalist.

The colleges of greatest interest to Kirk are Duke, Harvard, and Stanford. The amount of credit awarded for his examinations will depend not only on his scores but also on the university where he finally matriculates. If he goes to Duke, he may be awarded credit for one or more courses in each subject area with an examination score of 4 or 5. If he scores a 3 in any subject, he must complete a specified course in that subject at Duke with a grade of C or better before credit is awarded.

Suppose Kirk and Harvard choose each other. If he scores a 4 or 5 in at least three subject areas, he will probably be eligible for sophomore standing. He then may elect to complete the requirements for an A.B. degree in either three or four years. A three-year undergraduate program seems attractive to him at this point in his life, but even if he decides to remain for four years, entering as a sophomore will have increased his course options. Should Kirk matriculate at Stanford, most departments will award him ten credits for the examinations with scores of 4 or 5. A few will consider a score of 3.

Lisa, a sixteen-year-old senior in a northeastern public school, scored a 4 on the AP biology exam as a sophomore and a 5 on the AP European history exam as a junior. These scores are being held for her by the College Board until she is ready to have them sent to the colleges she chooses. This year Lisa is taking AP chemistry, English literature and composition, and Latin. She expects to earn more 4s and 5s on the exams to add to those she has already banked.

Undecided about a career choice, Lisa will seek an undergraduate degree in the liberal arts before specializing. She is confident; she plans to earn her degree in three years or less. Lisa is considering applying to the University of Virginia and to the University of Pennsylvania. At Virginia, scores of 4 or 5 earn from three to eight hours of credit. At Pennsylvania, policy regarding credit varies from one department to another, with each setting its own standard of achievement.

How extensive is AP? According to Maeroff (1983, p. 17), in 1982, 141,626 students from 5,525 high schools took 188,933 Advanced Placement examinations. Approximately 25 percent of the secondary schools in the country offer one or more AP courses. The distribution of these schools, however, is by no means even. Connecticut has the largest percentage of schools offering AP courses (52 percent in 1981); Maryland (48 percent) and Massachusetts (47 percent) are close behind. By way of contrast, in the Southwest Region of the College Board (Texas, Arkansas, Oklahoma, and New

Mexico) fewer than 8 percent of the schools offer AP courses.

Most schools offer AP courses in the regular classroom as a form of honors work. Where the number of students qualified and interested is not high enough, some schools offer AP preparation by providing supervised independent study or small seminars.

Robert Sawyer, director of the Talent Identification Program (TIP) at Duke University, says that TIP recently introduced by-mail courses for students who have no access to AP courses in their local schools.* Public schools in Andover, Massachusetts, contract with Phillips Academy as a cost-effective means of offering AP to their qualified students.

Other options are available for schools with few qualified students. For example, neighboring schools can pool their resources, including staff and students, to offer courses that a single school might not be able to offer on its own. In isolated areas students might study independently and telephone an instructor at a toll-free number for assistance as needed.

Some schools don't offer AP courses, not because they lack able students, but because their teachers are not adequately prepared or because the teachers lack confidence in their ability to handle college-level courses. The solution in either case is teacher training. According to Irwin Spear at the University of Texas at Austin, colleges of education have not addressed the training problem, and subject-area departments at the college level have rarely considered the preparation of teachers their mission. One approach to helping teachers increase both their competence and their confidence is summer workshops conducted in partnership by colleges of education and academic departments. Including a section of high-ability students would add zest to such workshops; both students and teachers would benefit from the arrangement. Generally, summer programs that combine teacher training with student sessions enjoy an enviable teacher/student ratio, with exciting results for both groups.

Whether a school selects teachers from its existing staff and trains them to teach AP courses or whether it hires new staff members, teachers must be selected with care if the program is to succeed. It should not surprise us that students have very definite ideas about teacher qualifications. College

---

* R. N. Sawyer, "Talent Identification Program: Duke University" (remarks at the National Science Board/National Science Foundation Commission of Precollege Education in Mathematics, Science, and Technology, New York, September 7, 1982).

students who took one or more AP courses in high school describe the best teacher this way:

> First, he has an infectious enthusiasm for the broad area in which a specific course falls. This means he can communicate the relationship of a particular course to the larger discipline and its relevance to other fields, and sometimes to the largest one—the human condition. . . .
>
> Second, he demands a great deal of competency of himself and of his students. He is continually increasing his own knowledge and skills and frequently expects students to do more at a higher level than they think is possible, until they have tried it. . . .
>
> Third, this teacher is not threatened by students who are brighter than he is. He can admit, without loss of ego or being overawed, that a student may be beyond him in a particular area, or indeed, shows more academic potential in all areas than he himself has demonstrated. (Casserly, 1968, p. 9)

What about the selection of students? The criteria for participation in AP programs vary from school to school but generally include such items as commitment to academic achievement, an A or B grade-point average, teacher and counselor recommendations, high performance on achievement tests, parental approval and support, and a sample of the student's writing.

Robin Crawford, college counselor at Phillips Academy, suggests that high-ability students who exhibit purposeful energy have the greatest chance for success in rigorous courses, AP or not. Some schools allow students to enroll on the basis of interest if they have an average of C or above. This modest requirement may be strengthened by requiring a commitment to take the AP examination.

Any discussion of AP turns sooner or later to grading. Bright students may learn that in AP and other honors classes it is more difficult to get the A's they have come to take for granted. Students planning to enter college have a natural and legitimate concern for the effect of their grade-point average on college admissions officers. In response to this concern many schools weight the grades to reflect the increased level of difficulty in advanced courses. This solution may not satisfy the student in a high school where the honor roll and other honors are determined by actual grades. Not all students find it more difficult to get A's in AP and other honors courses. Some report that teachers in these advanced classes assume the students are exceptionally able or they wouldn't be in the course. They grade generously.

Why do students elect one or more AP courses? What do they gain?

Given rising college costs, the most obvious answer is the dollars saved. It is less expensive to take a college-level course at the local high school than at college. If a student can earn enough college credit by this means to reduce the time spent earning an undergraduate degree, the savings are considerable. Whether the students go immediately into the job market or on to more advanced degrees, starting their careers a year or more earlier represents another savings.

Studying with others of similar interests and abilities has great appeal. The atmosphere of an AP class is stimulating. Moreover, students report that more rigorous courses don't necessarily require more time. They find the AP teachers more skilled in giving thoughtful assignments and less inclined to mete out busywork. AP students don't have to give up other activities.

Lisa and Kirk, mentioned earlier, find time to do what is important to them. Kirk has his part-time job. Although Lisa has not worked during her high-school years, she has been on the student council for two years and on the newspaper staff for three. Active in the drama club, she has the lead in a major production in her senior year. Both Kirk and Lisa find taking more demanding courses than many of their classmates encourages them to budget their time more carefully. Discipline and good organization are important by-products of their busy schedules.

Surprisingly, some parents urge their children to take AP courses but prefer that they not opt for college credit. They appreciate the increased rigor at the high-school level and value improved study habits, but think it is in the student's interest to make the transition to college easy. There is a danger, however, that such a decision will shift a year of wheel-spinning and inadequate demand from high school to college. A first-year student in college has the same need for academic challenge as a high school senior.

Concurrent Enrollment

In some ways the option of placing students in college courses before they complete high school is more direct than Advanced Placement courses, which use a special curriculum and offer credit by standardized examinations. Concurrent enrollment in high school and college takes many forms. Where schools and local colleges work out a cooperative plan, a college teacher may teach one or more college-level courses in area schools. Sometimes specially trained high-school teachers operating under the college's supervision are approved to teach courses on the high-school campus for college credit. One of the better known of such programs is Project Advance at Syracuse University, which offers college-level courses to some 4,000 high-school seniors in 77 high schools in New York, New Jersey, Massachusetts, and Michigan (Maeroff, 1983). It offers the advantage of keeping students in their high schools while they earn college credits on a Syracuse transcript, which the student can claim by entering Syracuse University or by transferring the credits to another university.

Students may enroll in college courses during the summer or on weekends at a number of universities as part of a program to encourage bright students to accelerate and enrich their education. The Governor's Schools in several states offer a similar opportunity (see the section "Programming for Excellence in the Summer"). Many community colleges offer courses on television, for which high-school students with special permission are eligible. And some colleges and universities offer courses by mail, either in preparation for Advanced Placement tests or for college credit.

The most common arrangement is that the student leaves the high school during the day, or at the end of the day, and goes to the college campus to take courses. This option usually requires some negotiating with high-school administrators and with the college admissions officers. A student may be able to receive high-school and college credit for the same course. Or the student may bank college credits on a provisional transcript to be awarded or transferred when the student matriculates.

Ideally the student enters this arrangement with careful counseling. Several concerns are involved. Even a precocious high schooler may need special attention to develop the study skills required by courses at an advanced level. On the other hand, many college courses are not sufficiently demanding for an unusually bright high-school student. And some, of course, would not fit the student's long-range academic plans.

Unfortunately not every school district or college makes such an obvious solution to the problems of the underchallenged high-school student easy to achieve. High schools and middle schools are often reluctant to turn their students over to the college for even part of the day. They may lose the student for purposes of state funding if they do so. High schools sometimes feel they are surrendering a student who could contribute to the social and extracurricular life of the high school. Or they may feel threatened, believing that if students elect to travel away from the high school campus for a part of their education, their doing so reflects on the ability of the public school to provide for the needs of all its students.

College tuition poses an additional problem. Sometimes special arrangements can be made. One year the Fort Worth Independent School District enrolled several students at Texas Christian University on a trial basis at the school district's expense. With a vision hardly typical, the district interpreted its responsibility to provide appropriate education for high-school students to include paying the tuition at the nearest college offering the appropriate math course. Eligible students included those who had completed the mathematics sequence in the public schools before their senior year. The students provided their own transportation to the university math class; the district paid for their tuition and books.

Concurrent enrollment is not limited to the upper high-school grades, nor does it necessarily entail college credit. Nathan spent two summers, between the seventh and eighth grades and between the eighth and ninth, taking Spanish at a nearby community college for twelve weeks each summer. He enrolled over the reluctance of the registrar and a secretary who insisted that the college did not accept seventh graders. He did not get college credit for the courses, despite earning A's and B's, but he was later able to move into fourth-year Spanish at his private high school.

Concurrent enrollment and other forms of acceleration have received fresh impetus and considerable publicity as a consequence of the talent searches at university centers around the country. The search for academically talented twelve-year-olds and seventh graders is covered in some detail in "Programming for Excellence in the Summer." The programs of academic enrichment or acceleration in association with the various searches include some courses for college credit offered on the campuses of these universities and on the campuses of other cooperating colleges and universities.

Sanford Cohn, formerly director of the Project for the Study of Academic Precocity at Arizona State University, now at Johns Hopkins, insists that students able and willing to handle college work successfully should receive college credit. In contrast, Joyce VanTassel-Baska, director of the Midwest Talent Search at Northwestern University, does not recommend college credit for students identified in the search. She says that the credit is expensive and that the students are too young for the credit to be useful to them. She prefers that students take proficiency tests for credit at their local secondary schools and then later take the Advanced Placement tests for college credit.

The goals of the talent searches and of concurrent enrollment generally are to help qualified students move more rapidly through the school system and to find both intellectual excitement and sound academic development as they mature. The particular advantage of these approaches to academic challenge is that they do not depend entirely on a local school system. The disadvantage is that they depend on the resourcefulness and initiative of the student. It is likely that many very able students are being missed simply because they are not aware of the opportunities. Some may not be able to afford even modest college tuition.

A further problem, more deep-seated philosophically, is that concurrent enrollment does not solve the real deficiencies of our school system; in fact it takes pressure off the schools to improve their quality. But it is a form of academic challenge widely available, and it is open to those students ready now. Moreover, it can be used to complement the International Baccalaureate, Advanced Placement, and other honors programs.

Early Entrance

A natural extension of the accelerated course work embodied in AP programs and concurrent enrollment is that the child who is academically ready can enter college early, even before the age when most students enter high school. Normally, individual arrangements must be made, involving close cooperation between the student's family and the college or university the youngster enters.

An extreme example of early entrance, or radical acceleration, is Jay, the youngest graduate of Boise State University, possibly the nation's youngest college graduate. Jay entered Boise State from the third grade at the age of eight. He became one of three ten-year-olds ever to score above 700 on the mathematics section of the SAT. At Boise State Jay completed his B.S. degree in math and computer science one month after turning twelve.*

More recently, nine-year-old Jenny, in Auburn, Maine, was the cause of some awkwardness when her parents enrolled her as a full-time student at the University of Maine. She had been advanced to third grade at the age of six, but dropped out because she was bored. Although Jenny had completed several college courses, local school board officials wanted her to

---

*W. P. Mech, "A Few of My Favorite Things" (presidential address to the National Collegiate Honors Council, Omaha, Nebraska, October 30, 1981).

take an achievement test to show she was learning before she continued her nontraditional education (*New York Times*, September 9, 1984).

Not all students who enter college early are as advanced as Jay and Jenny. Nor do they always face institutional obstacles. Increasingly, colleges and universities are seeking capable youngsters and providing a structure that welcomes them. A natural consequence of the Johns Hopkins Study of Mathematically Precocious Youth (SMPY) and Study of Verbally Gifted Youth (SVGY), established in the 1970s, was that many of their students enrolled early as regular college students at Johns Hopkins. A few entered when they were between eleven and thirteen years of age.

The Johns Hopkins experiment inspired the late Halbert Robinson to initiate an Early Entrance Program (EEP) at the University of Washington. The program opened in 1977 with 172 students. It is not a residential program; the students generally are from the Seattle area and live at home. Originally the students eased into the program by taking a course concurrently with their elementary or junior high school program. As they succeeded, they added a course or two each quarter until they were enrolled full-time at the university.

Although the EEP students generally performed well in their college work, in 1980 Robinson added a transition component, an educational program with a supportive peer group, to ensure that the young students would make the necessary adjustment and succeed in college. The transition component has become a separate school—a one-room school, if you will—on the university campus. Instead of being accepted directly into regular college courses, students now enter through the transition school. Students generally enroll in the transition school after the eighth grade. The ages vary from twelve to fourteen, the grades from seventh to ninth, depending on whether the students have been accelerated in their school years.

Now run by Nancy Robinson, the transition school has a curriculum especially designed to serve as "an educational bridge that can help [the students] make the transition between their former schools and the University of Washington."* Students study writing and literary criticism, history, mathematics, and a foreign language—usually German, by student

---

* *A Transition Program for Early Entrance to the University of Washington* (promotional material prepared by the Child Development Research Group, University of Washington, no date).

choice. The students have specially developed classes during the first quarter, then take one college course along with their transition courses in the second quarter. By the third quarter they are taking two college courses, and the following year they are full-time college students. In the meantime, they have a peer group and a supportive faculty in their one-room school. They can and do come back for reinforcement, or just to visit, after moving on to full-time college status.

The school employs three part-time teachers and one full-time teacher. "It is an expensive proposition," Nancy Robinson admits, "to run a one-room school for fifteen students when you need four teachers."* While the school tries to be self-supporting, it received important early support from the William H. Donner Foundation. It is a good example of productive cooperation between the schools, the university, and the private sector.

The Early Entrance Program at Washington offers an option some uncommonly able students need. "It is for the *bright, bright* who need radical acceleration," Nancy Robinson says. Robinson acknowledges there are other students, just as bright, who do well in high school and prefer to remain there. They enjoy their junior and senior years academically and socially. Sports are important, as are the school newspaper and the student council. But for some the extracurricular life is not important. For others the childhood and teen-age years are not happy. The Early Entrance Program provides an alternative way to get into the mainstream.

Michelle was such a student; we talked with her at the University of Washington. Michelle says she was always out of sync in school—not really ostracized, but not happy either. She skipped kindergarten and at the age of six worked with fourth graders most of the time. She was resented by other students. By the third grade she cried frequently in and out of the classroom. Michelle remembers the fifth grade as a miserable year when she felt this way: "Everyone hates me. I am different—an oddball, even among oddballs." In the seventh grade Michelle lost interest in learning and "went into neutral," failing some courses. The following year, desperate to be accepted, she cut her hair like the others and tried to act like them and so achieved a measure of acceptance.

Michelle entered the University of Washington in 1979, before the development of the transitional program. At the age of thirteen she took three regular freshman courses during the summer on a trial basis. She did so

---

*N. M. Robinson, personal communication, August 23, 1984.

well that she was later able to serve as a student instructor. Like some of the MacArthur Fellows quoted in our introductory section, she found teaching exhilarating. "That's my favorite thing," she beamed, "teaching really bright students."

People who worry about radical acceleration are usually concerned about the child's social development. "They are missing their childhood," the critics say. "And what about the senior prom?" Michelle grew weary of that question: "I'm sorry; the senior prom will just have to get along without me."

Concerning the social skills of Jay at Boise State, William Mech, who was his teacher and advisor, speaks with careful patience: "He is not especially talkative nor extroverted, giving an initial impression of shyness. In this respect, he's much like some of my own colleagues." Mech goes on to say that the traits by which we often identify a highly able learner—independence of thought, persistence of interests, and possible noncomformity—may cause the student to be perceived as socially awkward, even abrasive. But they have little to do with the student's age.

Many students with exceptional learning abilities will not find social acceptance among their age-mates without uncomfortable, perhaps even harmful behavior adjustments. If we add to their problems of growth by preventing them from progressing academically and intellectually at their own pace, we may do even more serious damage than if we take the minimal risk of putting them with older students, with whom they are at least intellectually compatible.

Conclusion

We have examined here three related ways schools and colleges can cooperate in providing intellectually mature secondary students an opportunity to do college-level work at an early age. These provisions are not mutually exclusive. A student could reasonably take one or more Advanced Placement courses, attend a course or two at a local university, and enter college early.

Among the benefits achieved when schools and colleges share a commitment to the education of able learners is that students advance at a pace appropriate to their ability and achievement. Getting into their careers a year or so early will bring professional and financial rewards to the young person. Society, too, will benefit from their earlier and additional professional contributions. It is important, moreover, that highly able students find and fit in with an intellectual peer group, whether it is a group of agemates or not.

Equally important in the long run are the benefits to the system—and hence to future students—of improved cooperation among diverse agencies. Colleges and lower schools help one another when they work together to develop fresh approaches and new materials to enrich the secondary classroom. A similar mutual assistance can grow out of the collegiality that can develop between professors in the academic disciplines and those responsible for training teachers. An adjunct to such cooperation among educational branches is the stimulation that results from participation and involvement by the community and funding agencies.

The compelling feature of the options we have been discussing—AP, concurrent enrollment, and early entrance—is that they take advantage of resources already in place. It is not always necessary to invent new ways to challenge our ablest learners. All that is required for these programs is that schools and colleges make present opportunities available to all students who are able to profit from them. So long as these agencies are resourceful, remain flexible, and keep their concern focused squarely on the benefits to individual students, the chances are good that the transition from school to college will be smooth. A smooth passage can strengthen and enrich the student's development rather than interrupt it. Our most able learners will then progress without institutional impediments from the beginning to the end of their formal education.

Recommendations

The following recommendations apply specifically to Advanced Placement programs.

▸ Contact the regional office of the College Entrance Examination Board for a complete list of subjects in which AP exams are offered.

▸ Determine by survey the level of student interest in the areas offered through the AP program and the potential number of student participants.

▸ Identify existing areas of teaching strength and areas where school improvement is desired.

▸ Select teachers who have sound professional knowledge of subject areas, who are able to use a wide variety of teaching strategies, and who are aware of the characteristics of high-ability students. Teachers should also demonstrate enthusiasm for the subject area.

▶ Select the first AP courses to be offered on the basis of student interests and teacher strengths.

▶ Obtain course descriptions and outlines from the College Board. Supplement these with locally developed curriculum.

▶ Encourage students to participate who have proved their academic ability, as demonstrated by achievement test scores and grades (preferably A or B) in the subject area of the course.

▶ Develop a grading system for AP courses. Give strong consideration to a weighted grading system that will reflect the increased difficulty of AP courses.

▶ Monitor the number of students who take AP examinations after completing the course(s) and, of these, the number who receive scores acceptable for college credit. Correlate the teacher-assigned grades with students' grades on AP exams.

▶ Conduct follow-up studies to determine students' success in college. The following recommendations apply specifically to concurrent enrollment.

▶ Select and counsel for college classes only students with the intellectual maturity to handle advanced work in an independent setting.

▶ Cultivate cooperation and joint planning between the institutions.

▶ Provide careful orientation to both sending and receiving institutions.

▶ Determine whether the college can offer appropriate-level work. For example, freshman English may be less appropriate for the high-ability student than some of the courses available at the high school.

▶ Develop a clear understanding about tuition and other costs. Know what the state requirements are for reimbursement. If funding is based on average daily attendance, know how many hours the student must be present in high school to avoid financial loss to the school. Remember, however, that appropriate education for the student must be the first goal; the reimbursement question is secondary.

▶ Arrange in advance whether credit will be awarded at the college, at the high school, or both.

▶ Arrange adequate counseling services at both the high school and college, knowing that the student will be coping with two academic environments and two social groups.

▶ Keep communication between the school and college open and extend that communication to parents and to the general public so that all students are aware of this option.

▶ Maintain continuous monitoring with respect to programming needs as well as student achievement. Consider adjusting the school curricular offerings if students must depend on the college persistently to meet their instructional needs.

PROGRAMMING FOR EXCELLENCE IN THE SUMMER

At an auditorium nested in pine trees and flanked by two lakes, a concert is in progress. Girls in blue corduroy knickers and boys in matching slacks listen attentively, applauding again and again. They are audience to their teachers at the National Music Camp in Interlochen, Michigan. Young performers themselves, they love good music.

We had embarked on an intensive tour of special summer programs for gifted and talented students throughout the country, and we would see faculty performing for students on more than one occasion. Students also performed for and were guided by faculty, of course, but we sensed that the reversal was significant on more than one level. Not only were the faculty teaching by example; they were developing a distinctive relationship with the students. A special camaraderie exists in the summer sessions.

At St. Andrews Presbyterian College in Laurinburg, North Carolina, a faculty recital brought a standing ovation from the students. The costumed faculty presented "Facade," the poetry of Dame Edith Sitwell set to music by Sir William Walton. Student response was as much to the performers as to the work.

Unable to get to all the outstanding sessions in the country, we visited the National Music Camp at Interlochen, Michigan; the National High School Institute at Northwestern University; two talent search programs, at Northwestern and at Duke; and Governor's Schools in Arkansas, North Carolina, South Carolina, and Virginia.

Many differences exist among the sessions around the country. Age levels vary widely. Selection criteria may be as casual as a recommendation from the student's home school, as required by the Gifted Students Institute, or as formal as SAT scores, as required by the four talent search sites. Course offerings vary from the arts to space science. Yet there are commonalities. Each session is the fruition of someone's dream. Each seeks a

Computer Magic

rare combination of high-ability students and superior faculty. Each tries to achieve a long-range impact from brief sessions, generally two to five weeks in length.

The National Music Camp at Interlochen

Interlochen embodies the dream of the late Joseph E. Maddy. A pioneer in instrumental music in the public schools, he wrote the first instrumental class method book. He became a professor of music at the University of Michigan, where he taught future teachers. His early accomplishments would have satisfied the average professional, but Maddy had an unconventional idea that was sparked by the enthusiasm of young musicians. In 1926 and 1927 Maddy organized and conducted high-school orchestras for educators' conferences. The students pleaded for a chance to work and play together longer than the few days afforded. Maddy promised them a camp.

> In June, 1928, at Interlochen, Michigan, in the midst of a magnificent stand of virgin pine trees between two lovely lakes, the National High School Orchestra

Camp opened its doors. On leased land, with the old Hotel Pennington, several cottages, 29 new camper cabins, a hospital, water and sewer system, the new Interlochen Bowl, and a $40,000 debt, this brave experiment was launched. The "world's foremost proving ground for youthful talent" was born.*

Later renamed the National Music Camp and still known by that name, it now offers ballet, modern dance, theater, and the visual arts in addition to music. A camping program rounds out the students' summer experience. In 1983 approximately 1,500 students, from the age of eight through college, convened at Interlochen for eight weeks of intensive study, practice, and play. The students come from all fifty states and from twenty other countries.

As we visited the camp we could feel Maddy's presence. He believed that the purpose of education is to educate, not to equalize. He held that competition is wholesome and that progress should be based on individual abilities, not limited by age. Interlochen continues to live up to the motto developed by Maddy: "Curriculum geared to talent, promotion geared to attainment."

Probably no other summer program offers the age range Interlochen does. College and secondary students are accustomed to being away from home, but imagine an eight-week residential session for eight-year-olds. We asked Edward J. Downing, director, about homesickness at such a young age. He responded that the student/teacher ratio is low and the students are kept very busy. "Besides," he smiled, "we do a lot of hugging down there to be sure the kids feel comfortable."

Commitment and a clear sense of priorities characterize both students and faculty at Interlochen. The students concentrate on their art. A typical high-school orchestra student is up at 7:00 A.M., eats breakfast, and is at orchestra rehearsal from 8:20 A.M. until 10:50 A.M. The balance of the day may include a conducting class, a theory class, and private practice. About once a week, the schedule includes a private lesson. At 4:30 P.M., free time for recreation and dinner begins. At 7:00 P.M. the student is back in a master class or a recital, and at 8:00 P.M. at a concert.

The students enjoy the special recreational facilities the camp affords. Skilled leaders supervise swimming, boating, canoeing, sailing, archery, and other outdoor recreational activities. But the students accept that they

---

*M. A. Stace, M. L. Bram, C. Bert, and C. Gierkey, *The First Fifty Years* (Interlochen: Interlochen Center for the Arts, 1978).

are there for a serious purpose, and the time allotted to study and practice is far greater than what is scheduled for leisure.

For the students' families, the educational opportunity may require a sacrifice, both in time away from their children and in tuition costs. Some scholarship assistance is available, but normally not more than 50 percent. Outstanding instrumentalists who play instruments needed to complete the high-school orchestra or the band may apply for work scholarships that require one hour of assigned work per day.

Whatever it takes, the students are eager for the opportunity afforded at Interlochen. About half the students who attend each year will return the next. In its faculty as well as its students, the camp depends on loyalty and dedication to the educational experience. Salaries are low, and the teachers pay for their own food and lodging. Yet they, too, come back year after year. The director of the ballet department has been coming for a decade; one of her dance instructors has been teaching at Interlochen for twenty-seven years.

The National High School Institute

Just two years after the founding of the music camp at Interlochen, two professors at Northwestern University established a program for able secondary students on their campus. Professor Floyd Arpan of the School of Journalism and Dean Ralph Dennis of the School of Speech conceived of a program that would "bring together gifted young people and superior teachers in an atmosphere of affection, knowledge, and trust."*

Each successive summer finds a new group of "Cherubs" on Northwestern's campus. The original goal is achieved again and again as superior students and teachers work together in six separate divisions: music, radio/television/film, theater arts, engineering science, forensics, and journalism.

Like those at Interlochen, students and teachers at the National High School Institute work hard. Classes begin at 8:00 A.M. and extend to as late as 10:00 P.M. And forget about five-day weeks! With so much to learn, it's six full days of work and study for five weeks. The high-school students are, after all, doing college-level work.

---

*D. Zarefsky, "Cherubs They Ain't" (address reprinted in *Cherubics*, newsletter of the National High School Institute, 1982).

Allison Good is general administrator of the institute. Each division has its own coordinator who designs the program, selects the staff, and enjoys a great deal of autonomy. The ratio of students to faculty is low, and only the finest instructors are considered. The theater arts faculty, for example, includes professional performers, designers, artists, and directors from theaters and universities throughout the country and from the major training schools in the United States and Canada: Carnegie-Mellon and Yale, the Guthrie Theatre of Minneapolis, the Court Theatre of Chicago, Julliard, North Carolina School of the Arts, and other major institutions.

Like Interlochen, the National High School Institute pays modest salaries. And yet more than 100 applicants competed for the thirty-one faculty associate positions in 1983.

Superior teachers and the reputation of Northwestern University attract gifted students. Applicants must have completed their junior year, rank in the top quarter of their high-school class, and meet a high standard of character, dependability, and intelligence. They must submit evidence of special ability or interest in their chosen field of study. Craig Kinzer, a former Cherub back now as a teacher, says of the 1983 Cherubs, "They are unusually bright. They have a hunger for knowledge like I've never seen before."

Students live in university residence halls supervised by experienced counselors. Many of the faculty members also live in the dormitories, and this practice enhances the camaraderie—the atmosphere of affection, knowledge, and trust.

Governor's Schools

Governor's Honors Programs or Governor's Schools began in North Carolina in the sixties. These summer programs are for high-ability students within the state, are typically state-funded, and enjoy the endorsement of the state's chief executive.

The Governor's School in Winston-Salem was a joint project of Governor Terry Sanford and novelist John Ehle initiated in the early sixties. Together they dreamed of a program that would bring together 400 rising high-school seniors on a college campus to work and study for eight weeks: "We wanted them to go back into the local schools and be dissatisfied. They were to come together, learn, and share experiences. They were to be chosen because of their special ability in some field, among them

natural science, mathematics, foreign languages, dance, voice, acting, instrumental music, and visual arts."*

Sanford had no state funds to support the project, so he and Ehle secured a $225,000 grant from the Carnegie Foundation and an equal amount
from other foundations and corporations. The $450,000 supported the
school for the first three years. At that time, it cost approximately $150,000
for each eight-week term with an enrollment of 400 students.

North Carolina now has two Governor's Schools, at St. Andrews Presbyterian College in Laurinburg and at Salem College in Winston-Salem.
Each has 400 students, but the term has been reduced to six weeks. At least
ten states conduct Governor's Programs during the summer, all modeled
more or less on North Carolina's.

Talent Searches

One of the most exciting recent developments in education of gifted learners is the systematic search for high academic aptitude among the nation's
young adolescents. It began at Johns Hopkins University in 1972 with a
search among seventh graders and twelve-year-olds for outstanding mathematical reasoning ability. With funding from the Spencer Foundation and
guided by the vision and energy of Julian Stanley, the Study of Mathematically Precocious Youth at Johns Hopkins became a movement that is
now, some twelve years later, a coordinated national (not federal) effort.

Four university centers—Johns Hopkins University, Duke University,
the University of Denver, and Northwestern University—conduct simul-
taneous searches in separate geographic areas that cover all fifty states and
most of the provinces of Canada. A talent search conducted at Arizona
State University from 1981 to 1984 has since been moved to Johns Hopkins.
Seventh and eighth graders are invited to take the Scholastic Aptitude Test
offered by the Educational Testing Service primarily for college-bound juniors and seniors. The scores of the twelve-year-olds are sent to the separate
talent search centers, and those who score exceptionally well are identified
as capable of doing accelerated academic work, often including work at the
college level.

---

*J. Ehle, "The Birth of Four Schools, the Death of One" (presentation to the Richardson
Conference, Dallas/Fort Worth, 1981).

A summer program of enriched academic work is associated with each of the talent searches. Students are provided with information about summer opportunities at other sites throughout the nation, but they frequently choose to attend the center that "discovered" them.

The first talent search at Duke was conducted in 1981. Robert Sawyer, director of the Talent Identification Program (TIP), refers to William Bevan as the godfather of TIP. Bevan, provost at Duke at the time TIP was developed, had worked with Julian Stanley when he began his search at Johns Hopkins, and his experience was important in starting the search at Duke. The search encompasses sixteen states, and approximately 20,000 seventh-grade students take the test. The numbers grow each year. Of the students who take the SAT, Sawyer says, roughly 40 percent score as high as or higher than the scores attained by college-bound seniors. Clearly, such high achievers can benefit from special educational opportunities. The summer programs are designed to meet part of that need.

The summer program at Duke provides courses for students identified in the talent search. Students may take either or both of two three-week sessions that offer courses in American history, chemistry, Latin, French, writing, and other academic subjects.

Duke University provides space for the talent search and facilities for the summer program as part of its commitment to young talent. "Duke has always been interested in bright people," Sawyer points out. "I think the basic reason is that our future as a nation may well depend upon how successful the Gifted Students Institute, this program, the one at Northwestern, and others are in identifying these kids and making sure that they get through those critical years."* Sawyer sees all of the summer programs as contributing to the need these youngsters have to see their abilities recognized and provided for. Frequently students participate in a variety of summer educational opportunities over a period of several years.

Erin is a case in point. She attended a session cosponsored by the Gifted Students Institute and Texas Christian University several years ago. The following year Erin attended a program sponsored by GSI and the University of Dallas. The next year found her back with GSI on a study tour of England. Then Sawyer discovered her. She attended the summer program at Duke and became an early-entrance freshman at the age of sixteen. The following year she served as a teaching assistant at Duke's summer pro-

---

* R. Sawyer, personal communication, 1983.

gram. Erin treats her acceleration casually. "I don't feel I missed anything. My roommates usually don't know how old I am unless I tell them. I fit in fine. I'm comfortable."

Joyce VanTassel-Baska, director of the Midwest Talent Search, credits Northwestern for much of the success of the summer program associated with the talent search. Northwestern's fine reputation for work with pre-college students, built in part by fifty years of the Cherubs program, is well earned. The university makes its facilities available for both the talent search and the associated summer program, just as it does for the National High School Institute. The college-level courses include precalculus mathematics, introduction to geology, chemistry, Latin I and II, writing skills, literary analysis, and American history.

Students in this program for academically precocious youth generally take their studies at Northwestern very seriously. Although most of them are only twelve to fourteen years old, they pay close attention to keep up with the fast-paced courses. They are still children, however. We observed a shoeless, blond, curly haired eleven-year-old in his soccer T-shirt finding it hard to sit still very long in his math class. Students in math work individually at their own pace. This youngster wanted and got a good share of the instructor's attention.

Students in the expository writing class do a great deal of group work. Getting a head start on compositions they will have to write in high school and college, they write twice daily. And then they sit together in groups, reading, criticizing, editing. In literary analysis, students learn to go beyond book reports to more thoughtful literary judgments. One youngster comments seriously about his novel, "I've never had a book affect me like this!"

The Center for the Advancement of Academically Talented Youth at Johns Hopkins University offers two three-week summer residential programs at the Dickinson College campus in Carlisle, Pennsylvania, and two at Franklin and Marshall College in Lancaster, Pennsylvania. Students who qualify through the Office of Talent Identification and Development may take one session or two, at one campus or both. Courses include some fourteen academic subjects in science, language, literature, and math.

The Rocky Mountain Talent Search offers a three-week summer institute for Talent Search participants at the University of Denver. Course offerings include creative writing, geography, and future studies, as well as more traditional academic subjects. If students who have attended these sessions

are asked to write on "How I Spent My Summer Vacation" when they return to school in the fall, they may astonish their classmates and teachers.
But perhaps not. Thousands of today's youth are choosing to spend part of
their summer vacations on college campuses "hitting the books."

Conclusion

A look back over the schools and summer programs mentioned here carries us over a long half-century. It reaches into many corners of the country. It covers a wide range of activities, from students graphing mathematical functions or parsing Latin sentences to student and faculty artists performing for each other.

We were particularly struck that each program we visited grew from the
distinct and personal vision of a single educator or small group who brought
together prople and resources to realize a dream of learning and achievement. The spirit of Joseph Maddy lives on at Interlochen. The mission of
Floyd Arpan and Ralph Dennis is reenacted each summer at Northwestern. An idea first pushed to realization by Terry Sanford and John Ehle is
carried on not only in North Carolina but in other states under the urging
of other governors. Julian Stanley's perception of the serious potential of a
few precocious youngsters has expanded to a national program identifying
and serving academically talented students in every part of the country.

We were aware as well that the students and their teachers are giving
their summers to an effort whose value is intangible. Parents often send
their children at considerable expense, trusting that the investment in love
and attention will result somehow in fulfillment and a better life. The
teachers and administrators contribute a level of intensity and intelligence
no money can buy. They do it because they have given their lives to an art,
a discipline, a form of exchange—discourse, if you will—that can only be
practiced under these special conditions.

Our national system of education has been examined under intense,
often harsh light in recent years. In particular, 1983 was a year of sustained
critique, as one report after another pointed to the flaws in the system,
expressing dissatisfaction with the achievements of students and teachers.
Certain strains come through these reports with noticeable persistence: we
need more effort from our students, stiffer grading standards, more homework; we must confer status on education by whatever means it takes—a

better reward system, more attractive teaching conditions—so as to enlist competent teachers with genuine dedication.

In summer programming for able students, excellence is already present and thriving. Youngsters at the Governor's Schools don't complain about lengthening their school year. Their teachers need not protest that they waste precious time in irrelevant paper-pushing and distracting disciplinary actions. These students and teachers are in it for the joy. The conditions are ideal for learning.

Time and again we listened as directors told us they were sure we would find theirs the best of all the summer programs. There was no braggadocio in their comments. They had selected a superior staff, the students were talented and eager, and all of them worked toward a common goal. Consequently, they believed in what they were doing and spoke confidently. Every director discovers that a special bond develops among students and staff. Every time it happens, faculty and students feel they are participating in a learning and sharing experience that is unique.

We are again reminded of those teachers under the lights, reading the poetry of Edith Sitwell to the accompaniment of a faculty chamber group before an audience of students. These are true mentors, modeling not so much particular skills or ideas or staging techniques, but a way of living and being. By this and a hundred other activities, thousands of young lives are being changed. The students will return in other years to meet with different teachers and students in new combinations. When they are ready to move on to higher education and eventually to independent discovery and creation, they will be well prepared. For these students will have experienced, at a crucial moment, the meaning and the thrill of the life of the mind. They will never be the same.

Recommendations

▶ Determine the geographic area to be served, whether the local region for day programs or state or national coverage for residential programs.

▶ Locate the population to be served by surveying students, school educators, parents, business and industry professionals.

▶ Consider competing summer programs in the same region.

▶ Determine the availability of special resources and personnel in both the educational and larger communities.

▶ Select staff with unusual care. The intensity of most summer programs puts a premium on the commitment and flexibility of the staff. Find experts wherever they are: colleges and universities, public school districts, business and industry.

▶ Select students on criteria appropriate to the content of the program, e.g., auditions for music or dramatic performance, achievement scores and teacher recommendations for accelerated academic subjects. Age and grade level will be determined by the program.

▶ Combine a teacher-education component with the student session when practicable. Summer programs offer excellent opportunities for educational experimentation and staff development.

▶ Make use of existing facilities and equipment. Often a program can be tailored to capitalize on available specialized facilities. Some colleges will contribute facilities or reduce their regular fees.

▶ Determine whether grades are to be given. For summer enrichment programs, grades may not be appropriate. Teachers may provide a narrative assessment instead.

▶ Survey students, faculty, and parents to determine their perceptions of the program's effectiveness. Follow-up assessments, particularly after some time has elapsed, are informative.

▶ Recognize that personal adjustment to a residential situation looms large. Homesickness is inevitable. The unfamiliar setting presents both opportunity and danger. The balance between freedom and supervision is delicate.

Resources

Persons interested in more information about the Governor's Programs should call their state education agency, their high-school principal, or their high-school guidance counselor.

For information about the Talent Search programs, write or call:

Rocky Mountain Talent Search	The Johns Hopkins University
School of Education	Center for the Advancement of
University of Denver	Academically Talented Youth
Denver, Colorado 80208	305 Latrobe Hall
Telephone: 303–753–2982	Baltimore, Maryland 21218
	Telephone: 301–338–8427

Midwest Talent Search Project
School of Education
Northwestern University
2003 Sheridan Road
Evanston, Illinois 60201
Telephone: 312–492–3782

Talent Identification Program
Duke University
01 West Duke Building
Durham, North Carolina 27708
Telephone: 919–684–3847

For information about the other programs discussed in this section, write or call:

National High School Institute
Northwestern University
1881 Sheridan Road
Evanston, Illinois 60201
Telephone: 312–492–3026

National Music Camp
Interlochen Center for the Arts
Interlochen, Michigan 49643
Telephone: 616–276–9221

Gifted Students Institute for
   Research and Development
3320 West Cantey
P.O. Box 11388
Fort Worth, Texas 76109
Telephone: 817–926–2461

SPECIALIZED SCHOOLS

Disenchantment with the nation's schools appears widespread. Many parents have given up. Students seem to lack motivation. Discipline has eroded. Teachers are thought to be ineffective, and those who are good are too busy policing corridors to concentrate on instruction. In recent years a number of national agencies and knowledgeable educators have put our schools under a microscope, trying to uncover the secret of excellence in education because they feel our future is at risk. Conclusions of these national studies are summarized briefly in our introductory section.

But the malaise is not universal, nor is it inevitable. In Ames, Iowa, at Project Pegasus; in Houston, Texas, at the Oaks Academy; and at Windsor Park Elementary School in Corpus Christi, Texas, parents are actively involved in their children's education. They visit regularly, conduct special activities for the children, and may even serve as volunteer teacher aides. At Houston's High School for the Performing and Visual Arts and at Cincinnati's School for the Creative and Performing Arts students stay for hours after school, and they return on weekends. At the Bronx High School of Science students have their laboratory period scheduled before or after their lunch period so that they can work straight through if they want to. Two of North Carolina's public secondary schools are residential; the school day is extended almost around the clock. At Cincinnati's Walnut Hills High School no one complains that all students are required to take three years of Latin.

Each of these schools is a specialized school for students of high ability. They all have selective admissions based on specific criteria. All have an element of self-selection, for the students or the parents choose this school over others available. Each of these schools is unique because each has a special purpose. From the laboratory school for three- and four-year-olds at Iowa State University, which studies gifted children and prepares teachers of the gifted, to the North Carolina School for the Arts, where the goal is to train professional performing artists, every one of these schools fulfills a specialized role.

Yet these specialized schools have common features, similar ways of fulfilling their special roles. All offer their students an intellectual or artistic peer group; each offers a curriculum tailored to the needs of the students selected and the special purpose of the school; every one offers more rapid pacing than is possible with a more heterogeneous group of students.

We have chosen the schools covered here for illustrative purposes. We will examine them in some detail, giving special attention to some of the philosophical concerns, problems, and benefits any community should consider if it plans to open a specialized school. We have been stringently selective in our coverage, as will be apparent to those who discover we have overlooked their favorite schools. For up-to-date information about other specialized public and private schools for the gifted, we suggest that the reader consult state education agencies and state associations for the gifted.

Project Pegasus

In Ames, Iowa, parents who want their children accepted by Project Pegasus must agree to participate in school activities. Instead of dropping them off at the door of the school, mothers and fathers come into the classroom with the children. They stay for a few minutes while the youngsters hang up coats and hats and review the activity choices selected by the children the previous day. This is a safety measure, according to Dianne Draper, director of the project, but it also smooths the transition from home to school. And it is an easy way for parents to keep in touch with their child's world away from home. Parents also participate in monthly meetings.

It is as a learning resource, however, that parents make the most exciting contribution to the project. A questionnaire invites parents to list ways they can contribute to the program: "Do you have a special skill that you can teach us? Are you a collector? Would you be willing to set up a temporary exhibit of your collection? Are you a musician? Would you be willing to provide music, live or on tape, for a study of instruments and music?"

The students in Pegasus are of an interesting ethnic mix. Partly because Ames is a university town, the children's parents may come from Greece, Nigeria, or Turkey. The head teacher, Marian Scott, explains that one year the school had a child whose father was Chinese-American: "The morning he came to school, we put out the map of China. He did some wok cooking and showed them character writing. This exposure to different countries doesn't happen much in other schools. Once when we were talking about the Netherlands, Scott's dad came in and told us about Dutch farms, and he played his accordion for the children. They loved that."

A program for gifted and talented preschoolers, Project Pegasus is sponsored by the Department of Education of Iowa State University as a part of its laboratory school. Only twenty three- and four-year-old youngsters—ten boys and ten girls—are accepted each year from the seventy-five to eighty who apply. Selection of the students for Project Pegasus is based on test results from the Stanford-Binet Testing Scale, the Peabody Individual Achievement Test, and the Starkweather (for creativity).

The even mix of sexes in the group selected does not precisely reflect the ratio of students who are nominated or apply for the program. As might be expected, more boys are nominated than girls (this phenomenon is discussed in the section "Discovering and Nurturing Talent"). The top girls score as high as the top boys on the selection tests, but among high-scoring children the boys outnumber the girls about five to two. Draper is unable to account for the difference in scores. She expresses concern that some parents don't want to nurture their daughters' talents, fearing that to do so would handicap them socially.

The educational goals of Project Pegasus are based to some extent on Renzulli's Enrichment Triad model, incorporating exposure to a wide range of intellectual activities, training in appropriate learning skills, and developing independent study projects (Renzulli, 1977). Specific objectives

of the learning activities are thinking and reasoning skills, task commitment, curiosity, creativity, social awareness, physical/motor abilities, and
the enhancement of individual talents. "We want to work with the cognitive development," Draper explains, "but we are also concerned about
social development, motor development. We want them to go outside and
exercise those muscles. Their emotional concerns and feelings are important as well, and that's part of how we organize our entire morning."

Draper believes that children learn best through play. To achieve a play-
like atmosphere the school has blocks, sand tables, and a water table. Some
visitors wonder why there are not more books, worksheets, and other academic trappings. But Draper points out that a good deal of learning goes
on when children use toys: "Look at this block construction. There's the
Sears Tower in Chicago, and look at the power lines the children have created. See the solar generator over there in the corner? This child has assumed the role of a lawyer working in the building; that child has become
an airline pilot flying over." There are books, of course: encyclopedias—
Childcraft, for example—dictionaries, and a variety of children's books.
"Once in a while," says Scott, "we will put out several books by one author. We do lots of talking about authors and do illustrations based on
their books."

Although there is no direct reading instruction, the children learn to
read anyway. They learn the book titles; they learn how to look things up
with adult help as needed. The typewriter and computer also teach reading
indirectly. All children have access to the typewriter and copy words from
teacher-made cards. They learn their letters this way, if they don't already
know them, and they become comfortable with the keyboard. Every child
receives some instruction on the computer, varied according to the child's
interest and abilities. The children are exposed to games, problem solving,
maps, and educational computer programs. And as time permits, the children learn elementary computer programming.

Math, too, is taught indirectly. For example, at the snack table, where
juice and crackers are set up for children, a daily menu above the table lists
the refreshments and the portions to which they may help themselves:
"CRACKERS [with drawing] $1+1+1+1+1=5$. JUICE [with drawing of
two half-filled glasses] two ½ glasses." Each day as the children serve
themselves and perhaps a friend or two, they read the day's menu, learn
some simple arithmetic, and develop independence and social awareness.

The Oaks Academy

At the Oaks Academy in Houston, Texas, kindergarten students write their own books from time to time. "Once there was a man named Aquaman. He lived in the ocean. One day he saw a oktopoose. He made frens with it." The teachers leave paper out on a table. The students can work together or work alone. For those who can't guess the spellings of words they want, the teacher takes dictation.

The Oaks Academy is an independent school for gifted children. It began small but has grown fast. From an enrollment of 13 in 1980 it had grown, by 1984, to 150 students from the age of three through the sixth grade. The goal of the founder, Lila Macaluso, is to add a grade each year until there is a complete preschool, elementary, and secondary educational program.

Macaluso also envisions a training center for teachers, with the school serving as a laboratory. She has a public school background, and her frequent consulting work with public schools throughout the state confirms her commitment to the public school system. Macaluso is convinced, however, that there is a need for alternatives like the Oaks Academy. Some gifted children fare well in public school settings. Others suffer boredom and loss of self-esteem. In a heterogeneous classroom their peers sometimes think they are weird. They may even think themselves weird. Macaluso talks about children who literally weep with joy at being surrounded with bright children more like themselves.

The screening to be accepted at the Oaks Academy is thorough. Two psychologists test each applicant, one administering an I.Q. test, the other giving a development or achievement test. If the child is of school age, a questionnaire is given to the sending school requesting additional information. And parents share in the process. If it is a two-parent family, both parents are expected to make appointments, which can be arranged at 7:00 A.M. or at 7:00 P.M. if necessary.

In the beginning many applicants were screened out and reluctantly turned away. The children did not fit the profile Macaluso was seeking. Now, thanks to local, state, and national publicity and word-of-mouth, more families understand that this is not just a private school but one with a special mission—serving gifted children.

Curriculum Director Diane Busche describes curriculum development at the Oaks as ongoing and eclectic. She and the teachers use the basal readers for skill development, but they draw from a variety of sources for what she describes as a "literature-based language experience program." She explains that a "language experience" approach without literature is limited to the vocabulary the children already have. "They need an infusion of literary language to help expand that vocabulary." The Junior Great Books Program in grades 2 through 6 taps the skills of volunteer parents as well as teachers and aides. As is recommended by the Great Books Foundation, pairs of specially trained leaders conduct the student discussions.

Spanish instruction begins in the preschool. The goal of the foreign language instruction is to acquaint students with a number of languages rather than to make them proficient in any one. Latin and French are included; occasionally an aide proficient in German and Russian adds to the foreign language offerings with lessons in those languages.

The new math is alive and well at the Oaks Academy, where they use the Comprehensive School Mathematics Program developed originally by Central Midwestern Regional Educational Laboratory in St. Louis in the 1960s. Busche says the children acquire a good understanding of fairly advanced mathematical concepts as early as kindergarten or first grade. Macaluso agrees that the program is especially appropriate for gifted youngsters. "It's not memorization, regurgitation. Those kids understand division and multiplication." At the upper levels the school backs up the new math with a more traditional approach to mathematics.

Like Project Pegasus in Ames, the Oaks Academy requires parents to participate actively in the school program. Macaluso thinks the ability to require parental participation is one advantage private education affords that public education doesn't. "The admission interview includes questions about what the parents' commitment is to their children's education. They can't expect us to do the whole job while the child is here from 8:00 A.M. until 3:00 P.M. We need to know what they are going to give, what they are already excited about that they can share."

The students, too, learn to share their talents for the benefit of all. Lee, a mature fifth grader, presented a lesson to third, fourth, and fifth graders on the day we visited. Like good teachers everywhere, she was well prepared, knew exactly what her objectives were, and had planned the activities she would use to achieve them.

Macaluso says that visitors to the school frequently want her to come help them start a similar school. "The plea is always 'Come help me get started.' But this isn't franchisable. My response is 'You can do it, too. It's not the building, it's the people. Find the right group of people with commitment to learn. Then grow.'"

Windsor Park Elementary School

In 1976 the Corpus Christi Independent School District converted the Windsor Park Elementary School into a school for the district's academically talented students for grades 1 through 6. Students were nominated by parents, teachers, and principals from both public and private schools in kindergarten through fifth grade. The screening procedures included achievement tests, a quick-scoring vocabulary test, and the Raven Progressive Matrices. Approximately 5 percent of the Mexican-Americans, blacks, and Anglo-Americans were accepted for each elementary grade level.

Ginger Harris, current principal of Windsor Park, insists that it is not and never was a school for geniuses. Laura Allard, who was the first principal, agrees, but likes to tell a story about one of the early students:

> The first day of the new school term a first-grade boy walked into my office, identified himself as Joseph, and asked, "Do you want to know how wide and long your office is in centimeters?" I said, "Why, of course I want to know." After a few moments of silence while piercing brown eyes traversed the length and width of the room, the small voice said, "It's 394 centimeters wide and 485 centimeters long." We got out a meter stick and discovered, to my astonishment, his estimate was correct. It was apparent that Joseph had unusual mathematics potential.

The Corpus Christi district has a continuum of skills in all content areas. Windsor Park students move up the continuum as they achieve mastery. Students are grouped and regrouped for instruction as necessary. It is an ongoing process, according to Harris. Joseph, for example, while still in the first grade worked successfully with the highest skill-level group in the sixth grade. Although some of his numbers were printed upside down, even backwards, the sixth graders did not scoff. He understood the mathematical concepts, and his answers were correct. Allard recalls, "He was clearly their intellectual peer. Yet he never played with the sixth graders on the playground because his intelligence told him he would be their football!"

In addition to the basics required by the district and by the state, students study Spanish daily at every grade level. Violin instruction is available to all interested sixth graders without cost to the parents. If space is available after interested sixth graders are accommodated, other students, beginning with the fifth grade, are invited to participate.

Each Friday two hours are devoted to special enrichment activities. These "Fabulous Fridays" include two kinds of enrichment activities. During one hour, the activities are an extension of the classroom; students study such subjects as marine biology, microbiology, and aeronautics. During the other hour students learn lifetime skills—from hobbies like stamp collecting and calligraphy to sports such as tennis. During a single year as many as 130 specialists and speakers volunteer their time for such activities. They are school personnel, parents, and other community leaders—the president of the chamber of commerce, the director of the Corpus Christi museum, well-known artists, poets, actors, lawyers, and farmers.

The school has an enviable staff. The pupil/teacher ratio is the same as in other district schools, and they have a principal and an assistant principal. The school also has a resource teacher, a counselor, a media specialist, two enrichment teachers, and three aides—all full time, their salaries paid by the state's special fund for gifted programs.

When Windsor Park was envisioned, the administration and the board deliberately chose one of the district's older buildings to avoid jealousy. Although old, the school has been well maintained. It is colorful and houses excellent equipment and materials. There are two enrichment centers and two libraries. "A good thing," says Harris. "These students read more books and consume more materials than students in any other school in the district."

Windsor Park is not inexpensive. Thirteen buses provide service to any qualified student who lives two miles or more from the school. The money for personnel, transportation, and special supplies is well spent, however. The children at Windsor Park develop greater self-esteem and independence, the principal believes, than they would in regular schools.

Walnut Hills High School

Since 1919 Walnut Hills High School (WHHS) in Cincinnati has functioned as a college preparatory school for academically talented students in grades 7 through 12. The nation's second oldest school of its type (only the Boston Latin School preceded it), Walnut Hills aims to offer a public-school education comparable to the best preparatory schools in the East.

"Today, it still provides one of the broadest programs of classical studies in the Midwest, requiring three years of Latin and a course in ancient and medieval history of all students," says Ward Ghory, the school's assistant principal.

Community interest in the school runs high. While district enrollment has declined, enrollment at WHHS has increased. With 2,550 students, it is the largest school in the Greater Cincinnati region. The success of the school can be attributed to the innovative faculty, the fine classical program, a strong parent group, and the chemistry of the student body itself. Like other magnet schools, WHHS attracts students from all ethnic, religious, and economic segments of the community. The common bond is their intellectual ability and their interest in pursuing a classical education. This is not fairyland; the students' diverse backgrounds present some problems, and there have been racial tensions over the years. But the educational and social benefits of sharing and learning are enormous, and in general the students appreciate their opportunity.

Identifying students for Walnut Hills is a two-step process. To get into the school, a student must successfully complete an admissions test and demonstrate above-average academic ability. Those who don't succeed at first may try again a second or third time. To take advantage of the school's strong emphasis on honors and advanced work, a student must meet more stringent requirements. The faculty looks at tested aptitudes, grades, and teacher recommendations. Students who clearly qualify enter the advanced classes; those who clearly don't qualify go into the regular classes. When the students' qualifications are marginal, the faculty prefers to risk allowing them to enroll in the advanced classes, depending on program availability, with appropriate backup procedures if they don't succeed.

Ghory explains how the second step of the identification procedure helps in integrating the diverse student body, "some of whom come from very polished, private-school backgrounds and some from very rough, inner-city kinds of backgrounds." The seventh grade offers the students an opportunity to find classes appropriate to their levels of ability. A few, roughly 6 percent, go into advanced classes. As the students adjust to the school's challenging instructional program, a larger number, approximately 20 percent, go into the eighth- and ninth-grade honors classes. By the tenth grade, approximately 35 percent of the students qualify for the advanced academic programs, and at the eleventh and twelfth grades approximately 40 percent of the students enroll in the Advanced Placement classes. And so each year a larger and larger number of students qualify for advanced classes, in part because the faculty orchestrates student progress.

School for Creative and Performing Arts

In another part of Cincinnati, housed in a bustling seventy-two-year-old building, with students spilling out of classrooms into the halls for some practice sessions, is the School for Creative and Performing Arts (SCPA), an elementary/secondary school that includes grades 4 through 12. This school takes a different approach to identification from that of its sister Walnut Hills School.

Students throughout the city compete for admission through auditions. Demonstrated ability in one or more of the arts, not intellectual ability, opens the door to this lively learning place. Indeed, some learning-disabled students enrolled in special academic classes at SCPA participate in the arts programs. Danny, for example, whose learning disabilities keep him in slow-paced academic classes, loves to dance. An average ballet student, he finds his place to shine in the top modern dance class.

Consideration of the Dannys of the world may help us see how the arts can enrich their school years and their adult years as well. The learning-disabled seventh grader in the average school may well suffer from low self-esteem when all school tasks are difficult for him. Imagine how that self-esteem can soar when he discovers he has a special talent valued by people the world over. No longer just a boy in the "slow" classes, he is a dancer!

A question sometimes raised about specialized schools has to do with motivation. Proponents of specialization claim that allowing students to concentrate their time and energy in their major areas of interest will encourage them to keep up their other academic work. Indeed, they claim that the specialized schools can save students who would otherwise find school alien to their interests. A visit to SCPA will convince any doubting Thomases. Aspiring young artists find here the motivation to complete their high-school education when many would not do so otherwise. Moreover, students put in a seven-hour day instead of the six-hour days most Cincinnati and suburban students enjoy.

The figures document a record of success. Keep in mind that these students are selected not on the basis of their intellectual ability, but because of their artistic talents. Even allowing that students who excel in the arts often rank high in other intellectual abilities, it is striking that 85 percent of SCPA's graduates have enrolled in sixty-four different colleges and universities. More than 45 percent of all SCPA graduates have been awarded college scholarships.

Although the SCPA offers an array of forty-eight courses in the arts, including the general categories of visual arts, creative writing, ballet, modern dance, drama, and music, the school's philosophy speaks directly to the issue of early specialization—that is, allowing students to zero in on a specific career interest at an early age. The academic areas receive equal attention with the arts. In 1981, 69 percent of SCPA's college-bound graduates enrolled in the arts. The other 31 percent majored in a wide range of liberal arts and preprofessional fields: engineering, premedicine, architecture, computer science, and the like.

Chris, a remarkably poised junior, aspires to a career in the arts; she takes both voice and dance, but she also takes a solid college preparatory program. She is not closing any doors at this stage of her life. Chris plans to enter prelaw in college. Her artistic talents and education will lead her to a lifetime appreciation of the arts if not to a career.

High School for the Performing and Visual Arts

Houston's High School for the Performing and Visual Arts (HSPVA) boasts a similar record of academic success for its arts students. Although the 600 students for this Houston school, in grades 9 through 12, are selected by audition and interview on the basis of their artistic rather than their intellectual ability, their academic course work is not neglected. If they choose to pursue a career in the arts, they will have the required basic skills to enter a college or professional training program. Should they decide to pursue other interests, they will have the academic background to do so. Norma Lowder, principal of HSPVA, has a ready answer for those who fear that schools like HSPVA encourage students to select and prepare for careers at too young an age: "There is no harm in opening a door for students if you don't close others."

The school ranks at the very top of the high schools in the district in standardized tests of verbal achievement and second or third from the top in mathematical achievement. Lowder says, "We frequently have as many National Merit and Achievement Finalists as we have finalists in the national Arts Recognition and Talent Search."

Like the faculty at Cincinnati's School for Creative and Performing Arts, Lowder cites motivation as the reason for the high academic achievement of the students. She says that HSPVA saves many students from becoming dropouts. They enroll at HSPVA because they love the arts, but they know they must do well academically to be allowed to perform. "Not to perform at HSPVA is a fate worse than death," she says.

Highly motivated students present few discipline problems. "Basically, we have no discipline problems and no suspensions at HSPVA," says Lowder. "We have no policemen in the halls, as you often see in other big-city schools." The students come from every racial, social, and economic background; yet there has never been a student fight. Quite an accomplishment in an urban center where racial unrest is well known.

What about the special facilities required for a specialized arts school? HSPVA recently moved into a new facility specially built for it. Instead of a gymnasium there are two ballet practice rooms equipped with barres, not basketball hoops. Instead of an auditorium the school has a theater, complete with box office. The lobby of the theater doubles as a lunchroom. Eleven music practice rooms, two art galleries. Impressive! But it was not always so at HSPVA. Just a few years back the students here were practicing in the halls just as the students do in Cincinnati. "The facilities enhance the program," says Lowder, "but we had an excellent program before we had this marvelous building."

Even more striking than the remarkable facilities is the commitment to excellence on the part of the young people and their dedicated faculty. A visitor to HSPVA can feel the excitement and the sense of purpose. Every student and all the teachers are there because they want to be. There are always more students eager for the opportunity to attend than there are openings for them. Those chosen know it is a privilege to attend. The faculty enjoy their work—a rare phenomenon in high schools these days.

Students and teachers everywhere must wish they could learn and work in an atmosphere like that at HSPVA, but one of the conditions that enables the school to bring together talented students from the entire city is the size of the city itself. There is a large talent pool from which to draw, and neighborhood schools are not likely to suffer because a relatively small number of students is taken from any one school.

Bronx High School of Science

The Bronx High School of Science (BHSS), one of the nation's best-known specialized schools, also draws students from the ample pool of a major urban center. There need be no concern about raiding talent from other schools.

The objectives of BHSS are to identify students who are gifted and well motivated in science and to develop these students to the point where they can carry through an original, creative, independent piece of scientific research. Students are screened for admission to BHSS by means of an entrance exam that has both verbal and mathematics segments. Standards are high.

An interesting feature of the program, however, makes the admissions and selection process adaptable to other high schools with less selective entrance requirements. It uses the ninth-grade year as a screen for the following years. All incoming ninth-year students participate in the model science program. From this pool of approximately 700 students a group of 100 students is selected to continue in the special research honors classes.

BHSS pays particular attention to teacher evaluation of students and the possibility of identifying an underachiever as a potentially gifted student who, with the right opportunity, could develop into a truly creative individual. Thus the selection process identifies students with high achievement and aptitude in science and mathematics who have demonstrated their ability in classroom and laboratory, both by examination and under direct observation.

Tenth-grade students learn by the Socratic method, with emphasis on recognizing problems and setting up hypotheses. Students who succeed in the tenth year and progress to the eleventh conduct their own research under the guidance of an individual teacher or a team of teachers.

Every student in the research honors program prepares an original research project to be submitted to the school's Science Congress, to the New York Biology Teachers Congress, to the Science Fair, and to the Westinghouse Science Talent Search. The best of the papers are published in the *Journal of Biology*, a student publication that highlights much of the creative work arising from the program. This kind of visibility, highlighting excellence in education, is important to the reputation of the school. It is important to students as well and helps them gain admission to the most competitive and rigorous colleges and universities.

The Bronx High School of Science demonstrates the wise use of community resources. The school provides opportunities for its students to work with researchers in industrial, medical, and university laboratories. The faculty has found research scientists willing to help students who have specific problems to solve, and thus mentor relationships develop in the most natural way. The researchers are often pleased and surprised by the knowledge, interest, and ability of the students.

North Carolina School of Science and Mathematics

In an article for the *New York Times* (October 12, 1980) Gene I. Maeroff wrote, "Imagine the Bronx High School of Science, New York's prestigious school for the mathematically gifted, opening its doors to selected students from across the state, providing them with dormitory space and charging no room, board, or tuition." Maeroff went on to say that the North Carolina School of Science and Mathematics (NCSSM) does just that. Maeroff's lead is a tribute to the Bronx High School of Science, of course. It also expresses admiration for the experiment then getting under way in Durham.

Established in 1978 at the urging of Governor James B. Hunt, NCSSM opened in the fall of 1980 with 150 students in the eleventh grade. Now serving some 400 students, the school hopes to reach and maintain a student body of about 600 eleventh and twelfth graders. In part because of the population distribution of North Carolina, a rural state with only small cities, students come from all over the state to the Raleigh–Durham–Chapel Hill area, known as the Research Triangle, where the state's education and research resources are most heavily concentrated.

Admission to NCSSM is highly selective. According to Sarah Hamilton, dean for academic affairs, sixteen separate criteria are used to screen students, including standardized tests, personal recommendations, writing samples, and out-of-class participation in science fairs and other projects. Rexford Brown reported in the *State Education Leader* (Winter, 1983) that the class just admitted had median SAT scores of 520 (verbal) and 600 (mathematics), and he added, "Not bad scores for students early in the tenth grade."

The curriculum at NCSSM is weighted toward rich math and science offerings, as one might expect—microbiology, astrophysics, calculus, organic chemistry. But the curriculum includes good grounding in the humanities and meets all the graduation requirements of any other state high school.

Like the Bronx High School of Science, NCSSM has an active mentor program. By arrangement with many of the businesses, research organizations, and universities in the area, students get practical experience under the guidance of individuals away from the campus. Dean Hamilton attributes the success of the mentor program to the caliber of the students who are offered as interns. Moreover, the area itself offers an unusually rich educational environment. Says Hamilton, "In the Research Triangle area we have more people asking us for interns than we have available students."

The heart of the curriculum is not single courses or even particular projects, but a set of skills. The students develop their abilities in writing and speaking, analyzing, computing, synthesizing, evaluating. These skills will carry them through the most rigorous university disciplines and through their lives. The school offers great promise for the best young scientific minds of North Carolina.

Because it is a public school, NCSSM is free to residents of North Carolina. The cost of educating each student is estimated at $6,000, well above the average for other public schools. The state pays 90 percent of the operating costs and 75 percent of the construction costs. Debate surrounds the issue of spending state funds in such magnitude for a selected population. The argument originally used by Governor Hunt and still urged by advocates of the school is that the money invested in this way pays dividends to the state as well as to the students who benefit directly. The private sector has contributed significantly to the school—perhaps as much as $8 million.

Other benefits to the state are less easy to quantify but significant. The school sponsors summer institutes for North Carolina teachers where innovations in curriculum and teaching methods are developed. The school has created a "ripple effect" on other public schools by stimulating healthy competition, advances in science and mathematics instruction, and renewed attention to the most able learners throughout the state. Most directly, 70 percent of the first graduating class chose to attend North Carolina colleges and universities, and there is every reason to expect that the majority will develop careers within the state, thus returning the investment the state has made in their education.

North Carolina School of the Arts

Fifteen years before the North Carolina School of Science and Mathematics opened, the state founded its first residential school for gifted and talented young people, the North Carolina School of the Arts (NCSA). This school, too, was created with the leadership and support of the governor. Terry Sanford, then governor and now president of Duke University, turned to John Ehle, North Carolina novelist, and to other leading figures in the arts. As the idea of the school developed, they engaged composer Vittorio Giannini to shape the dream and to become the school's first president. Plans for the school attracted both praise and criticism. Detractors were fond of calling it "Terry's toe-dancing school" or "Terry's tippety-toe school," but the idea found support among leaders in politics, civic affairs, and the arts. The project was funded in part by a $1.5 million challenge grant from the Ford Foundation.

That the school was seen as a plum and welcomed as a step forward for culture and for the state was demonstrated when the citizens of Winston-Salem, competing to have their city chosen as the site for the school, raised a million dollars in private contributions by means of a telephone campaign. In 1965 the school opened its doors to its first 250 students in the Gray High School building in Winston-Salem.

Those who worked for its founding envisioned a school that would train talented young artists to be professional performers. The school does not apologize for its career focus nor does it claim to develop creativity. Samuel Stone, director of development for NCSA, points out, "We are not training choreographers or composers, painters, or playwrights. Nor do we concern ourselves with teacher training." The students, taught by professional performing artists, learn to be dancers, actors, or musicians. They may also learn set and costume design.

Admission to the school is by audition or portfolio, although the students must present proof of ability to pursue both arts and general studies. The faculty looks for students with more than talent. Says Stone, "Talent alone, in the experience of our faculty, is not an adequate predictor of success in a professional career. A student may demonstrate talent in audition but may lack perseverance—that capacity, for example, that dancers need, to live on cottage cheese for the rest of their lives."

In some respects the school functions more nearly as a professional production company than as a conventional school or college. Part of its mis-

North Carolina School of the Arts

sion is to provide a home and to develop an audience for the lively arts. Over 560 public performances each year include dance productions, drama, orchestra and chamber music concerts, opera, television productions, and a variety of workshops. The students and faculty offer cultural events of professional quality to audiences that last year totaled over 163,000.

NCSA is a residential high school, and it is a college, functioning as a part of the state university system. Currently enrolling over 700 students, NCSA includes an educational span from the seventh grade through college and including three years of graduate school.

In addition to their concentration in the arts, all high-school students must take the general studies curriculum. General studies includes English, mathematics, science, foreign language, and social studies. Predictably, the liberal arts courses are slanted toward the arts, and the same high standards are not required in these classes as in the arts. A student must earn A's and

B's in the arts classes to be invited back the next term, but a C in a general studies class is acceptable.

Even though the emphasis is clearly on the arts, most of the students do well academically. Some students change their minds, for one reason or another, about pursuing a career in the arts and go on to academic pursuits in excellent colleges. Many of the high-school graduates compete successfully for acceptance at colleges like MIT, Yale, and Sarah Lawrence. Various reasons can be cited to explain this success. Although the students are selected for their artistic talent, they tend to be bright youngsters who can do well in many areas. In addition, the arts themselves have an intrinsic educational value. They offer a perspective of value in approaching the liberal arts or social sciences. And the concentration and intensity cultivated in the pursuit of the arts help to develop a discipline and intellectual drive that carry over into more academic fields.

Conclusion

Specialized schools for students of high ability have much to recommend them. A district unable to afford sophisticated science equipment for all of its high schools might be able to install such equipment in one school for those students who have the interest, the ability, and the motivation to benefit from it most. Faculty artists might be too few in number to train the district's aspiring musicians, dancers, actors, and artists if the students are scattered throughout the district. Bringing the talented students and the skilled teachers together on a single campus might then enable a district to meet the students' needs. And as anyone knows who has worked with groups of gifted students, the students gain inspiration from one another.

A specialized school, however, must be very clear and firm about establishing its purpose at the outset. All that the school does, everything it provides, must contribute in some way to its mission, carefully defined.

How to screen students will present a challenge. Who will select the students and what criteria will be used? Consideration must be given to the weight that will be accorded such elements as standardized and criterion-referenced tests, grades, work samples, and teacher recommendations. For arts schools, auditions must be scheduled and judges chosen. Whether the school's focus is on arts or academic disciplines, a decision must be made about whether students who fail the entrance screening the first time may try again.

Many districts open magnet schools as one means of achieving racial integration. A district that designs a specialized school to serve able learners, with a secondary goal of achieving racial integration, must recognize the implications this secondary purpose will have for selection. To succeed in its specialized educational mission, the school must be open to all on the basis of interest and demonstrated ability. If a racial or ethnic balance is a condition of starting the school, however, planners may have to develop special means to discover capable students in every group (see the section "Discovering and Nurturing Talent").

A specialized school can expect a mixed reaction from its public. Some may charge that a secondary school, unless it gives equal attention to all college preparatory courses, encourages students to focus on a career interest too early. Another issue is the impact a specialized school has on other schools in the district or state. If one school attracts the brightest and most talented students, other schools may perceive its recruitment as a talent raid. Unless the population served is large, this objection could scuttle the noblest of plans.

Finally, those who fear that specialized schools foster elitism should give thoughtful attention to the models presented here. Students from every socioeconomic stratum attend the schools. Family income is not a factor. Nor is race. Indeed, the specialized school may be truly egalitarian in a sense the neighborhood school, which has other values to recommend it, can never be. Students come together on the basis of interest and ability rather than by the circumstance of where they live, which tends to reflect ethnic and economic grouping.

As we lament the lack of student motivation, the apparent commitment to mediocrity in our schools, and the failure of parents and community to take an active role in preparing and advancing tomorrow's ablest citizens, we may find some encouragement in specialized schools. These are not the only schools across the country that have maintained or restored enthusiasm and community involvement, but they have achieved striking success, for they offer the most dramatic instance of meeting the special needs of very able learners.

Recommendations

▶ Determine the rationale for establishing a school—why it is needed and what its primary focus will be.

▶ Survey the student population to be served. Determine whether it will be limited to the local district, several area districts, the state, or some geographic region.

▶ Determine a selection procedure. If special attention is to be given to minorities, be sure special means are developed to discover talent in all groups. Decide whether students will be selected solely on the basis of specific talent or whether consideration will be given to other areas such as general intellectual ability. Entry-level requirements may be somewhat lower than those for advancement to higher levels.

▶ Develop a transportation policy. Consider, for example, whether busing will be needed.

▶ Determine the source(s) of funding. If funding is public, will the school be funded partially or entirely by the state?

▶ Select a location and facilities. Determine whether this is to be a separate school, a school within a school, or a residential school.

▶ Recruit the finest faculty possible for both the specialized and general curriculum. An outstanding faculty is far more crucial than the facilities, as important as they are.

▶ Develop a specialized curriculum to support the special purpose. The curriculum should provide the fundamentals students will need if they wish to pursue their specialty in college or in a professional training program.

▶ Develop a general curriculum that will prepare students to pursue other college and career interests as they choose.

▶ Establish a grading policy. Decide whether students must achieve a certain grade level in order to continue. Will the same level of achievement be required in the general and the specialized curriculum?

▶ Attend to public relations implications so that student recruitment will not be perceived as a talent raid.

WHAT NEXT:

Toward Comprehensive

Programming

In "What Works Best" we examined a number of promising practices, methods of meeting the needs of able learners that we regard as exemplary. We avoided endorsing particular practices as the best because conditions vary from region to region, from school district to school district. In this section we make our recommendations about finding and cultivating intellectual talent in a variety of settings. Precisely because we cannot anticipate the available resources or public acceptance of educational reform in any given district, we can't know the right way for a district to proceed in programming for its students of high ability. We must inevitably speak in general terms.

Certain issues, however, will always be of concern to educators trying to weave diverse but sequential experiences for able learners into the total educational program. Discovering those youngsters who are born with the potential for unusual development in one or another intellectual domain is crucial. Developing an educational continuum and a means to move along that continuum so that each child can find adequate and appropriate challenge at every stage must be regarded as the essential labor of the school or district.

We conclude by recommending a comprehensive approach to programming that will bring together all the resources of a community to meet as wide a range of abilities as the resources will allow. We illustrate the comprehensive approach by imagining an ideal district and showing how such a district might go about its task to develop a programming array that will uncover, encourage, and develop the priceless talents of its most capable students.

DISCOVERING AND NURTURING TALENT

Probably no topic in educating the gifted has received more attention than identification. Yet educators hold widely different opinions about what giftedness is and how it should be identified.

The terminology itself poses problems. Some educators use *gifted* and *talented* synonymously. Others distinguish intellectual giftedness from artistic talent. A great many see talent and giftedness as a continuum, with giftedness at the upper end. Indeed, the terms seem to be used this way most often by nonspecialists. We speak of many talented writers, scientists, or musicians, for example, and the few who are truly gifted. No one reverses the terms, however. We don't say an artist is gifted but not really talented.

Identification has become more complex as the focus of attention has expanded from a primary concern with general intellectual talent to include additional types of ability mentioned in the Marland report: specific academic aptitude, creative and productive thinking, leadership, psychomotor ability, and aptitude for the visual and performing arts (Marland, 1972). Howard Gardner, arguing for a theory of multiple intelligences in his book *Frames of Mind*, presents a convincing case that individuals are capable of unusual, even prodigious development in any of seven discrete intelligences: linguistic, musical, logical-mathematical, spatial, bodily-kinesthetic, interpersonal, and intrapersonal (Gardner, 1983). Gardner's personal intelligences are related to another talent to which Getzels and Dillon referred ten years earlier: ". . . a talent not so much for doing something as for being something or for 'living' something. The conception here is manifestly humanistic, the reference being to those talents anciently thought virtuous: the talent to love, to understand, to empathize, to be compassionate, to be of service; the talent of coping, of surviving, of getting along with grace and authenticity" (Getzels and Dillon, 1973, p. 705). The authors point out that although talents of this sort are discernible and useful to society, they are omitted from traditional definitions of talent and overlooked by those developing educational objectives. The skills rarely have currency value in our educational marketplace, nor are they testable by available psychometric methods.

Joseph Renzulli's definition of giftedness, based on the characteristics of high achievers, suggests that we should consider creativity and task com-

Young Scientist at Work

mitment along with above-average intelligence when we describe or identify the gifted (Renzulli, 1978).

It is widely recognized that a single measure, such as an I.Q. test, provides limited and sometimes misleading information about a child's intellectual capacity and may not be useful at all in identifying artistic and other
kinds of abilities. We must recognize that not only are there many kinds of
abilities but that each spans a continuum. No natural break in the continuum separates gifted students from others in any one ability or in collective abilities.

The focus of the Richardson Study differs from many in that we emphasize serving able learners, a student population larger than the 3–5 percent often singled out for special programming on the basis of standardized tests and other traditional identification and selection devices. We deliberately avoid assigning a specific percentage to students we call able learners because the level at which special programming is needed will vary from one district to another. In addition, many students have special learning abilities in some areas and not in others. To identify a single group as *the* gifted is to misunderstand the diversity of intelligence.

Furthermore, setting a cutoff level, a line that separates gifted children from others, can have distressing effects on children and their parents. A child identified as "gifted" in one school moves to another where he is no longer gifted. Children remaining in the same school sometimes face a similar trauma. Parents are notified that their child has been identified as gifted and, with their permission, will be placed in a special program with other gifted youngsters. At the end of the year the child may be tested again and the parents informed that the child no longer tests in the gifted range. An urban psychologist volunteers that a significant part of her practice consists of such cases.

Let's consider a different scenario, in which we assess student abilities and use the results case by case as a basis for appropriate programming decisions. John tests high in mathematical skills. He is capable of functioning well above his grade level. The teachers, principal, counselor, and perhaps a facilitator confer. Does John need a special class, or could some higher-level materials be made available to him? Could he go into a higher grade level for his math class? Could a local mathematician work with John out of school?

The parents are invited to share in making the decision about John's educational program. A program modification is selected, and John does fine for a while. Then for some reason he seems to reach a plateau. He and the program are reevaluated to see what adjustment is needed. He may be rescheduled into the regular class for a time. Since he was never labeled "gifted," he need not be labeled "ungifted." The school is simply meeting his needs, and his needs have changed.

It should be made clear that we are not simply moving a boundary down the scale so as to include more students. So long as a rigid screening is used to exclude students, some will be denied access to educational experiences because they just miss the cutoff. But if, as we suggest, the criteria for inclusion are made flexible, then no one should be denied access to programs that will serve their needs.

Interdependence of Discovering Talent and Nurturing Talent

We shall see that discovering talent and nurturing talent are interdependent. Educators cannot cultivate talents in any thoughtful, systematic way until they know what those talents are. Sometimes the program—that is, the nurturing—becomes a part of the discovery process. Shwedel and Stoneburner suggest, as a simple and succinct alternative to identification, combining tentative selection with continuous monitoring so that students can be placed in the classes and activities best suited to their needs and abilities (Shwedel and Stoneburner, 1983). As we have seen in the discussions of specialized schools and the International Baccalaureate, programs themselves can aid in the screening process. To remind the reader, requirements are somewhat lower for admission to Walnut Hills High School in Cincinnati than they are for admission to the school's advanced classes. The Bronx High School of Science uses the ninth grade year as a screen for the following years. Similarly, entrance requirements for the pre-IB program in Houston are less stringent than those of the IB program itself. In other words, a relatively large number of students enter the earlier or lower level of a particular program. Those students who have the talent and the motivation to move ahead do so. Guesswork is eliminated; students prove themselves, in a sense, for the next and greater challenge.

The interdependence of discovering and nurturing talent is clearly evident in work with young children. The minds of the very young are highly plastic and will respond to appropriate stimulation and cultivation. Merle Karnes recommends early identification of the potentially or functionally gifted so that parents can plan their child's educational program both at home and at school (Karnes, 1983).

J. McVicker Hunt underscores the importance of showing young parents how to help their offspring grow socially, emotionally, and intellectually. A parent is normally the child's first teacher. How well adults perform their parenting tasks depends on their own experiences as children, their socioeconomic level, and their educational background and training.

"I'd like to see an excellent film on good parenting practices made available to all new mothers," he says.*

In his own research Hunt found specific techniques, which parents can learn easily, that will produce happier, brighter children. For example, he urges that parents and caretakers should respond promptly to an infant's cries. Crying is the only way the newborn can communicate, and a quick response is reassuring. Infants gain trust in their caregiver and confidence in their own ability to get their needs attended to.

Referring to his ten-year study at the Orphanage of the Queen Farah Pahlavi Charity Society in Tehran, Hunt tells how he taught the caregivers to imitate the cooings of the infants in their charge. Later they were to initiate other sounds and encourage the babies "to follow the leader." After the infants learned to match the new sounds, the caregivers were instructed to name the parts of the babies' bodies as they washed them. Despite the simplicity of these procedures, the infants, at the age of eighteen and twenty-two months, had made impressive gains in achievement compared with the control group.

Howard Gardner's theory of multiple intelligences largely depends on the principle of early neural and functional plasticity. He argues that intellectual profiles should be drawn up in the first year or two of life. He suggests that high intellectual potential in any of the several intelligences will be manifest in a child's ability to recognize patterns in a given intellectual realm and to remember them:

> At a somewhat later age (all the way up through the preschool years!) it should prove possible to secure a contextually rich and reliable assessment of an individual's intellectual profile. The preferred route for assessment at this age is to involve children in activities which they themselves are likely to find motivating; they can then advance with little direct tutelage through the steps involved in mastering a particular problem or task. Puzzles, games, and other challenges couched in the symbol system of a single intelligence (or of a pair of intelligences) are particularly promising means for assessing the relevant intelligence. (Gardner, 1983, p. 386)

A belief in the importance of early nurturing led Bess Tittle in Dallas to start the Creative Learning Center (CLC), a school for children between

---

*J. McV. Hunt, *Toward Equalizing the Developmental Opportunities of Infants and Preschool Children* (the 1982 Kurt Lewin address, University of Illinois at Urbana-Champaign). Submitted to the Richardson Foundation, April, 1983.

the ages of two and eight. Designed for potentially gifted children from predominantly low-income families, the school opened in the late 1960s to an ethnic mix approximately 50 percent black, 25 percent Hispanic, 15 percent American-Indian, and 10 percent Anglo. One-third of the students were from nonpoverty homes.*

The screening process developed by Tittle and John Gladfelter, a clinical psychologist in Dallas who specializes in gifted children, relied heavily on objective observation based on some forty-two specific criteria, including characteristics of the child, sibling position in the family, and features of the home environment. Initial referrals came from professionals in the community who worked with low-income clients, such as public health doctors and nurses, county welfare case workers, ministers, day-care and nursery personnel, community center staffs, and others.

CLC adopted the philosophy of "throwing a wide net." Better to err by including a child who might eventually demonstrate only average ability than to exclude a youngster who would benefit from attending and whose life might be changed forever as a result.

The staff at CLC points to numerous success stories—children who have attended the Montessori-based school for a few crucial years and then have gone on to win scholarships to fine schools in the area and elsewhere. What is the staff's formula for discovering and educating potentially gifted, culturally diverse, low-income children? Catch them young, work with their families, and provide a rich educational program in a creative environment. Then watch the children blossom into independent, productive young people.

The Creative Learning Center, McVicker Hunt's work, and other examples are only illustrations. We are not suggesting that they should be duplicated elsewhere. We hope that readers will be able to adapt what is applicable, both in this section and elsewhere in the report, to local situations.

Studies related to females and their mathematical abilities call attention to an intellectual area in which educators have a special challenge in encouraging development. A two-year study by Armstrong quoted by C. K. Rekdal* found that women in engineering represent just one-tenth of 1

---

*B. Tittle, *The Creative Learning Center*. Paper submitted to the Richardson Foundation, May, 1983.

*C. J. Rekdal, *Females and Math: The Missing Link*. Paper submitted to the Richardson Foundation, May, 1983.

percent of the engineers in the United States. Only 2 percent of all physicists are women. The reason for this disparity is that these professional fields depend crucially on highly developed mathematical skills. When it comes to the intellectual domain of mathematical reasoning, it appears, females do not fare as well as males.

Are there genetic differences? Mary Meeker says, "As we at the SOI (Structure of the Intellect) Institute process thousands of test scores on boys and girls, and men and women from all over this country, Canada, and Australia, there is no question that the majority of boys do have figural, spatial, and symbolic superiority."* Girls, she goes on to say, are usually low in these areas, whereas they show early verbal superiority, and they read better and sooner than boys.

Parents compound the problem, according to Meeker. They treat girls differently than they do boys, especially in selecting toys. A little boy gets a tool box and a science kit. His sister gets a doll and a tea set. "So a girl suffers a double whammy!" Meeker says. The first may be genetic; the second comes from home conditioning. The lack of appropriate nurturing will cause mathematical skills that girls might have to lie dormant, at great cost to themselves and to society. Rekdal sees a direct cause-and-effect relationship between the lack of suitable experiences and girls' mathematical deficits, saying that girls develop negative attitudes toward math and as a consequence avoid math courses.

Since the National Commission on Excellence in Education found that thirty-five states required only one year of mathematics (*A Nation at Risk*, 1983), most states have raised their graduation requirements to at least two years of math (*The Nation Responds*, 1984). But will girls, even gifted girls, be ready for more stringent requirements? Will the changes overcome the differences in interest and aptitude? Girls may be intimidated by the new requirements unless parents and teachers work together to improve girls' mathematical skills and attitudes toward math during the preschool and elementary years.

The Disadvantaged and Culturally Diverse

Identifying student abilities and helping students develop those talents require knowledge, skill, and sensitivity. Children in some societal groups

---

*M. Meeker, Untitled paper presented to the Pennsylvania State Conference for Gifted, April, 1981.

may be overlooked unless unusual understanding and commitment are brought to the task. We present here two of those groups, the disadvantaged and culturally diverse, to illustrate the care that must be taken lest important talents go undiscovered.

When James Baldwin was a youngster attending public school in Harlem, he attracted the attention of a sympathetic teacher who observed his interest in writing plays and sensed the talent that would make him one of America's major writers. The teacher, an alert white woman, took young Baldwin to see a Broadway play over the objections of the boy's father. The elder Baldwin disapproved of the theater and thought of it as sinful. But young James, with the intuition of a precocious child, knew that his father would not keep him from going to the theater if a white lady showed up to take him (Baldwin, 1955).

This anecdote in *Notes of a Native Son* describes the damage the interference had on the balance of the Baldwin family. The father was defeated, in a way; the boy triumphed. James Baldwin despised his father for a time because of the defeat. He rejected the values of his own home—black, religious, poor—even though they helped to make him what he became.

Baldwin's experience raises problems associated with identifying able learners in communities that do not normally encourage intellectual gifts. It highlights the clash of values between the educational mainstream and some minority subcultures as well as the suspicion of and resistance to outside interference, which can thwart the best of intentions if educators are not sensitive to cultural differences within the communities where they work.

Dee Trevino, coordinator of the gifted and talented program in McAllen, Texas, knows firsthand how crucial respect for cultural diversity is. Located just six miles from the Texas-Mexico border, McAllen has a student population of more than 18,000 students. Of these, 85 percent have Spanish surnames, 80 percent are Spanish-language dominant. In addition, McAllen, one of the nation's fastest growing communities, is the poorest Standard Metropolitan Area according to the 1982 census figures.

McAllen faces the special problem of helping the large Mexican-American population absorb this country's culture without losing respect for its own. The students will always be bicultural; they need to know they can succeed in the larger world and still treasure their own heritage. Trevino and other staff members teach respect for both cultures by modeling it themselves.

Not the least of the problems is radical differences in economic status and standard of living. Maria's teacher thought she had been improperly identified as gifted because she didn't seem to catch on to very simple concepts in either language. When the teacher learned that Maria had a bed that year for the first time in her life, she realized that economic deprivation had kept from Maria some experiences that more privileged children take for granted.

The challenge in McAllen was to develop a procedure that would identify children with superior potential no matter what their language dominance or economic status. The measurements finally selected include the Otis-Lennon School Ability Test, the Raven Progresssive Matrices, the California Achievement Test, and three categories of the Renzulli-Hartman scales. The district emphasizes those measures such as the Raven and the Renzulli-Hartman Communication Characteristics, which are not dependent on English vocabulary or comprehension and therefore do not discriminate against Spanish-speaking children.*

While we are not recommending specific tests to discover talents in minority populations, the McAllen approach illustrates the need to adapt routine identification procedures. The salient achievement in McAllen is that students with outstanding abilities have been located in all the elementary schools. At least 60 percent of the students in the program are Mexican-American. Although the proportions in the gifted class do not match those of the total population, Trevino feels the district has achieved a reasonable balance. It is impossible, she points out, to eliminate economic factors totally. There are no poor Anglos in McAllen, and while some of the Mexican-American families are affluent, others, like Maria's family, live in abject poverty.

McAllen's success in identification is welcome. In 1978, Ernest Bernal, an educational consultant in Austin, Texas, estimated that traditional testing techniques identify only about one in three gifted Chicano children in Texas. Most selected by these means, he says, are highly acculturated students whose cognitive abilities match the patterns of the dominant ethnic group. Bernal lists seven characteristics of gifted Hispanic children used by residents in the barrios to identify their own brightest youngsters:

---

* de S. M. Trevino, *McAllen: G/T Identification*. Paper submitted to the Richardson Foundation, May, 1983.

1. Rapidly acquires English language skills once exposed to the language and given an opportunity to use it expressively.

2. Exhibits leadership ability, be it open or unobtrusive, with heavy emphasis on interpersonal skills.

3. Has older playmates and easily engages adults in lively conversation.

4. Enjoys intelligent (or effective) risk-taking behavior, often accompanied by a sense of drama.

5. Is able to keep busy and entertained, especially by imaginative games and ingenious applications, such as getting the most out of a few simple toys and objects.

6. Accepts responsibilities at home normally reserved for older children, such as the supervision of younger siblings or helping others do their homework.

7. Is "street wise" and is recognized by others as a youngster who has the ability to "make it" in the Anglo-dominated society. (Bernal, 1978, p. 15)

Bernal argues elsewhere* that to identify minority gifted students we need to satisfy at least two conditions that conventional testing methods fail to meet when used among minority populations: (1) the test must be appropriate to the student's repertoire, allowing the student to understand what is expected and eliminating particularly the language or dialect barriers; (2) the test must be interesting enough to the child to create motivation to complete the test.

He cautions us to avoid allowing multiple criteria to become multiple hurdles. This occurs, he says, when a school uses one measure (say a composite of achievement test scores) as a gross screening device, selects the highest-scoring children for further testing with a group-administered I.Q. test, and then selects from these an even smaller group to be given an individually administered I.Q. test. Such successive elimination results in underrepresentation of minorities.

But Bernal would not have us establish one standard for Anglos and then lower it to include a quota of minorities. The minority children then become "second-order gifted" or the "best of the worst." He goes on to point out that inappropriate testing methods lead us to miss not only

---

* E. Bernal, *Identifying Minority Gifted Students.* Paper submitted to the Richardson Foundation, May, 1983.

many very bright minority children but many other children, including low-income Anglos. His solution: adopt a more comprehensive definition of giftedness and expand our identification procedures so that various avenues to admission may be opened.

Philip Powell, a scholar with an interest in gifted youth, also recommends alternative ways to identify minorities and others outside the mainstream of middle-class culture. Begin with peer nominations, he suggests. Just as children at school can tell you who the smartest kid in the class is, so the street-wise youngster can identify his friend or foe outside the class as the smartest boy or girl around.

Powell also recommends personal interviews developed with the assistance of those who grew up in circumstances like those of the child being screened. He places heavy emphasis on the ability to see patterns and relationships. Abstract reasoning signals a high level of ability. A two-year-old skillfully playing checkers is demonstrating the ability to conceptualize. Powell would also have us include social competence—the ability to get along, to survive in an unfriendly environment—as an indication of giftedness.

He regrets the gifts and talents he saw wasted as he grew up in the ghetto environments on the South Side and the Near West Side of Chicago. The unidentified gifted in his neighborhoods were the young people who could handle themselves in any situation. Powell tells of the youngster who got by with B's in school but could reason with the best. The sign of his giftedness was his knack for survival. "He never got hurt too badly and made a considerable living hustling and otherwise using his wits. His test performance in school would never have impressed the white teachers, but he impressed us." *

Mary Frasier cites several special problems the gifted disadvantaged face:

1. They lack an educational tradition at home. Their aspirations tend to be low due to limited information and exposure.

2. These children are frequently encouraged to get a good education to improve their conditions, but seldom receive the direction and support necessary to accomplish this goal.

3. They face problems with peers, who may impede the steps needed to allow them to reach their potential.

---

* Powell, P. *Identification of Gifted Minorities and Poor Socioeconomic Groups.* Paper submitted to the Richardson Foundation, May, 1983.

4. They often do not have role models available to help them identify alternative ways to succeed.

5. They require negotiating skills to get others to respond to their needs and to recognize their above-average ability.*

Speaking from her own experience, Frasier warns against spending too much time and energy on the deficiencies of special populations. She insists that gifted children have much in common with other gifted children, whether they are black, Anglo, Hispanic, or Indian, low-income or high-income. She tells us that once we have identified the gifted from any of the special populations, we need to "give power to the kid." Instead of concentrating on the information youngsters need, we should pay attention to strategic skills. "The child needs power to manipulate the system," she says, "and I'm using 'manipulate' in a very positive sense to include decision-making skills."

Frasier's concern about decision-making skills and learning to negotiate through the system raises again the issue of nurturing the talents we uncover. Frasier turned to bibliotherapy as a way to help children develop their abilities. She defines bibliotherapy as help through books. "Hooked on books" herself from a young age, she finds that books offer youngsters, "locked by time and place in an uncongenial situation," one way to develop the skills and attitudes necessary to function effectively.

Book characters provide needed role models. Focusing on the problems of fictional characters also helps children deal with their own problems in nonthreatening ways. Frasier suggests that a teacher wishing to set up a bibliotherapy program should begin by categorizing the general areas in which the students face problems. These might include educational, career-vocational, social, personal, and other areas. The books can then be selected with the assistance of the librarian to match the children's needs. Frasier emphasizes that just reading the books is not enough. Children must participate in discussion and counseling for books to be effective in helping them solve their problems. It should be added that in the hands of a skillful professional, a child's response to bibliotherapy could serve as a

---

*M. Frasier, "Bibliotherapy: Educational and Counseling Implications for the Gifted Disadvantaged," in *Identifying and Educating the Disadvantaged Gifted/Talented: Selected Proceedings of the Fifth Biannual Conference on Disadvantaged Gifted/Talented*, ed. D. N. Smith (Los Angeles: National/State Leadership Training Institute on Gifted and Talented, 1982). Submitted to the Richardson Foundation, May, 1983.

Meeting Personal and Social Needs through Reading

means of identification, an indicator of emotional or intellectual potential. Especially among minorities and other special populations, discovering and nurturing unusual abilities are complementary activities—two sides of the same coin.

Conclusion

Not every James Baldwin has a teacher alert enough to perceive his undeveloped ability. Not every girl has teachers aware of the need to pay special attention to the development of her mathematical reasoning. And many school districts operating with the best of intentions fail to identify those abilities that slip through the conventional screening instruments.

We encourage attention to diverse abilities uncovered in a wide range of contexts, and we argue for eliminating arbitrary and rigid cutoff scores in the selection process. Districts should attempt to evaluate all children, assessing their discrete abilities insofar as those abilities can be separated. Developing an intellectual or skills profile for each will help the staff make a determination about those students whose abilities fall sufficiently below the average or soar so high above it that content and pacing must be adjusted for them.

The approach we recommend is not simple. It does not offer the teacher or counselor the convenience of "objective" scores when they decide which students will enter a special class. Since the assessment depends on uncovering talents and capabilities that may not surface in conventional testing, it requires uncommon attention and sensitivity.

We should replace the practice of identifying a narrow range of giftedness and small numbers of children with that of discovering many talents among many children. Throwing a wide net in early childhood and later allowing the program to be its own screen will improve our chances of discovering and nurturing many kinds of ability among populations excluded from opportunity, whether by ethnic and economic circumstances, by sex-role stereotyping, or by other limiting conditions. The goal, of course, is to see that no individual ability or potential withers for want of opportunity.

FLEXIBLE PACING

The conviction that students should move ahead on the basis of mastery may be the single most important concept for educators designing programs for able learners. Educators may question whether bright students should be allowed to move ahead with those who are older; they may prefer to bring advanced content down to the student. But surely all acknowledge that the content and pacing should match the student's abilities.

More often than not, teachers and administrators agree philosophically with the idea of flexible pacing, but they find it difficult to put into practice. Some have experienced cumbersome attempts to accommodate individual progress. In many situations the theory of self-paced instruction is reduced to the practice of substituting programmed packets for individualized instruction. Such results are discouraging.

For these reasons we pause here to look at several schools that demonstrate that flexible pacing need not be managed in an impersonal way. We visited a number of elementary schools and one senior high school where instruction based on age or grade and uniform pacing have been eliminated. These are schools with a track record of practical success in continuous progress.

Each of the schools we visited is committed to the philosophy that learning is an individual matter and that students learn at different rates. All bring students together in groups for instruction at least part of the time. As we look at their practices, however, we will see that the method of grouping differs from one school to another. Some give more attention to differing learning styles than others. Some have done away with grade labels altogether. But in each, students move ahead through the skills and content as they achieve mastery.

Any investigation of the nongraded school must include the elementary school of the University of California at Los Angeles, a laboratory school and once the home turf of John Goodlad. Goodlad and Anderson's *The Nongraded Elementary School* (1959) sparked the public's interest in the nongraded model and the philosophy undergirding it. Numerous educators claim the study as their bible and refer to it in any discussion of the nongraded concept.

Madeline Hunter, former principal of the UCLA lab school, emphasizes structure when she describes the model: "Nongrading is an organizational plan based on the premise that learning should be continuous; a student should not spend time on that which he already knows, nor should he proceed with gaps of essential unlearned material behind him."* Crucial to the program is the use of criterion-referenced indices to determine the presence of specific competencies and to assess progress through the learning sequence. The school is organized into four major phases: early childhood, then lower, middle, and upper elementary. The students progress from one phase to another as they accomplish the objectives at an acceptable level.

Within that general structure, grouping for instruction is not based primarily on gathering together students at the same level of achievement. Instead the staff is particularly concerned with the selection of the teacher whose teaching style is most compatible with the students' needs and with the most effective peer-group composition. They strive to give each student a variety of experiences: being the oldest, being the youngest; being the fastest student in a group, then the slowest; working with friends at one time and being separated from friends at another.

Nongrading at the University Elementary School at UCLA. Paper submitted to the Richardson Foundation, 1982.

Grouping for Instruction

The laboratory school at the University of Pittsburgh, under the direction of Margaret Wang, also employs an approach to continuous progress that includes a diagnostic-prescriptive monitoring system. Special training enables the teachers to evaluate and track each student's progress. It also enables the teachers to help the students develop self-management skills so that they can assume greater responsibility for their learning than students do in the more traditional school setting.

An important premise of Wang's Adaptive Learning Environments model is not only that children of different ages can learn together, but also that children of diverse abilities, from the slow learner to the highly gifted, can learn together *if*—and it's a big *if*—the teachers receive appropriate training and adequate support services.

Both lab schools report that constant testing and monitoring are the keys to the progress of individual students. A necessary concomitant is an efficient record-keeping system. As Wang points out, the record keeping must be designed to make minimal demands on the teacher's time and yet provide critical information about each student's learning. No single record-keeping method will work for all schools; each school and district must work out its own. It is essential, however, that precious instructional time not be lost to clerical tasks.

Despite the success of the lab schools at UCLA and Pittsburgh, the nongraded approach is not in wide use. In an interview (1981) Goodlad offered one explanation: the fact that more schools have not developed a nongraded approach has more to do with how change occurs than it does with the model. His staff welcomed visitors who wanted to learn about the lab school. Often the visitors were teachers not accompanied by administrators at the decision-making level. While teachers might admire the model, any kind of organizational change such as the nongraded school entails requires administrative support and leadership. Moreover, introducing new methods throughout a district presents problems not faced by an independent laboratory school. The question we wanted to answer was this: Can flexible advancement on a wide scale be achieved in a public school district in Anyplace, USA?

Plano, Texas, a suburb just north of Dallas, is a fairly typical lower- to upper-middle-class community. Although in other ways it is not particularly remarkable, the city has successfully developed a nontraditional, continuous approach to education. While the district has retained the usual first, second, and third grade labels for administrative purposes, the grade labels have little to do with the students' instructional levels. In large open classrooms students are grouped for instruction on the basis of achievement. When that is not possible—for example, when students are ready for high-school math before they have finished junior high—students can move between campuses for one or more periods every day. Kathy Hargrove, the district's gifted and talented coordinator, says, "Students are instructed where they are, not where they 'should be,' at each stage of their educational experience. Progress extends along a continuum. Students progress at the pace most appropriate for them."*

---

* *Continuous Progress in Plano.* Paper submitted to the Richardson Foundation, 1982.

We found that all these schools depend on carefully directed staff development. It is a sign of enlightened administration as well as commitment among the teachers that they have mastered the pedagogical methods of assessing skills with precision and monitoring progress efficiently.

Some time after visiting the elementary schools described here, we went to Canada to observe a continuous progress program in a high school. Bishop Carroll High School in Calgary, Alberta, demonstrates that continuous progress can work well at the secondary level. Developed as a public school primarily for Catholic students, Bishop Carroll is a three-year institution with a student population that ranges from 1,000 to 1,450, about one-fourth non-Catholic. The experimental high school opened in 1971 as part of a model school project directed by J. Lloyd Trump, of the National Association of Secondary School Principals, and William Georgiades, dean of the College of Education, University of Houston. Ralph A. Vigna, principal of Bishop Carroll, writes that the practices that distinguish this alternative school from other high schools in the city include differentiated staffing, team teaching, self-pacing, continuous progress, independent study, and the use of large and small groups.*

To graduate, students must meet requirements in nine subject areas: English language arts, fine arts, health fitness and recreation, mathematics, modern languages, philosophy and religious studies, practical arts, science, and social studies. Each course in these subject areas carries five credits toward graduation and is divided into units of work through which the students move at their own pace. While a minimum of 100 credits is required for graduation, the students at Bishop Carroll normally exceed that number. In general, students at Bishop Carroll High School complete 115–120 credits in about three years.

Because the school intends to place responsibility for learning directly on the students and to foster critical and independent thinking, the chief role of the teachers is as educational advisors. Each teacher is responsible for about thirty students. They guide the students in selecting their courses, help them plan their schedules, work with them to determine short- and long-range goals, assist them in undertaking the demands of independent study and continuous progress, and familiarize them with the operations of the nine resource centers and their curriculum.

---

*Ralph A. Vigna, *An Investigation of Learning Styles of Gifted and Nongifted High School Students* (Ph.D. diss., University of Houston, 1983).

Each student follows a personal performance schedule of independent study, planned with and approved by the teacher/advisor. The schedule includes time for independent study and group sessions. Large and small group sessions are the responsibility of subject-area teams. Students are not required to attend these sessions, but find them useful in completing the requirements in each subject area.

To provide such individualized programs and flexibility requires a great deal of personal attention to each student. The subject-area teachers are grouped in teams, and each team has a support staff that includes secretaries, general aides, and instructional assistants. Because record keeping and other clerical duties are assigned to nonteaching staff members, Bishop Carroll can operate at the same per-student cost as the other schools in the district.

Bishop Carroll's success is encouraging. Its approach to continuous progress can be imitated elsewhere with appropriate adaptations. The administrators of Bishop Carroll caution, however, that the model cannot be phased in gradually. It requires complete administrative reorganization as well as curriculum development. At the very least, flexible advancement on this scale would require a separate school within a school, of the sort that some magnet schools have adopted. Rather than undertake such reorganization, many schools will prefer more limited programs that still allow a measure of flexible advancement. The Advanced Placement program, early entrance, and concurrent enrollment, discussed previously in "What Works Best," all offer versions of flexible progression. Each is different from the others, but each, alone or in combination with others, offers a means of adjusting the pacing to student abilities.

Whatever approach a school or district selects, the issue of appropriate pacing should be thoughtfully addressed before additional programs are added. Julian Stanley, director of the Johns Hopkins Study of Mathematically Precocious Youth (SMPY), writes:

> While highly successful, SMPY's various procedures occur only because the age-in-grade, Carnegie-unit lockstep of schools, both public and (especially) private, makes such heroic measures essential. If schools were organized differently, SMPY would not have been necessary—nor, indeed, would the special provisions for most slow learners.
>
> In my opinion, age-grading for instruction in academic school subjects has crept insidiously upon us as we have moved from tutorial instruction and the one-room schoolhouse to the current situation. It needs to be reversed. (Stanley, 1980, p. 11)

Stanley goes on to recommend longitudinal teaching teams that span kindergarten through the twelfth grade. He believes that such an approach, however difficult to engineer, is the only hope for American education. "All else," he says, "will be sorry stopgaps."

ACCELERATION AND ENRICHMENT

Our attention to instructional pacing and individualized progress should not be taken to mean we advocate acceleration to the exclusion of enrichment. Such is not the case. Enrichment is central to the education of all children, including able learners. No matter how bright, students should not race through school without ample opportunities to explore widely and delve deeply along the way. A wise district will not make a choice between acceleration and enrichment, for such a choice limits educational opportunity.

In our introductory section we noted that the most widespread means of enriching the education of able learners is the part-time special class, the "pull-out" program. We explained why we think that option is not as useful as others. The second most prevalent practice reported in response to the Richardson Study questionnaire was enrichment in the regular classroom.

Although we observed some fine examples of enrichment in the regular classroom, we found that it, too, has limitations. A program of enrichment in the regular classroom frequently lacks clear goals, adequate substance, and carefully planned teaching strategies. As has been shown in "What's Happening," when modest criteria were applied to an evaluation of the data, only 16 percent of the reported enrichment programs qualified as "substantial," although 63 percent of the districts said they had such a program.

An enrichment program in regular classrooms in Richardson, Texas, seems to work well. In grades 1 through 3, a specially trained teacher goes into the regular classroom and teaches a demonstration class for all students while the regular teacher observes. The special teacher brings in materials for student learning centers. An example is a lesson on codes, printed on laminated colored sheets. Several gamelike activities teach children how to work with codes, substituting one symbol for another. Because one activity requires students to substitute numbers for letters and add the values of the letters, the materials also teach both verbal and math skills indirectly. Such materials are available to any student in the room. They are geared to the bright students' abilities, however, and emphasize higher-level thinking skills. The special teacher introduces new concepts and leaves follow-up lessons for the classroom teacher.

One value of this procedure to the regular teacher, according to Ruth Lawrence, consultant for gifted programs in Richardson, is the lesson in discovering and nurturing talent. The teacher often finds that a child perceived as a troublemaker offers unusual responses when properly challenged.

Developing learning centers requires more time than many classroom teachers have and rather specialized skills. But the enrichment for the child, and the training and resources the centers provide for the teacher, are an educationally sound combination. Some such model is clearly needed for teachers of heterogeneous classes.

Just as most teachers agree theoretically with appropriate pacing but find it difficult to manage without special training, most teachers also approve of differentiated enrichment activities but find them burdensome without a well-defined structure. One of the better-known and more widely accepted models of enrichment is Renzulli's Enrichment Triad Model. The model divides activities into three types: Type I—General Exploratory Activities, Type II—Group Training Activities, and Type III—Individual and Small Group Investigations of Real Problems (Renzulli, 1977).

The structure of Renzulli's model neatly captures Whitehead's Rhythm of Education: romance, precision, and generalization (Whitehead, 1929). But it also allows for differentiated activities in a heterogeneously grouped school setting. Renzulli says the first two types of enrichment are appropriate for all learners and the third is appropriate mainly for gifted learners.

Defining enrichment as "activities that are above and beyond the so-called 'regular curriculum,'" Renzulli maintains that all students, not just the gifted, benefit from appropriate kinds of enrichment. The gifted, with their greater persistence and facility, should learn to investigate real problems using the methods of real scholarship and research.

Responses from the MacArthur Fellows confirm Renzulli's position. In the Introduction we noted Michael Ghiselin's comment that there is no important connection between what is required of a student and what is needed by a scholar. Exploring real problems would remedy this problem and offer the additional benefit of heightened interest for the students.

COMPREHENSIVE PROGRAMS

Much of what we have to recommend can be summed up in the phrase "comprehensive programming." We use the term to suggest a collection of programmatic options designed for students of high ability. Such a program should be appropriate both for a range of abilities from higher than normal to truly gifted and for abilities in diverse intellectual domains. A comprehensive program should be integrated and thoughtfully articulated throughout. Ideally the provisions (not always separate programs) would begin at the kindergarten or preschool level and allow students to move through sequential curricula at an appropriate pace to commencement from high school and beyond.

We would like to see programs that offer both acceleration and enrichment or a differentiated curriculum. We would also like to see a balance of attention to all learning needs, allowing students to progress rapidly in those subject areas and skills where they have highly developed aptitude and at the same time helping them to strengthen those skills where they have a weakness. The goal we have in mind is not fully realized in any system we examined during the course of our study. We will describe briefly, however, two school districts struggling consciously and intelligently, toward that ideal—programming at all levels—hoping, as all educators hope, that no bright mind or exceptional talent will be wasted for lack of a program to stimulate and challenge every ability.

The development of the program for the gifted in Marshall, Texas, illustrates an important first step in planning a comprehensive program for able learners: assessment of what is already in place. The district is small; it serves 6,000 students. When comprehensive planning began some seven or eight years ago, the Marshall Independent School District took stock. At the secondary level the district already had honors and Advanced Placement courses. At the middle school there were enriched courses in language arts for the most successful students. Elementary-school children were being placed and moved at variable rates along a continuum of skills. The school district focused its attention first on the elementary level and added enrichment in critical and creative thinking. The planners saw that their first task was to strengthen the individual elements and tighten the links between them.

Nancy McClaran, director of resources and coordinator of language arts and second languages in the Marshall Independent School District, describes K–8 continuous progress as central to providing appropriate instruction for all students, including the able learners. The reading program for grades K–8 places students on levels commensurate with their reading achievement, as measured by a placement test and a locally developed series of reading tests based upon the school district's continuum of skills. Literature studies enrich the reading instruction. Students who master the skills early take advanced reading courses, including the Junior Great Books Program.

In math, as well, the students are placed according to their achievement on the district's continuum of skills. Seventh and eighth graders who move through the schedule of skills early are placed in enriched, accelerated classes so that they move on to algebra before they go to high school. They are given enrichment activities, including access to a microcomputer.

Fifth and sixth graders, located on two middle-school campuses, have one teacher trained in teaching the gifted and talented at both campuses, teaching at each school for half a day. As an example of an enrichment activity that engenders independence and leadership skills among middle-school students, McClaran cites interviews with prominent public figures. Working in small groups, the students make contact with outstanding personalities, write letters, pose questions, and conduct telephone interviews. The interviewers use a speaker phone in the classroom so that the entire class can hear the interviews and contribute questions. Students have talked with writers, psychologists, and their congressman. On one occasion a student interested in cartooning lined up an interview with political cartoonist Ben Sargent, of the *Austin American-Statesman*.

Seventh and eighth graders attend Marshall Junior High. Those identified as gifted and talented have a special class in language arts that occupies a two-period block. They concentrate part of each period on reading and writing. In addition, they study skills of philosophical inquiry, using materials developed by the Institute for the Advancement of Philosophy for Children.

Specific academic aptitude qualifies students to take honors classes at the secondary level in English, mathematics, science, or social studies. The English honors courses prepare students for the Advanced Placement tests in language and composition in the junior year and in literature and composition in the senior year.

In addition, able secondary students may pursue interests outside the regular offerings through independent study. Students may apply by proposing a course of study and a plan for its completion. If a proposal is accepted, the student works independently under the supervision of a teacher with special qualifications in the area proposed. In one such project, a girl named Emily produced a slide-tape program on the poetry of Emily Dickinson, illustrating the poetic imagery with artistic still photography. Now the slide-tape program is used regularly by Marshall High School classes studying Dickinson's poetry. Emily's project would qualify nicely as a Renzulli Type III activity, an investigation of a real problem or a real-world situation.

Able students may sit for examination in specific courses without taking the courses. Satisfactory performance on the examination earns credit without grade points and enables the successful student to advance to a higher-level course. The Marshall district also provides for concurrent college enrollment. An instructor from Marshall Junior College teaches a course in American history to advanced seniors. College credit is awarded upon their graduation from high school.

According to McClaran, "Continuous modifications are made in an effort to offer a varied program that meets the interests and challenges the aptitudes of gifted students." This district, though small, is making a sustained effort to provide a comprehensive program for all its able learners.

Programming for Chicago's brightest students presents challenges smaller districts do not encounter. At the same time, the large city has resources most small communities lack. One of the nation's largest school systems, the Chicago public schools serve a population of more than 400,000 students. To meet their needs requires careful organization. Richard Ronvik directs the city's program with the assistance of four coordinators, each serving five of the school system's twenty districts.

More than 200 Chicago schools make some special provision for gifted students. The locally developed options vary widely, from traditional Advanced Placement to training in the arts. There are, in addition, a number of all-city programs administered by the central gifted office, either in local schools throughout the city or in facilities away from the schools: an astronomy program at the Adler Planetarium, an Advanced Placement history of art program at the Art Institute, and a museology program also at the Art Institute. Students study animal behavior and zoo ecology at the Lincoln Park Zoo, science at the Museum of Science and Industry, and aquatic science at the Shedd Aquarium.

Ronvik acknowledges that Chicago's museum programs are not well in-

Talcott Mountain Science Center

tegrated into the curriculum even though the gifted staff members work with teachers to coordinate them. In any case, he says, these programs serve low-incidence gifted students. "We search the entire city for perhaps twenty kids for one program."

Chicago also has a variety of magnet schools designed to meet the special needs and interests of able learners. An example is at Kenwood Academy near the University of Chicago, serving students from the predominantly black and Hispanic neighborhood in grades 9 through 12. The academic magnet program at Kenwood Academy attracts high-ability students from the entire city. It is in one sense a school within a school, but it avoids some of the typical problems of a magnet because the same administrators serve both groups of students, and the magnet students are frequently in the same classes as the neighborhood students. Not all classes are the same, however. For example, some seniors take classes at the University of Chicago. The university has for years cooperated with Kenwood in this manner without charging the school or the individual students. The district may arrange for payment of tuition, however, in order for students to receive college credit.

Lincoln Park High School hosts not one but several magnet programs. Included are math and science, the arts, and the International Baccalaureate.

Another city-wide program is fast-paced courses. Students are recruited with letters from the Academic Talent Search list and by social workers and psychologists in the gifted program. Classes are held one half-day per week in cooperation with Chicago's many universities, generally on the university campuses. Students enroll in fast-paced algebra, language arts, Latin, biology, or social studies.

The Chicago schools are not without their problems, and we do not mean to minimize the difficulties associated with a large urban population. Nor would we suggest that the small district in Marshall, Texas, has avoided or eliminated all the impediments to sound education. Nonetheless, the Marshall and Chicago systems illustrate in different ways some common elements of effective, comprehensive programming for able learners. One element is thoughtful assessment of the current program and then building on what is available already. There is no need, usually, to disrupt an active program. By adding program options and coordinating them with current offerings, the district can often enrich the opportunities of the most promising students with a minimum of dislocation.

Another element is the attempt to offer programs throughout the system. In both cities the programming for the gifted is arrayed across the district and from the earliest elementary grades through the upper grades of high school. At each level the teachers are aware of the whole package, and the students benefit from the coordinated structure. Furthermore, the programming for the gifted is seen as only one part of the district's approach to meeting the educational needs of all students.

One key to the success of a comprehensive program is the wise use of community resources and cooperation with neighboring institutions that share a concern for sound education. Chicago is fortunate to have so many colleges and museums to enrich the education of the city's youth. Marshall has a junior college nearby and a number of interested persons in public life. And parents everywhere are a valuable resource. They have an interest in the schools that goes beyond simply augmenting the education of their own children, and often they will share their special knowledge and talents to the benefit of the community schools. The private sector as well, as we have suggested in our discussion of mentoring and internships, can be a powerful ally and partner.

Among the principal values of having colleges and universities close at hand is the role such institutions can play in staff development. Apart from their function in preparing prospective teachers and the continuing education of current teachers in advanced degree programs, colleges and universities can be and should be made to see their dependence on and their ability to help area school districts. We have spoken at some length about cooperation across the school-college boundary in "a Shared Commitment."

The model of the Yale–New Haven Teachers Institute is especially interesting (*Teaching in America: The Common Ground*, 1983). Through the institute, Yale helps the local school system with curriculum and staff development. Since 1978 the Yale–New Haven Teachers Institute has sought to breach the barrier between town and gown in a program that enables about eighty teachers a year from the city's secondary schools to study with senior professors at the university.

Teachers participate in the seminars for several months each year. The topics are determined by a panel of teachers, assuring relevance to teacher needs and interests. Teachers develop curriculum units containing objectives, strategies, suggested classroom activities, and bibliographies. Although the teachers themselves determine what goes into their units, based on the topics studied in the seminars, they write and rewrite under the guidance of professors in the academic disciplines. The completed units are combined, published, and made available to teachers throughout the New Haven district.

Such cooperation among institutions must be encouraged and cultivated in every communty that seeks a broad and comprehensive program for all its students, including its most able learners.

AN IMAGINED DISTRICT

To illustrate an ideal comprehensive program, we would like to invent an imaginary district whose provisions for able learners would include many of the components that are in place in the districts described throughout this report. The program would, of course, be unique to the district because what is suitable for one district may not be possible or even desirable in another. But we want to consider how a hypothetical district might go about constructing its comprehensive program, keeping its own needs carefully in mind.

Imagine a district in a mid-sized city—a city of about 400,000 with a student population approaching 60,000. The city has a mix of ethnic cultures and socioeconomic strata that make it unexceptional among American cities. The school district consists of some sixty elementary schools, twenty middle schools, and ten high schools. We need not be more specific about the imaginary city and school district, for we do not intend to present a concrete agenda for action, only some generalized procedures.

First will come a period of assessment, a district-wide effort involving top administrators and all teachers, community leaders and the private sector, as well as the parents of children in the community. They will examine current testing programs and select others as needed, gradually developing a full continuum of skills in each basic area, particularly for the elementary and middle grades. Longitudinal teaching teams of the sort Stanley recommends, preferably covering the whole K–12 grade range, will make decisions about material to be covered and pacing throughout the schools.

The district will examine programs already in place that serve able learners. How do educators, parents, and the community feel about these programs? What community resources are being tapped? Are they used wisely? This assessment will require some serious soul-searching. What are the strengths the district can build on? Where are the greatest weaknesses, and what services are needed to overcome those weaknesses?

Providing flexible progress for all students will be a tough and continuing challenge. The district must tackle that issue head-on at all levels to make sure all schools not only allow students to advance as they achieve mastery, but provide specific procedures to monitor and assist their advancement. The secondary schools may prefer alternative practices to achieve flexible advancement. They may include Advanced Placement courses, concurrent enrollment, and early entrance to college among the options.

The size of a school district and community values have an important bearing on the range and variety of options the district adopts. If enough members of the community value education with an international perspective, the district will begin the study of a second language at the kindergarten level. They will perhaps concentrate their elementary foreign language program in one or two elementary schools. Those students with exceptional interest and ability in languages will have an opportunity to pursue other languages as they move through school. At the secondary level at least one high school will offer the International Baccalaureate.

Knowing that students and their families respond well to options, the district will have at least one secondary school that concentrates on the performing and visual arts. The district will recognize the strong motivational force inherent in a performing arts choice, and they will also know that many students will change career goals, possibly several times, during their educational development. They will, as a consequence, make a strong liberal arts focus and solid college preparation a part of their performing and visual arts curriculum.

The district should find as the comprehensive program takes shape that they are building on student strengths and buttressing areas where students are weak. Some students will be able to profit from early exposure to the work place and professional supervision. The mentor and internship programs described earlier in our report will be put in place as they find support in the community.

It is unlikely that these developments will take place one at a time in sequential order. The district may launch some of its programming options while student assessment is still in progress. If teachers and administrators remain alert and responsive, admitting students to any services and programs from which they can benefit should present no problem.

In all this activity the parents will play an important role. Not only will they be kept informed; they will be invited to share in educational planning and the educational process. We have found that such involvement is frequently required in the private schools with excellent results. The parent-school partnership can characterize public schools as well.

Mindful of the research that verifies the importance of early learning, the district will give special attention to low-income and disadvantaged families, sponsoring frequent seminars on parenting and reaching out in creative ways to the parents of young children, involving them in the cultural and educational life of the school.

The district will surely recognize that not all education takes place during regular school hours, so it will offer a series of Saturday enrichment classes. These may be offered in cooperation with an area cc¹lege, by parents, or by other talented individuals in the community.

Summer should bring a needed change of pace, a time for exploration, study, and travel. It can be a time for curriculum and staff development. But the summer is long and boring for some bright students. The district therefore will offer enrichment and fast-paced courses to those interested. Administrators and teachers will be aware of opportunities available within the community. They will publicize other summer programs available throughout the country so the families can choose other options if they wish and if they have the resources.

Our imaginary district, as it serves its able learners well, will discover that the education of all children in the district has been elevated in the process. Good news may not travel as fast as bad, but the word will spread that the district has a superior educational program. Requests may pour in from educators throughout the country for the privilege of visiting. The district will be cordial, eager to share what it has accomplished as well as to continue learning from others. Remembering the importance of cooperation among teachers, administrators, board members, and parents, the district will require visitors to come in teams.

The district and the comprehensive program we have sketched here represent an ideal. We know that change is not easy. We acknowledge that a single approach will not meet the educational needs of a central Detroit, a Dearborn, and a Grosse Pointe. We are aware as well that no single district can fulfill the goal of making comprehensive programming the rule across the land. But we also know, because we have talked with teachers and administrators throughout the country, that there is a joy in even modest success, a thrill that comes with seeing more and more students develop their talents.

The task cannot be finished, of course. There will be no time when the district can sit back and feel its work is done. For the ideal we recommend is not an end state but a process. It depends on constant assessment, awareness of developments in educational theory, and adjustment to changes in the community. But so long as our ideal district or any other district remains attuned and ready to adjust, and so long as whole communities keep in mind the learning needs of every student, we can be confident that improvement is possible. In that way what we imagine can become real.

SUMMARY OF RECOMMENDATIONS

From the beginning of the Richardson Study we have had in mind an audience of several layers. At one level are the private foundations and public agencies that fund educational programs or guide state and local funding for the public school system. At another level are the professional educators—school teachers, administrators, and others actively involved in the nation's educational enterprise. A third level of audience, overlapping the other two, is made up of those who will most benefit from improved education, the young people themselves, their parents, and interested teachers and community members with an investment in the sound education of our ablest learners.

In presenting a summary of recommendations that have emerged from our study, we concentrate on one fairly limited element of one audience: schools and districts that are initiating a comprehensive program for their able learners or are contemplating a change in the programs currently in effect. We address those who will assume a decision-making role in such developments.

Many of our recommendations have implications for all learners, especially those recommendations that suggest reconsidering classroom strategies, record keeping, ability grouping, and flexible pacing. Insofar as these practices allow for more individualization, they will enable us to do a better job with all students.

Administration

▶ Develop a written philosophy for the education of able learners that is consistent with the goals and values of the school district and community. This fundamental first step should include a careful consideration of all the recommendations that follow.

▶ Select a coordinator or coordinators during the early planning stages. As the person responsible for the success of the program, the coordinator should participate in the planning.

▶ Assess the current program for able learners. Those elements that serve their needs well may be retained and expanded as other options are added.

▶ Adopt flexible pacing at all levels. Recognize that not all students learn at the same rate; allow students to advance as they master content and skills, at whatever pace is most natural and offers the steadiest challenge for each.

Discovering Talent

▶ Broaden the process for assessing student abilities. This recommendation is implicit in our adoption of the term "able learners," intended to include a larger population than those customarily identified as "gifted students."

▶ Assess the abilities of all students and use the results as a basis for appropriate programming decisions.

▶ Recognize that there is neither a single kind of intelligence nor a single instrument for measuring intelligence. Rather there are multiple intelligences and multiple measures.

▶ Encourage parents, primary teachers, and others responsible for the supervision of children to note their abilities and interests early and to provide appropriate stimulation. Remember that discovering talent and nurturing talent are interdependent activities.

▶ Observe the ability of children to solve problems or fashion products over an extended period as an indicator of interest and ability.

▶ Use puzzles and games that young children find motivating to discover their talents. A child's ability to recognize patterns in a given intellectual realm will indicate potential in that intelligence and aid in developing an intellectual profile. Pay close attention to the child's ability to use other symbol systems as well as the verbal.

▶ Give thoughtful attention to special groups such as minorities. Avoid tests that are dependent on English vocabulary or compehension. Supplement testing with checklists of characteristics valued by the subcultures. The screener should understand and respect each population and, if possible, speak the child's native language.

▶ Use a wide range of testing strategies, including out-of-level testing. If students' abilities are to be assessed with standardized instruments, be sure they have a good congruence or "match" with the objectives of the curriculum and programming.

▶ Throw a wide net, keeping entrance requirements fairly modest and tentative. Avoid arbitrary cutoffs. The goal is to include all students who can benefit from enriched programming rather than exclude any who are marginal. Monitor regularly and let those with talent and motivation move ahead.

▶ Avoid labeling any group of children as *the gifted*. To do so implies that some children are gifted in every area and other children gifted in none.

▶ Provide a psychologically safe environment. Teach students to value their abilities and to use their individual strengths.

Program

▶ Recognize the importance of counselors in several capacities: participating in student assessment, ministering to the affective needs of students, guiding program selection of students, and counseling in career and college choices.

▶ Build a comprehensive program as you would piece together a mosaic. Do not expect all elements to be in place at once.

▶ Take care that programs are sequential, carefully integrated, and articulated throughout the system.

▶ Offer program options that reach through and beyond the normal institutional boundaries: across disciplines, across grade levels, and across levels of intelligence.

▶ Encourage independence through projects that culminate in real products and employ the methods of inquiry used by real scholars.

▶ Develop specific plans for concurrent enrollment at all levels—elementary/middle, middle/high school, and high school/college.

▶ Recognize that a few students will benefit from the opportunity to leave school and enter college early.

▶ Make use of community resources, including the private sector. For example, include one-to-one mentoring relations between students and business and professional leaders, or offer internships at the secondary level so that students can examine one or more career interests as an aid to informed academic and career choices.

▶ Cooperate with area museums, arts organizations, and civic groups to increase educational options available outside the school walls.

▶ Encourage students to participate in some of the fine educational programs available after school, on Saturdays, and during the summer.

▶ Consider specialized schools if the population of the community and the district's resources will support them. Although an ambitious undertaking, a residential school can serve a wider area than a single school district, and the school can be a laboratory for teaching strategies and curriculum content.

▶ Recognize that racing through the curriculum is not the primary goal of a well-conceived educational program. Balance acceleration with enrichment activities for diverse types and degrees of intelligence.

Staff Development and Teacher Support

▶ Consider staff development a continuous process for teachers, consultants, and administrators.

▶ Develop teaching strategies that are appropriate to the learning styles of able students, and encourage a wide range of thinking and questioning skills.

▶ Arrange for joint planning among teachers at different levels with careful attention to the K – 12 sequence in each content area.

▶ Help teachers develop a manageable record-keeping system that allows them to monitor student progress without undue loss of instructional time.

▶ Provide the regular classroom teacher adequate support services— clerical support, for example, or a resource teacher—so that enrichment is available to able learners in the regular classroom.

▶ Use nearby colleges or universities as a resource for ongoing staff development and for innovations in curriculum as well as for educational research.

Evaluation

▶ Plan the evaluation design as the program is being developed. It is necessary, for example, to establish baseline data in order to monitor progress.

▶ Conduct comprehensive and regular program evaluation to assure accountability. The evaluation design must answer questions about the success of individual program elements and about their impact on student growth and achievement.

▶ Employ an external evaluator or team of evaluators to reinforce internal evaluation, to assure objectivity, and to add credibility.

AFTERWORD:

Some First Efforts at

Implementation

THE PYRAMID PROJECT

In the Foreword Valleau Wilkie, executive vice-president of the Richardson Foundation, expresses a hope he has harbored from the beginning of the study "that the report will become the basis for specific programs that our foundation and others can support." Determined that the study and the report should not be relegated to a long shelf-life and little use, the Sid W. Richardson Foundation has taken the initiative of funding a model program in Texas. A second project will soon be inaugurated in Ardmore, Oklahoma, with initial funding from the Noble and Kerr foundations. Others, we hope, will follow.

We present here a brief description of the Pyramid Project, being undertaken in the Dallas/Fort Worth metropolitan area. It illustrates that the analysis and recommendations of our study provide a sound conceptual framework for a real and practical programming approach. While we don't suggest that the Pyramid Project defines the only way our recommendations can be realized in action, we take courage from its commitment to develop a comprehensive approach to meeting the needs of all able learners, including the gifted and talented. It is gratifying to note that even before the study is published, its findings and its recommendations are going to work.

The Gifted Students Institute for Research and Development, with June Cox as its executive director, has entered into the five-year Pyramid Project with four Dallas/Fort Worth Metroplex school districts: Cedar Hill (in a suburb of Dallas), Birdville (in a suburb of Fort Worth), Arlington, and Fort Worth. The districts were selected, in part, because they represent a wide range of sizes. Cedar Hill has a student population of 2,300; Birdville, 16,300; Arlington, 36,900; Fort Worth, 65,000.

Each of the four districts has appointed teachers and administrators to serve on a steering committee. They began by gathering information about the current status of their services to bright students to help determine what specific services each district could most profitably add. The information will also provide a baseline for documenting the project's successes and failures when the project is evaluated.

Informed by past experience and with the benefit of preliminary reports from the Richardson Study, each district has developed a five-year plan. Each is charged with determining where it wants to be at the end of the five years and what efforts are necessary in the intervening years to accomplish the task.

The premise that students should move ahead as they master content and skills is basic to the pyramid concept, illustrated in Figure 2. Whether the districts accelerate the educational process by moving bright students to higher grade levels in their areas of accomplishment or by bringing advanced material down to the students, this provision is expected to meet the needs of many able learners in the regular classroom.

While breaking the age-in-grade lockstep will meet the needs of large numbers of able learners (represented by the broad base of the pyramid), a smaller number of students (represented by the mid-section of the pyramid) will require special classes. In large districts, such as Fort Worth, special schools will serve an even smaller proportion of the students (represented by the top of the pyramid) who either are exceptionally gifted or have specialized interests and talents.

The participating districts will select programming options and classroom strategies primarily from those represented in this study. To illustrate, the Fort Worth district will provide for the largest number of its talented learners (the base of the pyramid) by adjustments in the regular classroom. The district plans to provide enrichment with portable classroom learning centers and to provide for flexible pacing by cluster grouping and curriculum compacting. At the building level the Fort Worth schools will use such techniques as block class scheduling and modular scheduling so as to permit cross-grade grouping. They will offer enrichment in resource centers in special areas like the library or a separate computer room.

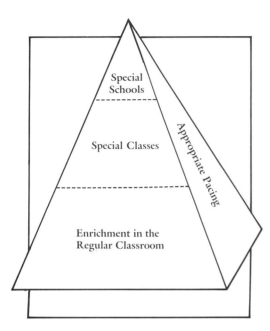

Figure 2. The Pyramid Concept

Moving up the pyramid to levels at which the more specialized needs of fewer superior students can be served, the system will offer honors classes and will allow dual enrollment at elementary and middle schools, at middle and high schools, and at high schools and area colleges. The district's existing magnet schools are specialized schools designed to serve even smaller proportions of the district's ablest learners. One magnet will soon be offering the International Baccalaureate, and the district hopes to have a school for the performing and visual arts by the end of the five-year program.

To support these programming adaptations the Fort Worth district has worked out a plan for assessment of students' abilities and special needs so that students can be placed properly and exposed to the right opportunities for acceleration and enrichment. The plan also provides for continuing staff development, which will allow longitudinal team planning, interdisciplinary planning, and cooperation among parents, administrators, and teaching personnel.

The distinguishing feature of the Pyramid Project is its comprehensiveness. The provisions for the ablest learners will be thoughtfully coordinated with the regular curriculum and will provide appropriate instruction for all students daily. If the project is successful in these four districts, it will meet the needs of talented K–12 youngsters in all content areas and at all levels of ability, from the above average to the highly gifted. No children will be excluded from any provision that meets their needs.

The Gifted Students Institute will be the coordinating and fiscal agent for this project, which will require major funding from a number of sources—an estimated $3,500,000 over the project's five years. The Richardson Foundation has provided the first grant, hoping to attract additional funding. Most of the funds will be expended on staff development, evaluation, and dissemination. Because of the emphasis on staff development, the participating districts should enjoy a real improvement in educational awareness, preparedness, and vision. They expect to be able to continue their programs at the same high level when the project comes to an end.

STATE AND REGIONAL CONFERENCES

The Pyramid Project provides a model response from one audience for this report, educational policy makers at the district level. An important additional audience is those agencies, both public and private, that provide funding for education.

To encourage the development of comprehensive programs for able learners throughout the country, the Richardson Foundation has initiated a number of state and regional conferences bringing business and foundation executives and state legislators together with educators, parents, and others with an interest in education. Participants review the findings of the study and the progress of the Pyramid Project in Texas. The first such conference was hosted by Winrock International in Arkansas. Participants came from Arkansas, Oklahoma, and Texas. It was as a direct result of this meeting that the Ardmore public schools secured funding to develop their project based on the pyramid concept.

Public funding and state legislation are also crucial, for public education is funded primarily at the state level. By including legislators and personnel from the state education agencies as conference participants, the foundation seeks to stimulate thoughtful discussions of the need for broad-based support for this segment of the student population. The Richardson Foundation hopes this study will serve and inform such discussions. For our part, we are pleased to see projects resulting from the study already off the ground.

Appendices

APPENDIX A
Conferences

RICHARDSON CONFERENCE
Amfac Hotel and Resort, Dallas/Fort Worth International Airport,
March 26–27, 1981

Staff

Valleau Wilkie, Jr., Sid W. Richardson Foundation, Fort Worth, Texas
June Cox, Sid W. Richardson Foundation, Fort Worth, Texas

Speakers

John Ehle, Novelist, Winston-Salem, North Carolina
John Silber, President, Boston University, Massachusetts

Participants

Laura Allard, Gifted Students Institute, Arlington, Texas
Alexinia Y. Baldwin, State University of New York, Albany
Richard Benjamin, Fort Worth Independent School District, Texas
Ernest Bernal, Creative Educational Enterprises, Inc., Austin, Texas
Barbara Clark, California State University, Los Angeles
Sanford J. Cohn, Arizona State University, Tempe
Neil Daniel, Texas Christian University, Fort Worth
Betty Fuller, Hurst-Euless-Bedford Independent School District,
    Euless, Texas
Juliana Gensley, National Association for Gifted Children,
    Calabasas, California
J. W. Getzels, University of Chicago, Illinois
Marvin Gold, *G/C/T* and *Chart Your Course*, Mobile, Alabama
Milton J. Gold, Teachers College, Columbia University, New York,
    New York
Smith Goodrum, Mars Hill College, North Carolina
Eleanor G. Hall, University of Wisconsin, Green Bay, Wisconsin
Judith Judy, Texas Association for the Gifted and Talented, Temple
Leonard J. Lucito, Georgia State University, Atlanta

Harold C. Lyon, Jr., Department of Health, Education and Welfare, Washington, D.C.

Ann McGee-Cooper, Texas Woman's University, Dallas

June Maker, University of New Mexico, Albuquerque

William R. Nash, Texas A&M University, College Station

Al Oliver, University of Pennsylvania, Broomall

Charles Patterson, Texas Association for Gifted and Talented, Killeen

Annamarie Roeper, Gifted Consultant, Franklin, Michigan

Margaret Russell, Arlington Independent School District, Texas

Robert Sawyer, Duke University, Durham, North Carolina

K. R. Seeley, University of Denver, Colorado

Ann Shaw, Texas Education Agency, Austin, Texas

Dorothy Sisk, University of South Florida, Tampa

Cornelia Tongue, Department of Public Instruction, Raleigh, North Carolina

Jearnine Wagner, Learning About Learning, San Antonio, Texas

Miniconferences

The following series of miniconferences was held at the Americana Hotel and at the Fort Worth Club in Fort Worth, Texas, and at the Mandalay Four Seasons Hotel in Irving, Texas, on:

June 6–9, 1981

October 9–11, 1981

February 11–12, 1982

June 6–8, 1982

September 21–23, 1982

December 15–17, 1982

February 13–15, 1983

April 22–24, 1983

May 29–31, 1983

September 12–14, 1983

October 27–31, 1983

December 12–14, 1983

November 1–2, 1984

Those who participated in one or more meetings are listed below.

Staff

Valleau Wilkie, Jr., Sid W. Richardson Foundation, Fort Worth, Texas
June Cox, Sid W. Richardson Foundation, Fort Worth, Texas

Committee Members

Richard Benjamin, Fort Worth Independent School District, Texas
J. W. Getzels, University of Chicago, Illinois
Marvin Gold, *G/C/T*, Mobile, Alabama
Dorothy Sisk, University of South Florida, Tampa

Adjunct Committee Members

Laura Allard, Gifted Students Institute, Arlington, Texas
Charles Patterson, Killeen Independent School District, Texas
Ann Shaw, Texas Education Agency, Austin

Writers/Authors

June Cox, Sid W. Richardson Foundation, Fort Worth, Texas
Neil Daniel, Texas Christian University, Fort Worth
Bruce Boston, Wordsmith, Inc., Fairfax, Virginia

Consultants

Ernest Bernal, Creative Educational Enterprises, Inc., Austin, Texas
Jewell Bindrup, Utah Department of Education, Salt Lake City
Bruce Boston, Wordsmith, Inc., Fairfax, Virginia
Steven M. Brown, Madison Elementary School District, Phoenix, Arizona
Sanford J. Cohn, Arizona State University, Tempe
Robert L. Crawford, Phillips Academy, Andover, Massachusetts
Donald R. Davis, Executive High School Internship Association, Springfield, Illinois
Dennis Day, Highland Park High School, Dallas, Texas
Mary M. Frasier, University of Georgia, Athens
Martha Fulbright, Weslaco Independent School District, Texas
Ward J. Ghory, Walnut Hills School, Cincinnati, Ohio
Kathy Hargrove, Plano Independent School District, Texas
Paul E. Heckman, University of California, Los Angeles
Betty Herbert, Houston Independent School District, Texas

Marie Laine, O. D. Wyatt High School, Fort Worth, Texas

Norma Lowder, High School for the Performing and Visual Arts, Houston, Texas

Leonard J. Lucito, Georgia State University, Atlanta

Nancy McClaran, Marshall Public Schools, Texas

Mary McElroy, Houston Independent School District, Texas

Gayle Mineweaser, Southfield Public Schools, Michigan

William R. Nash, Texas A&M University, College Station

H. Gilbert Nicol, International Baccalaureate North America, New York, New York

Terry O'Banion, Dallas County Community College District, Texas

A. Harry Passow, Teachers College, Columbia University, New York, New York

Paul Plowman, California State Department of Education, Sacramento

Philip M. Powell, University of Texas, Austin

C. K. Rekdal, Medina Resource Center, Bellevue, Washington

Joseph Renzulli, University of Connecticut, Storrs

Gail Riley, Hurst-Euless-Bedford Independent School District, Bedford, Texas

Irving Sato, Leadership Training Institute, Los Angeles, California

Ann Shaw, Texas Education Agency, Austin

Joan Shelley, Carrollton–Farmers Branch Independent School District, Carrollton, Texas

Irwin Spear, University of Texas, Austin

Samuel M. Stone, North Carolina School of the Arts, Winston-Salem

Mike Stuart, Chamber of Commerce, Dallas, Texas

Bess Tittle, Free-Lance Writer, San Diego, California

de Saussure M. Trevino, McAllen Independent School District, Texas

Joyce VanTassel-Baska, Northwestern University, Evanston, Illinois

William G. Vassar, Connecticut State Department of Education, Hartford

Margaret C. Wang, University of Pittsburgh, Pennsylvania

Elizabeth Wendell, Albuquerque Public Schools, New Mexico

Betty H. Yarborough, Darden School of Education, Norfolk, Virginia

Other Participants

Don Achziger, Mesquite Independent School District, Texas

John W. Arnn, Jr., Texas Christian University, Fort Worth

Connie Baker, Sherman Public Schools, Texas
Paul Baker, Arts Magnet School, Dallas, Texas
Nancy Bower, Arlington Independent School District, Texas
Toni Brown, Fort Worth Independent School District, Texas
I. Carl Candoli, Fort Worth Independent School District, Texas
Harris Cantrell, Ysleta Independent School District, El Paso, Texas
Piers L. Chance, City Center Development Company, Fort Worth, Texas
Frances Chaney, Fort Worth Independent School District, Texas
M. E. Chappell, Sid W. Richardson Foundation, Fort Worth, Texas
Barbara Clark, California State University, Los Angeles
Donna Clopton, West Texas State University, Canyon
Cathy Collins, Texas Christian University, Fort Worth
Don Cook, State Board of Education, Mesquite, Texas
Ruth Cowan, Oakland Center, Lawrenceville, Georgia
Pat Denton, Fort Worth Independent School District, Texas
Dorys Dickey, Judson Independent School District, Converse, Texas
Charles Evans, State Representative, Hurst, Texas
Anne Ferrell, Irving Independent School District, Texas
Betty Fuller, Hurst-Euless-Bedford Independent School District, Euless,
    Texas
Juliana Gensley, National Association for Gifted Children, Calabasas,
    California
Milton J. Gold, Teachers College, Columbia University, New York,
    New York
Smith Goodrum, Mars Hill College, North Carolina
Shirley Hall, Advisory Committee on Gifted and Talented Education to
    the State Board of Education, Weatherford, Texas
Trudy H. Herolz, Houston Independent School District, Texas
JoAnn Houston, Grapevine-Colleyville Independent School District,
    Grapevine, Texas
Mary Frances Hull, Education Service Center, Fort Worth, Texas
Judith Judy, Texas Association for the Gifted and Talented, Temple
Elaine F. Klos, Fort Worth Association for Gifted and Talented, Texas
Chita Kramer, Grand Prairie Independent School District, Texas
John R. Lamond III, Tarrant County Community College Board Member,
    Fort Worth, Texas
Lee Anne Lamond, Birdville Association for Gifted and Talented, Fort
    Worth, Texas

Mollie Lasater, Board Member, Fort Worth Independent School District, Texas

Suzanne Lasko, Board Member, Fort Worth Independent School District, Texas

Grace Lichtenstein, Free-Lance Writer, New York, New York

Vance Littleton, Corpus Christi Independent School District, Texas

Annette Lowry, Fort Worth Independent School District, Texas

Harold C. Lyon, Jr., Department of Health, Education and Welfare, Washington, D.C.

John W. McFarland, Texas Woman's University, Denton

Ann McGee-Cooper, Author/Consultant, Dallas, Texas

June Maker, University of New Mexico, Albuquerque

John Mangieri, Texas Christian University, Fort Worth

Terry Masters, MasterSchool, Austin, Texas

Mickey Mayer, Education Service Center, Richardson, Texas

Al Oliver, University of Pennsylvania, Broomall

Elene Ondo, Alice Carlson Elementary School, Fort Worth, Texas

Marjorie Powell, Westcliff Elementary School, Fort Worth, Texas

Billy R. Regan, Houston Independent School District, Texas

Anne Roberts, Lincoln Instructional Center, Dallas, Texas

Annamarie Roeper, Gifted Consultant, Franklin, Michigan

Margaret Russell, Arlington Independent School District, Texas

Sandra Santillo, Dallas Independent School District, Texas

K. R. Seeley, University of Denver, Colorado

J. D. Shipp, Fort Worth Independent School District, Texas

Paul M. Stevens, State Board of Education, Fort Worth, Texas

Willis M. Tate, Southern Methodist University, Dallas, Texas

Cornelia Tongue, Department of Public Instruction, Raleigh, North Carolina

Jearnine Wagner, Learning About Learning, San Antonio, Texas

Donald G. Williams, Birdville Independent School District, Fort Worth, Texas

Linus Wright, Dallas Independent School District, Texas

Jocelyn Wuester, Board Member, Fort Worth Independent School District, Texas

Questionnaire Consultants

Alexinia Y. Baldwin, State University of New York, Albany
Eleanor G. Hall, University of Wisconsin, Green Bay
Frances A. Karnes, University of Southern Mississippi, Hattiesburg
A. Harry Passow, Teachers College, Columbia University, New York, New York

Data Analysts

Robert Demaree, Texas Christian University, Fort Worth
Bennett Fletcher, Texas Christian University, Fort Worth
LaVerne Knezek, Texas Christian University, Fort Worth
Brenda Mitchell, Consultant, Garland, Texas

RICHARDSON STUDY REVIEW CONFERENCE

Sponsored by the Aspen Institute for Humanistic Studies, the Wye Institute, and the Sid W. Richardson Foundation, Wye Plantation, Queenstown, Maryland, November 27–29, 1984

Participants

Laura Allard, Texas Association for the Gifted and Talented, Austin
Joan Beck, *Chicago Tribune*, Illinois
Richard Benjamin, Ann Arbor Public Schools, Michigan
Richard B. Bessey, Corning Glass Works Foundation, New York
Bruce Boston, Wordsmith, Inc., Fairfax, Virginia
M. E. Chappell, Sid W. Richardson Foundation, Fort Worth, Texas
June Cox, Sid W. Richardson Foundation, Fort Worth, Texas
Neil Daniel, Texas Christian University, Fort Worth
Ruth Duskin Feldman, Free-Lance Writer, Highland Park, Illinois
Gordon E. Forward, Chaparral Steel, Dallas, Texas
Marvin Gold, *G/C/T* Publishing Company, Inc., Mobile, Alabama
Kenneth Hope, John D. and Catherine T. MacArthur Foundation, Chicago, Illinois
Arthur A. Houghton, Jr., Carmichael Farm, Queenstown, Maryland
Stephen Kaagan, Commissioner of Education, Montpelier, Vermont
Merle B. Karnes, University of Illinois, Champaign
Brenda Sheperd Mitchell, Consultant, Garland, Texas

Patricia Bruce Mitchell, National Association of State Boards of Education, Alexandria, Virginia

Anne Hodges Morgan, Kerr Foundation, Inc., Oklahoma City, Oklahoma

James G. Nelson, Wye Institute, Inc., Queenstown, Maryland

Lynn Olson, *Education Week*, Washington, D.C.

Charles Patterson, Killeen Independent School District, Texas

David Perkins, Harvard Project Zero, Cambridge, Massachusetts

Ann G. Shaw, Texas Education Agency, Austin

Dorothy Sisk, University of South Florida, Tampa

Frederick J. Weintraub, Council for Exceptional Children, Reston, Virginia

John F. White, Aspen Institute for Humanistic Studies, New York, New York

Anthony B. Wight, Aspen Institute for Humanistic Studies, New Haven, Connecticut

Brian L. Wilcox, Legislative Assistant, Washington, D.C.

Valleau Wilkie, Jr., Sid W. Richardson Foundation, Fort Worth, Texas

Edward L. Williams, Winrock International, Morrilton, Arkansas

Auditing Participants

Catherine Chappell, Fort Worth, Texas

Doris Gluck, Gifted Students Institute, Fort Worth, Texas

Nina Houghton, Queenstown, Maryland

Charles Radcliffe, National Association of Gifted Children, Washington, D.C.

Margie Snyder, Los Angeles, California

Paul H. H. Snyder, Atlantic Richfield Company, Los Angeles, California

Joan White, New York, New York

MacArthur Fellows Who Responded

Name (Age)	Field/Current Affiliation
George Archibald (37)	Ornithology, Conservation/ International Crane Foundation
R. Stephen Berry (51)	Chemistry, Energy Research/ University of Chicago
Joseph Brodsky (41)	Poetry/Columbia University; Mt. Holyoke College
John Cairns (59)	Molecular Biology/Harvard School of Public Health
William C. Clark (34)	Ecology and Environmental Studies/ Institute for Energy Analysis; Oak Ridge Associated Universities
Joel E. Cohen (37)	Population Sciences/Rockefeller University
Robert Coles (51)	Research Psychiatry/Harvard University; University Health Services
Richard Critchfield (50)	Journalism
Philip D. Curtin (60)	History (Africa)/Johns Hopkins University
Robert Darnton (43)	History (Enlightenment and French Revolution)/Princeton University
Shelly Errington (36)	Anthropology (Southeast Asian Cultures)/University of California, Santa Cruz
David L. Felten (34)	Anatomy, Neurobiology/University of Rochester Medical Center
Randall Forsberg (40)	Defense and Disarmament Studies/ Institute for Defense and Disarmament Studies

Name/(Age)	*Field/Current Affiliation*
William Gaddis (59)	Fiction
Howard E. Gardner (38)	Developmental Psychology/Boston University Medical Center; Harvard University
Henry Gates (30)	English, Afro-American Studies/ Yale University
Alexander George (63)	Political Science/Stanford University
Michael T. Ghiselin (42)	Biology, History of Science/ California Academy of Sciences
Shelomo D. Goitein (82)	History (Medieval Mediterranean)/Institute for Advanced Study, Princeton
Ian Graham (57)	Archaeology (Mayan)/Peabody Museum of Archaeology and Ethnology, Harvard University
Mott Greene (37)	History of Geology/University of Washington
James E. Gunn (44)	Astronomy, Astrophysics/Princeton University
Robert Hass (42)	Poetry, Criticism, and Translation/ St. Mary's College of California
David Hawkins (68)	Education, Philosophy/Mountain View Center for Environmental Education, University of Colorado
Ada Louise Huxtable (60)	Architecture Criticism
Robert W. Irwin (55)	Visual Arts
Ruth Prawer Jhabvala (56)	Fiction, Screen Writing
Bela Julesz (54)	Experimental Psychology/Bell Laboratories
Leszek Kolakowski (55)	Political Philosophy, History of Philosophy/Committee on Social Thought, University of Chicago

Name/(Age)	*Field/Current Affiliation*
Paul Oskar Kristeller (78)	Renaissance Studies/Columbia University
Sylvia Law (41)	Law, Human Rights/New York University
Brad Leithauser (29)	Poetry, Law/Amherst College
Michael Lerner (40)	Public Health/Commonweal
Matthew Meselson (53)	Molecular Biology, Arms Control/Fairchild Biochemical Laboratories, Harvard University
Richard A. Muller (38)	Experimental Physics/University of California, Berkeley
Douglas D. Osheroff (35)	Experimental Physics/Bell Laboratories
Elaine H. Pagels (38)	History of Religion/Princeton University
Paul Richards (38)	Theoretical Seismology, Geophysics/Lamont-Doherty Geological Observatory of Columbia University
Alice M. Rivlin (52)	Economics, Public Affairs/Brookings Institution
Francesca Rochberg-Halton (30)	Assyriology/Oriental Institute, University of Chicago
Robert S. Root-Bernstein (27)	Biochemistry, History of Science/Salk Institute for Biological Studies
Richard Rorty (50)	Philosophy of Language/University of Virginia
Lawrence Rosen (39)	Anthropology, Law/Princeton University
John Sayles (32)	Fiction, Film-Making
Judith Shklar (55)	Political Philosophy/Harvard University

Name/(Age)	*Field/Current Affiliation*
Charles Simic (45)	Poetry, Essays/University of New Hampshire
John E. Toews (39)	Intellectual History/University of Washington
James E. Turrell (40)	Visual Arts/Skystone Foundation
Robert Penn Warren (76)	Poetry, Fiction, Literary Criticism
Adrian Wilson (59)	Typography, Book Design, Rare Books
Edward Witten (30)	Theoretical Physics/Princeton University
Carl Woese (55)	Molecular Biology/University of Illinois

APPENDIX C

THE RICHARDSON STUDY

FOLLOW-UP QUESTIONNAIRE

The Sid W. Richardson Foundation in Fort Worth, Texas, is continuing its national study of elementary and secondary programs for gifted students. We are collecting data on programs that are identified as special programs for the gifted and also on other provisions for the most able and talented students which may not be identified as "Gifted Programs."

This follow-up questionnaire, though rather lengthy, should require only a few minutes of your time since not all of it will be applicable to any one district. You will notice that the programs are identified by a Roman numeral in the margin and that they are separated by double lines. We request that you complete the General Information section at the beginning and any of the other sections which apply to your district or school. The results of the study will be available nationally to all who are concerned with this important issue.

An addressed envelope, requiring no postage, is enclosed for your convenience.

GENERAL INFORMATION

School District*_____
Name of District or School

Check here if you are responding for an individual school. _____

Name of person completing questionnaire_____

Person's title _____Telephone No. _____ / _____
AC

Address_____
Street

City	State	Zip

A. What is the total population of the area served by your school district?

____(1) Less than 50,000   ____(2) 50,000-100,000   ____(3) 100,000-200,000

____(4) 200,000-300,000   ____(5) 300,000-400,000   ____(6) 400,000-500,000

____(7) More than 500,000

B. Please list the number of certified staff members in your district.

____(1)

C. What percentage of teachers have as their highest degree:

____(1) B.S., B.A.   ____(2) M.S., M.A., M.Ed.   ____(3) Ph.D, D.Ed.

D. Is the school: ____(1) Public   ____(2) Private

____(3) Parochial   ____(4) Other. Please specify. _____

E. Is the student population:

____(1) All male   ____(2) All female   ____(3) Co-educational

*If you are responding for an individual school, please equate the word district with school each time it appears in the questionnaire.

F. Please list the number of students enrolled in:

___(1) Pre-School ___(2) Elementary (Inc. K.)

___(3) Middle/Junior High ___(4) Senior High

G. The student ethnic ratio is:

___(1) % Anglo ___(2) % Black ___(3) % Hispanic

___(4) % Asian ___(5) % Native American

___ Other. Please specify. _____

H. What percentage of students receive a free or reduced-price lunch?

___(1) None ___(2) List the percentage who do.

I. Check the procedures included in identifying students for special programs or provisions for gifted students.

___(1) None ___(2) I. Q. tests ___(3) Achievement tests

___(4) Grades ___(5) Teacher nomination ___(6 Peer nomination

___(7) Other. Please specify. _____

J. Are there special requirements for teachers in these programs?

___(1) No ___(2) Yes. Please specify. _____

_____

K. The following staff members participate in inservice training on a regular basis:

___(1) None ___(2) Teachers in gifted/talented programs

___(3) All teachers ___(4) Counselors ___(5) Administrators

___(6) Other. Please specify. _____

L. Is a staff member at the supervisory or administration level responsible for the gifted program?

___(1) Yes. Specify title. _____ ___(2) No

M. Check the following resources your program uses.

___(1) Library ___(2) Museum ___(3) Industry ___(4) Government Agency

___(5) Mentors ___(6) Others. Please specify. _____

_____

N. Does the district have a written philosophy for educating gifted students?

___(1) Yes ___(2) No

O. Goals for gifted/talented students are written:

___(1) For the district level ___(2) For the building level ___(3) Not at all

P. An advisory group for the gifted/talented program includes:

___(1) Students ___(2) Parents ___(3) Teachers ___(4) Administrators

___(5) Others. Please specify. _____ ___(6) Does not exist

Q. Special procedures for evaluating the gifted/talented program are established:

___(1) At the district level ___(2) At the building level ___(3) Neither

R. What is the per pupil expenditure in your district?

____(1) Less than $1,500   ____(2) $1,500-$2,000   ____(3) $2,000-$2,500

____(4) $2,500-$3,000   ____(5) $3,000-$3,500   ____(6) $3,500-$4,000

____(7) $4,000-$4,500   ____(8) $4,500-$5,000   ____(9) More than $5,000

S. Are special additional budgetary provisions made for gifted/talented students?

____(1) Yes   ____(2) No

T. If special funding is available for gifted/talented, check any of the following sources which apply.

____(1) State   ____(2) Local   ____(3) Federal   ____(4) Private

____(5) Other. Please specify. _____

U. Please list the program or school in your district which you recommend for a visit from an outside observor.

Name of school_____

Address_____

                                  Street

_____

           City   State   Zip

Person to contact_____ Position_____

Telephone No. _____ / _____
           AC

I ENRICHMENT IN THE REGULAR CLASSROOM. The teacher, with or without special assistance, provides enrichment activities for gifted students in a heterogeneous classroom. We include individualized instruction in this category

V. How many students participate in the enrichment activities?

____(1) All of the class   ____(2) Those identified as gifted/talented

____(3) Those identified as gifted/talented plus others, but not including the entire class.

W. How much time is allotted to enrichment activities per week?

____(1) Less than 3 hours   ____(2) 3-5 hours   ____(3) More than 5 hours

X. Which content areas are enriched?

____(1) Math   ____(2) Science   ____(3) English/Language Arts

____(4) Social Studies   ____(5) Multidisciplinary

____(6) Other. Please specify. _____

Y. Are the curricular materials used in the enrichment activities:

____(1) The same as those used in the basic program

____(2) Different from those used in the basic program

Z. What strategies are used in the enrichment activities?

____(1) Group instruction   ____(2) Individualized instruction

____(3) Special projects   ____(4) Puzzles and games

____(5) Other. Please specify. _____

II   PART-TIME SPECIAL CLASS. The gifted student is with a heterogeneous class part of the time but is with students of similar ability part of the time. At the elementary level, this provision might be described as a "pull-out" program; at the secondary level it would include honors classes. Resource rooms are considered later as a separate category.

AA.   How many days per week does the special class meet?

_____(1) 1 day per week   _____(2) 2-4 days per week   _____(3) 5 days per week

BB.   What is the length of each class session?

_____(1) Less than 1 hour   _____(2) 1-2 hours   _____(3) More than 2 hours

CC.   Which content areas are studied in the special class?

_____(1) Math   _____(2) Science   _____(3) English/Language Arts

_____(4) Social Studies   _____(5) Multidisciplinary

_____(6) Other   Please specify. _____

DD.   What strategies are used in the special class?

_____(1) Group instruction   _____(2) Individualized instruction

_____(3) Special projects   _____(4) Puzzles and games

_____(5) Other.   Please specify. _____

EE.   Do the regular classroom teacher and the special class teacher co-ordinate their curricular plans:

_____(1) Regularly   _____(2) Occasionally   _____(3) Not at all

FF.   Is a student required to make up work covered in the regular classroom during his/her absence?

_____(1) Yes   _____(2) No

III FULL-TIME SPECIAL CLASS. At the elementary level, this might be a self contained or departmentalized classroom of high-ability students. At the secondary level, this might be a single course in which the student's curriculum is enriched and accelerated. See XV for situations where two or more classes are integrated and fast-paced.

GG.   Which content areas are studied in the special class?

_____(1) Math   _____(2) Science_____(3) English/Language Arts

_____(4) Social Studies   _____(5) Multidisciplinary

_____(6) Other.   Please specify. _____

HH.   Are the curricular materials the same as those studied in regular classes?

_____(1) Yes   _____(2) No

II.   How are students assigned to special classes?

_____(1) Specific selection criteria   _____(2) Self-selection

JJ.   Is the amount of curricular material covered:

_____(1) About the same as in the regular classes   _____(2) Greater than in the regular classes

IV INDEPENDENT STUDY. A student chooses certain areas or investigation and assumes a high degree of responsibility for meeting objectives.

KK. How much school time is allotted to independent study?

_____(1) Less than 3 hours per week   _____(2) 3-5 hours per week

_____(3) More than 5 hours per week

LL. In which content areas do students engage in independent study?

_____(1) Math   _____(2) Science   _____(3) English/Language Arts

_____(4) Social Studies   _____(5) Multidisciplinary

_____(6) Other.   Please specify. _____

MM. What resources do the students use in independent study?

_____(1) Staff   _____(2) Library   _____(3) Community   _____(4) Laboratory

_____(5) Other.   Please specify. _____

NN. How is a student's independent study progress evaluated?

_____(1) Self   _____(2) Teacher

_____(3) Other.   Please specify. _____

V ITINERANT TEACHER. A teacher with special skills in gifted education teaches gifted students in more than one school on a regular basis.

OO. How many schools do itinerant teachers serve?

_____(1) Less than 5   _____(2) 5-10   _____(3) More than 10

PP. Do itinerant teachers teach in:

_____(1) The regular classroom teacher's room

_____(2) A permanent classroom assigned for the purpose

_____(3) In a variety of settings

QQ. Do the regular classroom teacher and the itinerant teacher co-ordinate their curricular plans:

_____(1) Regularly   _____(2) Occasionally   _____(3) Not at all

RR. What is the average number of miles driven by an itinerant teacher per week, exclusive of the distance to and from home?

_____(1) Less than 50 miles   _____(2) 50-100 miles   _____(3) More than 100 miles

VI MENTORSHIPS. We define mentorships as a program which assigns gifted students to work or study with adults who have special knowledge or skills in the student's areas of interest. We include the High School Executive Internship Program in this category.

SS. How much school time is allotted to a student to work with a mentor?

_____(1) None; it is an out-of-school program   _____(2) Less than 3 hours per week

_____(3) 3-5 hours per week   _____(4) More than 5 hours per week

TT. Is Carnegie credit awarded for work with mentors?

_____(1) Yes   _____(2) No   _____(3) Sometimes

UU. How are mentors selected?

___(1) On a voluntary basis ___(2) Specific criteria ___(3) Recommendations

VV. Who are the mentors?

___(1) School staff ___(2) University faculty ___(3 Business and professional people

___(4) Other. Please specify. _____

WW. Do mentors receive special training?

___(1) Yes ___(2) No

XX. Are mentors paid?

___(1) Yes ___(2) No

VII RESOURCE ROOMS. This might be a corner of the library or an entire room where gifted students go individually or in groups to explore special areas of study.

YY. How much time per week does a student spend in a resource room?

___(1) Less than 3 hours ___(2) 3-5 hours ___(3) More than 5 hours

ZZ. Is time scheduled in the resource room:

___(1) The same each week ___(2) Varied from week to week

AAA. Who is in charge of the resource room?

___(1) Special teacher of the gifted ___(2) Librarian

___(3) Aide ___(4) Parent ___(5) Community volunteer

BBB. What materials are available in the resource room?

___(1) Books ___(2) Films ___(3) Packets

___ Other. Please specify. _____

CCC. What equipment is available in the resource room?

___(1) Laboratory equipment ___(2) Shop tools

___(3) Other. Please specify. _____

DDD. Where is the resource room located?

___(1) In a separate room ___(2) In the library

___(3) Other. Please specify. _____

VIII SPECIAL SCHOOLS. These include magnet schools which focus on a single discipline as well as these which include the entire spectrum. Also included are residential schools for the gifted.

EEE. Is the special school:

___(1) Residential ___(2) Non-residential

FFF. Does the special school have a:

___(1) General curriculum

___(2) Special area of concentration. Please specify. _____

GGG. Is the school considered a magnet?

___(1) Yes ___(2) No

HHH. How are students selected?

___(1) Self-selected ___(2) Specific criteria

III. Is the school considered a school for gifted students?

___(1) Yes ___(2) No

JJJ. Do students pay tuition?

___(1) Yes ___(2) No

KKK. How long has the school been in existence?

___(1) Less than 5 years ___(2) 5-10 years ___(3) More than 10 years

IX EARLY ENTRANCE. We define early entrance as a policy of allowing students to enter a school earlier than the normal age for that district.

LLL. At what level(s) is the provision for early entrance made?

___(1) Kindergarten ___(2) First Grade

___(3) Middle/Junior High School ___(4) Senior High School

MMM. How many students entered these levels last year due to early entrance policy? List the numbers please.

___(1) Kindergarten ___(2) First Grade

___(3) Middle/Junior High School ___(4) Senior High School

NNN. On what basis were early assignments made? Check all which apply.

___(1) Ability test ___(2) Achievement test ___(3) Teacher recommendation

___(4) Parental request ___(5) Other. Please specify. _____

OOO. Of the number accepted last year as early entrants, how many continued for at least one full year? List numbers at the appropriate levels please.

___(1) Kindergarten ___(2) First Grade

___(3) Middle/Junior High School ___(4) Senior High School

PPP. Last year how many students left high school prior to graduation to enter college or university?

___(1) None ___(2) List the number, please.

QQQ. How long has the early-entrance policy existed in your school (or district)?

___(1) Less than 5 years ___(2) 5-to 10 years ___(3) More than 10 years

X CONTINUOUS PROGRESS. We define continuous progress as a provision for students to progress through the curriculum of one or more subject area as the required skills are mastered.

RRR. At what level(s) is continuous progress in operation?

___(1) Pre-School ___(2) Elementary (Inc. K)

___(3) Middle/Junior High School ___(4) Senior High School

SSS. In what content areas does continuous progress allow students to advance at their own pace?

___(1) Math   ___(2) Science   ___(3) Social Studies

___(4) Language Arts (Inc. Reading)   ___(5) English   ___(6) Foreign Language

___(7) Other.   Please specify. _____

TTT. On what basis does a student move from one level to another?

___(1) Standarized tests   ___(2) Teacher made tests

___(3) Demonstrated competency   ___(4) Other. Please specify. _____

UUU. What percentage of students are functioning above grade level in one or more content areas this year?

___(1) Less than 5%   ___(2) 5%-10%___(3) 11%-20%   ___(4) More than 20%

VVV. How would you describe the continuous progress program?

___(1) Group instruction   ___(2) Individual instruction

___(3) Other.   Please specify. _____

WWW. How long has the continuous progress program been in operation?

___(1) Less than 5 years   ___(2) 5-to 10 years   ___(3) More than 10 years

---

XI NONGRADED SCHOOL. We define a nongraded school as one in which the usual labels, such as first grade have been removed, and students progress at their own pace. Thus, one child might complete what is normally covered in one grade in less than the usual amount of time, and another child might require more than the usual amount of time to gain the skills generally acquired in one year in a graded school situation.

XXX. At what level(s) is your school (or district) nongraded?

___(1) Pre-School   ___(2) Elementary (Inc. K)

___(3) Middle/Junior High   ___(4) Senior High

YYY. Do some students complete the level(s) checked in fewer years than is normally required?

___(1) Yes   ___(2) No

ZZZ. If you answered "Yes," how many students:

___(1) Received additional enrichment only

___(2) Were offered curricula from the next higher level but did not leave the first school

___(3) Moved on to the next higher school

AAAA. How long has your school (or district) been nongraded?

___(1) Less than 5 years   ___(2) 1-to 10 years   ___(3) More than 10 years

---

XII MODERATE ACCELERATION. We define moderate acceleration as any kind of provision which allows a student to complete the grades K-12 in less than thirteen years but more than ten.

BBBB. How many students were in last year's graduating class?

___(1) Less than 100   ___(2) 100 - 500   ___(3) More than 500

CCCC. Of this number, how many spent fewer than 13 years but more than ten in grades K-12?

_____(1) Less than 2%   _____(2) 2% - 5%   _____(3) More than 5%

DDDD. How long has your school had a policy which allowed or encouraged moderate acceleration?

_____(1) Less than 2 years   _____(2) 2 - 5 years   _____(3) More than 5 years

---

II RADICAL ACCELERATION. We define radical acceleration as any kind of provision which allows a student to complete grades K-12 in fewer than 11 years.

EEEE. How many students were in last year's graduating class?

_____(1) Less than 100   _____(2) 100 - 500   _____(3) More than 500

FFFF. Of this number, how many spent fewer than 11 years in grades K-12?

_____(1) Less than 1%   _____(2) 1% - 2%   _____(3) More than 2%

GGGG How long has your school had a policy which allowed or encouraged radical acceleration?

_____(1) Less than 2 years   _____(2) 2 - 5 years   _____(3) More than 5 years

---

V COLLEGE BOARD ADVANCED PLACEMENT. As the name specifies, we refer to the Advanced Placement of the College Board.

HHHH How long has your school offered College Board Advanced Placement Courses?

_____(1) Less than 5 years   _____(2) 5 - 10 years   _____(3) More than 10 years

IIII. In what content areas does your school offer Advanced Placement courses?

_____(1) American History   _____(2) Art-History   _____(3) Biology   _____(4) Chemistry

_____(5) English Composition/Literature   _____(6) English Language/Composition

_____(7) European History   _____(8) French   _____(9) German   _____(10) Latin

_____(11) Mathematics   _____(12) Music   _____(13) Physics   _____(14) Spanish

JJJJ. How many students completed at least one Advanced Placement course last year?
List the number, please.

_____(1) Sophomores   _____(2) Juniors   _____(3) Seniors

_____(4) Others.   Please specify. _____

KKKK. How many students took at least one Advanced Placement examination last year?
List the number, please.

_____(1) Sophomores   _____(2) Juniors   _____(3) Seniors

_____(4) Others.   Please specify. _____

LLLL. What percentage of the examinations received a score of:

_____(1) "3"   _____(2) "4"   _____(3) "5"

MMMM. How were the Advanced Placement opportunities offered?

_____(1) Conventional classes   _____(2) Independent study

_____(3) Seminars   _____(4) Correspondence courses

_____(5) Other.   Please specify. _____

XV   FAST PACED COURSES. We define fast paced courses as an arrangement which allows a student to complete two or more courses in a discipline in an abbreviated time span.

NNNN.   Last year, how many students were enrolled in such courses in:

_____(1) Mathematics   _____(2) Foreign language   _____(3) Science

_____(4) Other.   Please specify. _____

XVI   CONCURRENT OR DUAL ENROLLMENT.   We define concurrent or dual enrollment as an arrangement which allows a student to enroll in classes on two campuses. For example, a middle/junior high student who takes one or more classes at the high school or a high school student who takes one or more classes on a college campus.

OOOO.   How many students enrolled in classes on two campuses last year? Please specify the numbers.

_____(1) Middle/Junior High and Senior High combination

_____(2) Middle/Junior High and College combination   _____(3) Senior High and College combination

PPPP.   Of the number who enrolled in classes at both the middle/junior high and senior high, what percentage satisfactorily completed the class?

_____(1) Less than 50%   _____(2) 50 - 75%   _____(3) 76% - 99%   _____(4) 100%

QQQQ.   Of the number who enrolled in classes at both the middle/junior high and college, what percentage satisfactorily completed the class?

_____(1) Less than 50%   _____(2) 50% - 75%   _____(3) 76% - 99%   _____(4) 100%

RRRR.   Of the number who enrolled in classes at a senior high school and college, what percentage satisfactorily completed the class?

_____(1) Less than 50%   _____(2) 50% - 75%   _____(3) 76% - 99%   _____(4) 100%

OTHER.   If your school has a provision or program for gifted students not listed in any of the above sections, please describe it briefly.

_____

_____

_____

_____

THANK YOU!

June Cox, Director of Research
Sid W. Richardson Foundation
309 Main Street
Fort Worth, Texas 76102

Survey Responses from Districts

$(N = 1,172)$*

A. What is the total population of the area served by your school district?

	N	%
1. Less than 50,000	951	(81)
2. 50,000–100,000	126	(11)
3. 100,000–200,000	46	(4)
4. 200,000–300,000	14	(1)
5. 300,000–400,000	6	(1)
6. 400,000–500,000	3	(<1)
7. More than 500,000	12	(1)
No. of Districts Reporting	1,158	(99)

B. Please list the number of certified staff members in your district.

No. of Districts Reporting	1,054 or 90%
Median	154.8
Mean	383.2
Range	1–16,034

C. What percentage of teachers have as their highest degree:

	Median %	Mean %	Districts Reporting
1. B.S., B.A.	60.5	58	910
2. M.S., M.A., M.Ed.	37.2	40	938
3. Ph.D., Ed.D.	0.4	1	917

D. Is the school:

	N	%
1. Public	1,129	(96)
2. Private/Independent	0	(0)
3. Parochial	9	(1)
4. Other	1	(<1)
No. of Districts Reporting	1,139	(97)

---

*Percentage of districts answering each item is based on the total number of districts responding to the questionnaire—1,172. Not every district answered each question.

E. Is the student population:

	N	%
1. All male	2	(<1)
2. All female	1	(<1)
3. Coeducational	1,166	(99)
No. of Districts Reporting	1,169	(100)

F. Please list the number of students enrolled in:

Levels of Enrollment	N	Mean	Median	Range
Preschool	0	–	–	–
Elementary*	32	1,373.0	820.5	32–11,000
Middle/Junior High	7	1,301.0	707.0	120–3,900
Senior High	13	6,403.6	3,400.0	120–24,000
Preschool, Elementary	3	2,480.0	1,565.0	525–5,350
Preschool, Middle/Junior High	1	1,530.0	1,530.0	1,530–1,530
Preschool, Senior High	0	–	–	–
Elementary, Middle/Junior High	65	2,234.4	1,100.0	30–23,068
Elementary, Senior High	58	8,878.0	1,519.5	120–167,616
Middle/Junior High, Senior High	10	4,109.2	2,651.0	305–11,100
Preschool, Elementary, Middle/Junior High	19	2,697.6	1,212.0	27–23,807
Preschool, Elementary, Senior High	11	4,981.2	1,338.0	150–23,147
Elementary, Middle/Junior High, Senior High	609	6,502.3	2,800.4	31–127,586
Preschool, Elementary, Middle/Junior High, Senior High	231	11,331.7	3,760.0	194–400,673
No. of Districts Reporting	1,059	(90%)		

G. The student ethnic ratio is:

	Mean %
1. Anglo	(83)
2. Black	(8)
3. Hispanic	(5)
4. Asian	(1)

*Elementary included kindergarten in all cases.

5. Native American (1)
6. Other (<1)
    No. of Districts Reporting 989 or 84%

H. What percentage of students receive a free or reduced-price lunch?

	N	%
1. None	55	(5)
2. List the percentage who do.	Median Percentage = 20.2	
No. of Districts Reporting	931	(79)

I. Check the procedures included in identifying students for special programs or provisions for gifted students.

	N	%
1. None	33	(3)
2. I.Q. tests	956	(82)
3. Achievement tests	1,058	(90)
4. Grades	585	(50)
5. Teacher nomination	1,063	(91)
6. Peer nomination	298	(25)
7. Self	67	(6)
8. Parent	246	(21)
9. Creativity measure	74	(6)
10. Other	255	(22)
No. of Districts Reporting	1,160	(99)

J. Are there special requirements for teachers in these programs?

	N	%
1. No	449	(38)
2. Yes, inservice training, education, or experience specified	385	(33)
3. Yes, state certification in gifted and talented	136	(12)
4. Yes, attributes such as well-read, willing, high I.Q., time, and others	118	(10)
5. Yes, nothing specified	40	(3)
No. of Districts Reporting	1,128	(96)

K. The following staff members participate in inservice training on a regular basis:

	N	%
1. None	75	(6)
2. Teachers in gifted/talented programs	651	(56)
3. All teachers	753	(64)
4. Counselors	439	(37)
5. Administrators	598	(51)
6. Other	103	(9)
No. of Districts Reporting	1,148	(98)

L. Is a staff member at the supervisory or administration level responsible for the gifted program?

	N	%
1. Yes (no title specified)	69	(6)
2. Yes—principal, vice-principal, assistant principal	104	(9)
3. Yes—director of G/T programs, directors of special programs, etc.	412	(35)
4. Yes—superintendent, assistant superintendent, supervisor, administrator, assistant administrator	154	(13)
5. Yes—gifted/talented teacher, resource room teacher	11	(1)
6. Yes—teacher	4	(<1)
7. Yes—general curriculum directors, elementary or secondary instruction directors	160	(14)
8. Yes—other (director of funding, counselor, psychologist)	58	(5)
9. No	164	(14)
No. of Districts Reporting	1,136	(97)

M. Check the following resources your program uses.

	N	%
1. Library	1,070	(91)
2. Museum	662	(56)
3. Industry	592	(51)
4. Government agency	395	(34)
5. Mentors	591	(50)
6. Community	107	(9)
7. Parents	43	(4)

8. University or college	113	(10)
9. Others	226	(19)
No. of Districts Reporting	1,113	(95)

N. Does the district have a written philosophy for educating gifted students?

	N	%
1. Yes	847	(72)
2. No	301	(26)
No. of Districts Reporting	1,148	(98)

O. Goals for gifted/talented students are written:

	N	%
1. For the district level	841	(72)
2. For the building level and/or individual level*	272	(23)
3. Not at all	135	(12)
No. of Districts Reporting	1,126	(96)

P. An advisory group for the gifted/talented program includes:

	N	%
1. Students	149	(13)
2. Parents	632	(54)
3. Teachers	738	(63)
4. Administrators	720	(61)
5. Counselors	18	(2)
6. Others	113	(10)
7. Does not exist	295	(25)
No. of Districts Reporting	1,108	(95)

Q. Special procedures for evaluating the gifted/talented program are established:

	N	%
1. At the district level	808	(69)
2. At the building level and/or individual level*	271	(23)
3. Neither	174	(15)
No. of Districts Reporting	1,127	(96)

---

*"And/or individual level" was added because respondents wrote this in.

R. What is the per pupil expenditure in your district?

	N	%
1. Less than $1,500	260	(22)
2. $1,500–$2,000	335	(29)
3. $2,000–$2,500	213	(18)
4. $2,500–$3,000	124	(11)
5. $3,000–$3,500	49	(4)
6. $3,500–$4,000	20	(2)
7. $4,000–$4,500	4	(<1)
8. $4,500 or more	19	(2)
No. of Districts Reporting	1,024	(87)

S. Are special additional budgetary provisions made for gifted/talented students?

	N	%
1. Yes	860	(73)
2. No	264	(23)
No. of Districts Reporting	1,124	(96)

T. If special funding is available for gifted/talented, check any of the following sources which apply.

	N	%
1. State	749	(64)
2. Local	578	(49)
3. Federal	173	(15)
4. Private	42	(4)
5. Grants*	21	(2)
6. Other	22	(2)
No. of Districts Reporting	980	(84)

I. **Enrichment in the Regular Classroom.** The teacher, with or without special assistance, provides enrichment activities for gifted students in a heterogeneous classroom. We include individualized instruction in this category.

The number of districts responding to at least one question in this section was 737, or 63% of the 1,172 participating districts.

---

* "Grants" was added as a source because 21 respondents wrote it in. Federal grants were counted in both "Federal" and "Grants" categories.

V. How many students participate in the enrichment activities?

	N	%
1. All of the class	195	(26)
2. Those identified as gifted/talented	121	(16)
3. Those identified as gifted/talented plus others, but not including the entire class	413	(56)

W. How much time is allotted to enrichment activities per week?

	N	%
1. Less than 3 hours	431	(58)
2. 3–5 hours	258	(35)
3. More than 5 hours	84	(11)

X. Which content areas are enriched?

	N	%
1. Math	423	(57)
2. Science	329	(45)
3. English/Language Arts	451	(61)
4. Social Studies	277	(38)
5. Multidisciplinary	317	(43)
6. Arts and Music	38	(5)
7. Other	66	(9)

Y. Are the curricular materials used in the enrichment activities?

	N	%
1. The same as those used in the basic program	94	(13)
2. Different from those used in the basic program	487	(66)
3. Both	143	(19)

Z. What strategies are used in the enrichment activities?

	N	%
1. Group instruction	468	(64)
2. Individualized instruction	603	(82)
3. Special projects	650	(88)
4. Puzzles and games	422	(57)
5. Other	104	(14)

II. Part-Time Special Class. The gifted student is with a heterogeneous class part of the time but is with students of similar ability part of the time. At the elementary level, this provision might be described as a "pull-out" program; at the secondary level it would include honors classes. Resource rooms are considered later as a separate category.

The number of districts responding to at least one question in this section was 836, or 71% of the participating districts.

AA. How many days per week does the special class meet?

	N	%
1. 1 day per week	414	(50)
2. 2–4 days per week	298	(36)
3. 5 days per week	210	(25)

BB. What is the length of each class session?

	N	%
1. Less than 1 hour	261	(31)
2. 1–2 hours	350	(42)
3. More than 2 hours	275	(33)

CC. Which content areas are studied in the special class?

	N	%
1. Math	347	(42)
2. Science	313	(37)
3. English/Language Arts	423	(51)
4. Social Studies	261	(31)
5. Multidisciplinary	521	(62)
6. Arts and Music	32	(4)
7. Other	120	(14)

DD. What strategies are used in the special class?

	N	%
1. Group instruction	737	(88)
2. Individualized instruction	698	(83)
3. Special projects	772	(92)
4. Puzzles and games	528	(63)
5. Other	148	(18)

EE. Do the regular classroom teacher and the special class teacher coordinate their curricular plans:

	N	%
1. Regularly	172	(21)
2. Occasionally	519	(62)
3. Not at all	114	(14)

FF. Is a student required to make up work covered in the regular classroom during his/her absence?

	N	%
1. Yes	364	(44)
2. No	291	(35)
3. Sometimes	138	(17)

III. **Full-Time Special Class.** At the elementary level, this might be a self-contained or departmentalized classroom of high-ability students. At the secondary level, this might be a single course in which the student's curriculum is enriched and accelerated. See XV for situations where two or more classes are integrated and fast-paced.

The number of districts responding to at least one question in this section was 395, or 34% of the participating districts.

GG. Which content areas are studied in the special class?

	N	%
1. Math	250	(63)
2. Science	208	(53)
3. English/Language Arts	276	(70)
4. Social Studies	168	(43)
5. Multidisciplinary	122	(31)
6. Arts and Music	18	(5)
7. Other	42	(11)

HH. Are the curricular materials the same as those studied in regular classes?

	N	%
1. Yes	53	(13)
2. No	308	(78)
3. Sometimes	33	(8)

II. How are students assigned to special classes?

	N	%
1. Specific selection criteria	335	(85)
2. Self-selection	18	(5)
3. Both	38	(10)
4. Other	3	(1)

JJ. Is the amount of curricular material covered:

	N	%
1. About the same as in the regular classes	33	(8)
2. Greater than in the regular classes	338	(86)
3. Both or other	8	(2)

IV. **Independent Study.** A student chooses certain areas of investigation and assumes a high degree of responsibility for meeting objectives.

The number of districts responding to at least one question in this section was 603, or 51% of the participating districts.

KK. How much school time is allotted to independent study?

	N	%
1. Less than 3 hours per week	345	(57)
2. 3–5 hours per week	245	(41)
3. More than 5 hours per week	57	(9)

LL. In which content areas do students engage in independent study?

	N	%
1. Math	250	(41)
2. Science	282	(47)
3. English/Language Arts	254	(42)
4. Social Studies	234	(39)
5. Multidisciplinary	329	(55)
6. Other	94	(16)

MM. What resources do the students use in independent study?

	N	%
1. Staff	547	(91)
2. Library	583	(97)

3. Community	510	(85)
4. Laboratory	286	(47)
5. Computer	20	(3)
6. Other	88	(15)

NN. How is a student's independent study progress evaluated?

	N	%
1. Self	386	(64)
2. Teacher	566	(94)
3. Projects	4	(1)
4. Other	123	(20)

V. Itinerant Teacher. A teacher with special skills in gifted education teaches gifted students in more than one school on a regular basis.

The number of districts responding to at least one question in this section was 428, or 37% of the participating districts.

OO. How many schools do itinerant teachers serve?

	N	%
1. Less than 5	308	(72)
2. 5–10	94	(22)
3. More than 10	24	(6)
4. Multiple answer	3	(1)

PP. Do itinerant teachers teach in:

	N	%
1. The regular classroom teacher's room	30	(7)
2. A permanent classroom assigned for the purpose	226	(53)
3. In a variety of settings	231	(54)

QQ. Do the regular classroom teacher and the itinerant teacher coordinate their curricular plans:

	N	%
1. Regularly	117	(27)
2. Occasionally	269	(63)
3. Not at all	43	(10)

RR. What is the average number of miles driven by an itinerant teacher per week, exclusive of the distance to and from home?

	N	%
1. Less than 50 miles	309	(72)
2. 50–100 miles	77	(18)
3. More than 100 miles	30	(7)

VI. **Mentorships.** We define mentorships as a program which assigns gifted students to work or study with adults who have special knowledge or skills in the student's areas of interest. We include the High School Executive Internship Program in this category.

The number of districts responding to at least one question in this section was 380, or 32% of the participating districts.

SS. How much school time is allotted to a student to work with a mentor?

	N	%
1. None; it is an out-of-school program	129	(34)
2. Less than 3 hours per week	143	(38)
3. 3–5 hours per week	82	(22)
4. More than 5 hours per week	45	(12)

TT. Is Carnegie credit awarded for work with mentors?

	N	%
1. Yes	54	(14)
2. No	251	(66)
3. Sometimes	32	(8)

UU. How are mentors selected?

	N	%
1. On a voluntary basis	259	(68)
2. Specific criteria	127	(33)
3. Recommendations	184	(48)

VV. Who are the mentors?

	N	%
1. School staff	210	(55)
2. University faculty	166	(44)

3. Business and professional people   321   (84)
4. Other   77   (20)

WW. Do mentors receive special training?

	N	%
1. Yes	75	(20)
2. No	284	(75)
3. Sometimes	10	(3)

XX. Are mentors paid?

	N	%
1. Yes	34	(9)
2. No	325	(86)
3. Sometimes	10	(3)

VII. Resource Rooms. This might be a corner of the library or an entire room where gifted students go individually or in groups to explore special areas of study.

The number of districts responding to at least one question in this section was 511, or 44% of the participating districts.

YY. How much time per week does a student spend in a resource room?

	N	%
1. Less than 3 hours	267	(52)
2. 3–5 hours	217	(42)
3. More than 5 hours	56	(11)

ZZ. Is time scheduled in the resource room:

	N	%
1. The same each week	293	(57)
2. Varied from week to week	197	(39)
3. Both	18	(4)

AAA. Who is in charge of the resource room?

	N	%
1. Special teacher for the gifted	338	(66)
2. Librarian	69	(14)
3. Aide	18	(4)
4. Parent	2	(<1)
5. Community volunteer	0	(0)

BBB. What materials are available in the resource room?

	N	%
1. Books	478	(94)
2. Films	344	(67)
3. Packets	357	(70)
4. Other	132	(26)

CCC. What equipment is available in the resource room?

	N	%
1. Laboratory equipment	170	(33)
2. Shop tools	39	(8)
3. Computer	112	(22)
4. Audiovisual equipment	116	(23)
5. Other	70	(14)

DDD. Where is the resource room located?

	N	%
1. In a separate room	295	(58)
2. In the library	107	(21)
3. Other	98	(19)

VIII. Special Schools. These include magnet schools which focus on a single discipline as well as those which include the entire spectrum. Also included are residential schools for the gifted.

The number of districts responding to at least one question in this section was 52, or 4% of the 1,172 participating districts.

EEE. Is the special school:

	N	%
1. Residential	5	(10)
2. Nonresidential	43	(83)

FFF. Does the special school have a:

	N	%
1. General curriculum	36	(69)
2. Special area of concentration	17	(33)

GGG. Is the school considered a magnet?

	N	%
1. Yes	35	(67)
2. No	17	(33)

HHH. How are students selected?

	N	%
1. Self-selected	12	(23)
2. Specific criteria	41	(79)

III. Is the school considered a school for gifted students?

	N	%
1. Yes	18	(35)
2. No	32	(62)

JJJ. Do students pay tuition?

	N	%
1. Yes	2	(4)
2. No	49	(94)

KKK. How long has the school been in existence?

	N	%
1. Less than 5 years	25	(48)
2. 5–10 years	16	(31)
3. More than 10 years	10	(19)

IX. Early Entrance. We define early entrance as a policy of allowing students to enter a school earlier than the normal age for that district.

The number of districts responding to at least one question in this section was 317, or 27% of the 1,172 participating districts.

LLL. At what level(s) is the provision for early entrance made?

	N	%
1. Kindergarten	248	(78)
2. First Grade	120	(38)
3. Middle/Junior High School	46	(15)
4. Senior High School	51	(16)

MMM. How many students entered these levels last year due to early entrance policy? List the numbers, please.

	Median No.	Mean No.	Range	Districts
1. Kindergarten		8	1–150	
2. First Grade		5	1–60	
3. Middle/Junior High School		9	1–120	
4. Senior High School		8	1–40	

NNN. On what basis were early assignments made? Check all which apply.

	N	%
1. Ability test	259	(82)
2. Achievement test	89	(28)
3. Teacher recommendation	114	(36)
4. Parental request	204	(64)
5. Other	105	(33)

OOO. Of the number accepted last year as early entrants, how many continued for at least one full year? List numbers at the appropriate levels, please.

	Median No.	Mean No.	Range	Districts
1. Kindergarten		8	1–140	
2. First Grade		6	1–60	
3. Middle/Junior High School		16	1–150	
4. Senior High School		7	1–40	

PPP. Last year how many students left high school prior to graduation to enter a college or university?

	Districts	%
1. None	113	(36)

	Median No.	Mean No.	Range	Districts
2. List the number, please.		9	1–140	

QQQ. How long has the early-entrance policy existed in your school (or district)?

	N	%
1. Less than 5 years	112	(35)
2. 5–10 years	82	(26)
3. More than 10 years	75	(24)

X. Continuous Progress. We define continuous progress as a provision for students to progress through the curriculum of one or more subject areas as the required skills are mastered.

The number of districts responding to at least one question in this section was 370, or 32% of the 1,172 participating districts.

RRR. At what level(s) is continuous progress in operation?

	N	%
1. Preschool	24	(6)
2. Elementary (inc. K)	297	(80)
3. Middle/Junior High School	196	(53)
4. Senior High School	147	(40)

SSS. In what content areas does continuous progress allow students to advance at their own pace?

	N	%
1. Math	315	(85)
2. Science	87	(24)
3. Social Studies	73	(20)
4. Language Arts (inc. Reading)	269	(73)
5. English	94	(25)
6. Foreign Language	64	(17)
7. Arts and Music	2	(1)
8. Other	12	(3)

TTT. On what basis does a student move from one level to another?

	N	%
1. Standardized tests	152	(41)
2. Teacher-made tests	168	(45)
3. Demonstrated competency	322	(87)
4. Other	30	(8)

UUU. What percentage of students are functioning above grade level in one or more content areas this year?

	N	%
1. Less than 5%	86	(23)
2. 5%–10%	76	(21)
3. 11%–20%	72	(19)
4. More than 20%	89	(24)

VVV. How would you describe the continuous progress program?

	N	%
1. Group instruction	225	(61)
2. Individual instruction	237	(64)
3. Other	16	(4)

WWW. How long has the continuous progress program been in operation?

	N	%
1. Less than 5 years	148	(40)
2. 5–10 years	137	(37)
3. More than 10 years	51	(14)

XI. Nongraded School. We define a nongraded school as one in which the usual labels, such as first grade, have been removed and students progress at their own pace. Thus, one child might complete what is normally covered in one grade in less than the usual amount of time, and another child might require more than the usual amount of time to gain the skills generally acquired in one year in a graded school situation.

The number of districts responding to at least one question in this section was 36, or 3% of the 1,172 participating districts.

XXX. At what level(s) is your school (or district) nongraded?

	N	%
1. Preschool	3	(8)
2. Elementary (inc. K)	31	(86)
3. Middle/Junior High School	4	(11)
4. Senior High School	3	(8)

YYY. Do some students complete the level(s) checked in fewer years than is normally required?

	N	%
1. Yes	22	(61)
2. No	11	(31)

ZZZ. If you answered "Yes," how many students:

	Mean No.	Range	Districts
1. Received additional enrichment only	450	100–800	
2. Were offered curricula from the next higher level but did not leave the first school	153	3–500	
3. Moved on to the next higher school	25	25–25	

AAAA. How long has your school (or district) been nongraded?

	N	%
1. Less than 5 years	7	(19)
2. 1–10 years*	16	(44)
3. More than 10 years	8	(22)

XII. **Moderate Acceleration.** We define moderate acceleration as any kind of provision which allows a student to complete the grades K–12 in less than thirteen years but more than ten.

The number of districts responding to at least one question in this section was 324, or 28% of the 1,172 participating districts.

BBBB. How many students were in last year's graduating class?

	N	%
1. Less than 100	82	(25)
2. 100–500	146	(45)
3. More than 500	89	(27)

---

*Categories 1 and 2 overlap. They are not changed here because the respondents answered according to these categories.

CCCC. Of this number, how many spent fewer than thirteen years but more than ten in grades K–12?

	N	%
1. Less than 2%	247	(76)
2. 2%–5%	43	(13)
3. More than 5%	17	(5)

DDDD. How long has your school had a policy which allowed or encouraged moderate acceleration?

	N	%
1. Less than 2 years	40	(12)
2. 2–5 years	74	(23)
3. More than 5 years	174	(54)

XIII. Radical Acceleration. We define radical acceleration as any kind of provision which allows a student to complete grades K–12 in fewer than eleven years.

The number of districts responding to at least one question in this section was 123, or 11% of the 1,172 participating districts.

EEEE. How many students were in last year's graduating class?

	N	%
1. Less than 100	38	(31)
2. 100–500	41	(33)
3. More than 500	44	(36)

FFFF. Of this number, how many spent fewer than eleven years in grades K–12?

	N	%
1. Less than 1%	102	(83)
2. 1%–2%	12	(10)
3. More than 2%	3	(2)

GGGG. How long has your school had a policy which allowed or encouraged radical acceleration?

	N	%
1. Less than 2 years	23	(19)
2. 2–5 years	24	(20)
3. More than 5 years	46	(37)

XIV. College Board Advanced Placement. As the name specifies, we refer to the Advanced Placement of the College Board.

The number of districts responding to at least one question in this section was 352, or 30% of the 1,172 participating districts.

HHHH. How long has your school offered College Board Advanced Placement courses?

	N	%
1. Less than 5 years	138	(39)
2. 5–10 years	93	(26)
3. More than 10 years	110	(31)

IIII. In what content areas does your school offer Advanced Placement courses?

	N	%
1. American History	205	(58)
2. Art History	40	(11)
3. Biology	137	(39)
4. Chemistry	147	(42)
5. English Composition/Literature	264	(75)
6. English Language/Composition	121	(34)
7. European History	66	(19)
8. French	76	(22)
9. German	34	(10)
10. Latin	21	(6)
11. Mathematics	238	(68)
12. Music	34	(10)
13. Physics	85	(24)
14. Spanish	75	(21)

JJJJ. How many students completed at least one Advanced Placement course last year?

	Median No.	Mean No.	Range	Districts
1. Sophomores		51	1–500	
2. Juniors		114		
3. Seniors		65	1–805	
4. Others		0	0–0	

KKKK. How many students took at least one Advanced Placement examination last year? List the number, please.

	Median No.	Mean No.	Range	Districts
1. Sophomores		59	1–520	
2. Juniors		40	1–530	
3. Seniors		46	1–711	
4. Others		39	1–150	

LLLL. What percentage of the examinations received a score of:

	Median %	Mean %	Districts
1. 3		(43)	
2. 4		(27)	
3. 5		(21)	

MMMM. How were the Advanced Placement opportunities offered?

	N	%
1. Conventional classes	267	(76)
2. Independent study	65	(18)
3. Seminars	21	(6)
4. Correspondence courses	15	(4)
5. Other	19	(5)

XV. **Fast-Paced Courses.** We define fast-paced courses as an arrangement which allows a student to complete two or more courses in a discipline in an abbreviated time span.

The number of districts responding to this section was 78, or 7% of the 1,172 participating districts.

NNNN. Last year how many students were enrolled in such courses in:

	Median No.	Mean No.	Range	Districts
1. Mathematics		60	1–1,000	
2. Foreign language		18	1–65	
3. Science		123	2–800	
4. Other		149	1–1,000	

XVI. Concurrent or Dual Enrollment. We define concurrent or dual enrollment as an arrangement which allows a student to enroll in
classes on two campuses. For example, a middle/junior high student
who takes one or more classes at the high school or a high school
student who takes one or more classes on a college campus.

The number of districts responding to at least one question in this
section was 318, or 27% of the 1,172 participating districts.

OOOO. How many students enrolled in classes on two campuses
last year? Please specify the numbers.

	Median No.	Mean No.	Range	Districts
1. Middle/Junior High and Senior High combination		12	1–90	
2. Middle/Junior High and College combination		8	1–66	
3. Senior High and College combination		17	1–290	

PPPP. Of the number who enrolled in classes at both the mid-
dle/junior high and senior high, what percentage satisfactorily
completed the class?

	N	%
1. Less than 50%	2	(1)
2. 50%–75%	2	(1)
3. 76%–99%	29	(9)
4. 100%	107	(34)

QQQQ. Of the number who enrolled in classes at both the middle/
junior high and college, what percentage satisfactorily completed the class?

	N	%
1. Less than 50%	3	(1)
2. 50%–75%	1	(<1)
3. 76%–99%	4	(1)
4. 100%	17	(5)

RRRR. Of the number who enrolled in classes at a senior high school and college, what percentage satisfactorily completed the class?

	N	%
1. Less than 50%	4	(1)
2. 50%–75%	3	(1)
3. 76%–99%	77	(24)
4. 100%	167	(53)

Other. If your school has a provision or program for gifted students not listed in any of the above sections, please describe it briefly.

The number of districts responding to this section was 116, or 10% of the 1,172 participating districts. These responses were reviewed on an individual basis.

Criteria Used for Selecting Districts with Substantial Programs

An objective evaluation of gifted/talented programs offered by school districts requires that (1) specific criteria be defined to serve as a basis of comparison, (2) necessary information about each site be collected, and finally (3) the results be compiled into a form from which a conclusion can be drawn.

The questionnaires used in this survey outlined components of sixteen G/T program offerings. The research staff and study director considered certain question and answer options to be essential components of a strong program offering; that is, if a district responded to these questions in the manner indicated, it would have a "substantial" program. The objective was to identify the substantial programs offered in the 1,172 districts.

The advisory committee for this study, a group of distinguished individuals selected for their expertise to give advice and guidance to the study, reviewed the list of questions drawn from each of the sixteen program sections of the questionnaire. This review was carried out as a form of validation of these criteria: (1) whether the questions/items selected from the questionnaire were necessary components of a substantial program offering and (2) whether other questions/items that were not selected should be integrated in the list. Revisions made by this group were incorporated in the final criteria, which follow. A district must have answered all questions listed below for a particular section to have the respective substantial program offering.

The following questions are designated by letters corresponding with the same descriptions that appear in the questionnaire.

I. Enrichment in the Regular Classroom
V. How many students participate in the enrichment activities?
   2. Those identified as gifted/talented
   OR
   3. Those identified as gifted/talented plus others, but not including the entire class

W.   How much time is allotted to enrichment activities per week?
    2. 3–5 hours
    OR
    3. More than 5 hours

X.   Which content areas are enriched?
    At least one of these must be checked.
    1. Math
    2. Science
    3. English/Language Arts
    4. Social Studies
    5. Multidisciplinary
    6. Arts and Music
    7. Other

Y.   Are the curricular materials used in the enrichment activities:
    2. Different from those used in the basic program
    OR
    3. Both the same as those used in the basic program and different from those used in the basic program

II. Part-Time Special Class

AA.   How many days per week does the special class meet?
    1. 1 day per week

AND

BB.   What is the length of each class session?
    3. More than 2 hours

OR

AA.   How many days per week does the special class meet?
    2. 2–4 days per week

AND

BB.   What is the length of each class session?
    1. Less than 1 hour
    OR
    2. 1–2 hours
    OR
    3. More than 2 hours

OR

AA.   How many days per week does the special class meet?
    3. 5 days per week

AND

BB. What is the length of each class session?
  1. Less than 1 hour
  OR
  2. 1–2 hours
  OR
  3. More than 2 hours

CC. Which content areas are studied in the special class?
  At least one of these must be checked.
  1. Math
  2. Science
  3. English/Language Arts
  4. Social Studies
  5. Multidisciplinary
  6. Arts and Music
  7. Other

DD. What strategies are used in the special class?
  At least one of these must be checked.
  1. Group instruction
  2. Individualized instruction
  3. Special projects
  4. Puzzles and games
  5. Other

EE. Do the regular classroom teacher and the special class teacher coordinate their curricular plans:
  1. Regularly
  OR
  2. Occasionally

III. Full-Time Special Class

GG. Which content areas are studied in the special class?
  At least one of these must be checked.
  1. Math
  2. Science
  3. English/Language Arts
  4. Social Studies
  5. Multidisciplinary

6. Arts and Music
7. Other

HH.   Are the curricular materials the same as those studied in regular classes?
2. No
OR
3. Sometimes

JJ.   Is the amount of curricular material covered:
2. Greater than in the regular classes

IV. Independent Study

KK.   How much school time is allotted to independent study?
2. 3–5 hours per week
OR
3. More than 5 hours per week

LL.   In which content areas do students engage in independent study?
At least one of these must be checked.
1. Math
2. Science
3. English/Language Arts
4. Social Studies
5. Multidisciplinary
6. Other

MM.   What resources do the students use in independent study?
At least two of these must be checked.
1. Staff
2. Library
3. Community
4. Laboratory
5. Computer
6. Other

NN.   How is a student's independent study progress evaluated?
At least one of these must be checked.
1. Self
2. Teacher
3. Projects
4. Other

V. Itinerant Teacher

OO.   How many schools do itinerant teachers serve?
    1. Less than 5
    OR
    2. 5–10

QQ.   Do the regular classroom teacher and the itinerant teacher coordinate their curricular plans:
    1. Regularly
    OR
    2. Occasionally

RR.   What is the average number of miles driven by an itinerant teacher per week, exclusive of the distance to and from home?
    One of these must be checked.
    1. Less than 50 miles
    2. 50–100 miles
    3. More than 100 miles

VI. Mentorships

SS.   How much school time is allotted to a student to work with a mentor?
    3. 3–5 hours per week
    OR
    4. More than 5 hours per week

TT.   Is Carnegie credit awarded for work with mentors?
    Only for districts with high schools.
    1. Yes

UU.   How are mentors selected?
    2. Specific criteria
    OR
    3. Recommendations

VV.   Who are the mentors?
    At least one of these must be checked.
    1. School staff
    2. University faculty
    3. Business and professional people
    4. Other

WW. Do mentors receive special training?
One of these must be checked.
1. Yes
2. No
3. Sometimes

XX. Are mentors paid?
One of these must be checked.
1. Yes
2. No
3. Sometimes

VII. Resource Rooms

YY. How much time per week does a student spend in a resource room?
2. 3–5 hours
OR
3. More than 5 hours

ZZ. Is time scheduled in the resource room:
One of these must be checked.
1. The same each week
2. Varied from week to week
3. Both

AAA. Who is in charge of the resource room?
One of these must be checked.
1. Special teacher of the gifted
2. Librarian
3. Aide
4. Parent
5. Community volunteer

BBB. What materials are available in the resource room?
At least two responses from this question and the next one, CCC, must be checked.
1. Books
2. Films
3. Packets
4. Other

CCC. What equipment is available in the resource room?
See question BBB *above.*
1. Laboratory equipment
2. Shop tools
3. Computer
4. Audiovisual equipment

VIII. Special Schools

EEE. Is the special school:
1. Residential
OR
2. Nonresidential

FFF. Does the special school have a:
1. General curriculum
OR
2. Special area of concentration

GGG. Is the school considered a magnet?
1. Yes
OR
2. No

HHH. How are students selected?
1. Self-selected
OR
2. Specific criteria

III. Is the school considered a school for gifted students?
1. Yes
OR
2. No

JJJ. Do students pay tuition?
1. Yes
OR
2. No

KKK. How long has the school been in existence?
One of these must be checked.
1. Less than 5 years
2. 5–10 years
3. More than 10 years

IX. Early Entrance

LLL.   At what level(s) is the provision for early entrance made?
At least one of these must be checked.
1. Kindergarten
2. First Grade
3. Middle/Junior High School
4. Senior High School

MMM.   How many students entered these levels last year due to early entrance policy? List the numbers, please.
At least one of these must be answered.
1. Kindergarten
2. First Grade
3. Middle/Junior High School
4. Senior High School

NNN.   On what basis were early assignments made? Check all which apply.
At least one of these must be checked.
1. Ability test
2. Achievement test
3. Teacher recommendation
4. Parental request
5. Other

X. Continuous Progress

RRR.   At what level(s) is continuous progress in operation?
At least one of these must be checked.
1. Preschool
2. Elementary (inc. K)
3. Middle/Junior High School
4. Senior High School

SSS.   In what content areas does continuous progress allow students to advance at their own pace?
At least one of these must be checked.
1. Math
2. Science
3. Social Studies
4. Language Arts (inc. Reading)

    5. English

    6. Foreign Language

    7. Arts and Music

    8. Other

TTT.   On what basis does a student move from one level to another?
At least one of these must be checked.

1. Standardized tests
2. Teacher-made tests
3. Demonstrated competency
4. Other

VVV.   How would you describe the continuous progress program?
At least one of these must be checked.

1. Group instruction
2. Individual instruction
3. Other

WWW.   How long has the continuous progress program been in operation?
One of these must be checked.

1. Less than 5 years
2. 5–10 years
3. More than 10 years

XI. Nongraded School

XXX.   At what level(s) is your school (or district) nongraded?
At least one of these must be checked.

1. Preschool
2. Elementary (inc. K)
3. Middle/Junior High School
4. Senior High School

YYY.   Do some students complete the level(s) checked in fewer years
than is normally required?

1. Yes

ZZZ.   If you answered "Yes," how many students:

2. were offered curricula from the next higher level but did not
leave the first school

OR

3. moved on to the next higher school

AAAA.   How long has your school been nongraded?
One of these must be checked.
1. Less than 5 years
2. 1–10 years
3. More than 10 years

XII. Moderate Acceleration

BBBB.   How many students were in last year's graduating class?
One of these must be checked.
1. Less than 100
2. 100–500
3. More than 500

CCCC.   Of this number, how many spent fewer than thirteen years but more than ten in grades K–12?
2. 2%–5%
OR
3. More than 5%

DDDD.   How long has your school had a policy which allowed or encouraged moderate acceleration?
2. 2–5 years
OR
3. More than 5 years

XIII. Radical Acceleration

EEEE.   How many students were in last year's graduating class?
One of these must be checked.
1. Less than 100
2. 100–500
3. More than 500

FFFF.   Of this number, how many spent fewer than eleven years in grades K–12?
2. 1%–2%
OR
3. More than 2%

GGGG.   How long has your school had a policy which allowed or encouraged radical acceleration?
2. 2–5 years

OR

3. More than 5 years

XIV. College Board Advanced Placement

HHHH.   How long has your school offered College Board Advanced
         Placement courses?
         One of these must be checked.
         1. Less than 5 years
         2. 5–10 years
         3. More than 10 years

IIII.   In what content areas does your school offer Advanced Place-
         ment courses?
         At least three content areas must be checked.
         1. American History
         2. Art History
         3. Biology
         4. Chemistry
         5. English Composition/Literature
         6. English Language/Composition
         7. European History
         8. French
         9. German
         10. Latin
         11. Mathematics
         12. Music
         13. Physics
         14. Spanish

JJJJ.   How many students completed at least one Advanced Place-
         ment course last year? List the number, please.
         At least one of these must be answered.
         1. Sophomores
         2. Juniors
         3. Seniors
         4. Others

KKKK.   How many students took at least one Advanced Placement ex-
         amination last year? List the number, please.
         At least one of these must be answered.

1. Sophomores
2. Juniors
3. Seniors
4. Others

LLLL.   What percentage of the examinations received a score of:
1. 3
2. 4
3. 5
At least 10% must have scored 3, 4, or 5.

MMMM.   How were the Advanced Placement opportunities offered?
One of these must be checked.
1. Conventional classes
2. Independent study
3. Seminars
4. Correspondence courses
5. Other

XV. Fast-Paced Courses. Since only one question was asked regarding fast-paced courses, no criteria for a substantial program were established.

XVI. Concurrent or Dual Enrollment

PPPP.   Of the number who enrolled in classes at both the middle/junior high and senior high, what percentage satisfactorily completed the class?
2. 50%–75%
OR
3. 76%–99%
OR
4. 100%
AND

OOOO.   How many students enrolled in classes on two campuses last year? Please specify the numbers.
1. Middle/Junior High and Senior High combination
OR

QQQQ.   Of the number who enrolled in classes at both the middle/junior high and college, what percentage satisfactorily completed the class?

      2. 50%–75%

      OR

      3. 76%–99%

      OR

      4. 100%

      AND

OOOO. How many students enrolled in classes on two campuses last year? Please specify the numbers.

      2. Middle/Junior High and College combination

OR

RRRR. Of the number who enrolled in classes at a senior high school and college, what percentage satisfactorily completed the class?

      2. 50%–75%

      OR

      3. 76%–99%

      OR

      4. 100%

      AND

OOOO. How many students enrolled in classes on two campuses last year? Please specify the numbers.

      3. Senior High and College combination

Patterns of G/T Programs and Practices in 1,172 Districts

	Pattern				
Program/Practice	A	B	C	D	E
1. ENRICH	*	*	*	*	*
2. PT SP CL	**	**	**	**	**
3. FT SP CL	**	**		*	**
4. IND STUDY	*	**	**	**	*
5. ITINERANT	**		**	**	
6. MENTORS		*	*	*	
7. RESOURCE	**		*	**	**
9. EARLY ENT	**	**			
10. CONT PROG	**	**	*		*
12. MOD ACCEL	*	*	*		
13. RAD ACCEL					
14. AP COURSES	*	*	*		
16. CONC ENROL		**	**		
No. of Districts	47	60	35	41	46
% of 1,172 Districts	4.0	5.1	3.0	3.5	3.9

Note: An asterisk denotes that 50% or more of the districts reported the program or practice; a double asterisk signifies a substantial program by 50% or more of the districts. Programs 8, 11, and 15 are omitted due to insufficient data.

F	G	H	I	J	K	L	M	N	O
✶	✶	✶	✶	✶		✶	✶	✶	✶
✶	✶	✶✶		✶✶	✶✶	✶	✶	✶	✶
		✶✶						✶✶	
✶✶	✶✶		✶	✶					
		✶✶		✶✶		✶✶			
	✶			✶					
	✶✶	✶			✶✶				
			✶✶						
✶✶	✶		✶✶						
✶			✶						
✶									
✶									
✶✶	✶✶		✶✶				✶✶		
20	33	56	78	73	90	121	70	111	291
1.7	2.8	4.8	6.7	6.2	7.7	10.3	6.0	9.5	24.8

APPENDIX G

Correlations between Selected Variables and the G/T Options Chosen by School Districts

Variable		G/T Option			
	ENRICH	PT SP CL	FT SP CL	IND STUDY	ITIN-ERANT
A Population Served		+	+		
Grade 1 Elementary Only			−	−	
Grade 2 Elem, Jr Hi Only					
Grade 3 Elem, Jr Hi, Sr Hi	+		+	+	+
Total Enrollment			+		+
% Anglo			−		
Black, Over 20%	−				
Other Ethnic, Over 10%			+		
I3 Achievement Tests		+			
I5 Teacher Nomination					
J No Spec Teacher Requirement		−	−		−
J Teacher Inservice Required		+	+		+
J State Certification Required	−				+
K2 G/T Teachers		+	+		+
L G/T Director			+		+
L No G/T Monitor		−			
M2 Museum Resources		+	+		+
M3 Industry Resources		+		+	+
M4 Government Resources		+		+	
M6 Other Resources					

G/T Option

MEN-TORS	RE-SOURCE	SP SCHOOL	EARLY ENT	CONT PROG	NON-GRADED	MOD ACCEL	RAD ACCEL	AP COURSES	CONC ENROL
+		+	+		+		+	+	
−								−	−
				+					
+	+	+	+	+	+	+	+	+	+
+		+	+			+	+	+	+
		−	+						
	+								
		+							
			−						
	−		−						
			+						
	+								
	+	+						+	
+	+	+							
+	+	+						+	
+	+							+	
+	+						+		

Variable	G/T Option				
	ENRICH	PT SP CL	FT SP CL	IND STUDY	ITINERANT
N Written Philosophy for G/T		+	+		+
O1 District G/T Goals		+	+		+
O2 Building G/T Goals	+				
P1 Students on Advisory Group				+	
P2 Parents on Advisory Group		+			+
Q1 District Evaluation of G/T		+	+		+
R Per Pupil Expenditure	+			+	
S Budgetary Provisions for G/T Students	−	+	+		+
G/T Funding State and Local Sources Only		+	+		+
G/T Services Mandated					+
Teacher Certification Mandated					+
Region 3					+
Region 4	−			−	
Region 5		−			−
Region 6			+		
Region 7					

G/T Option

MEN-TORS	RE-SOURCE	SP SCHOOL	EARLY ENT	CONT PROG	NON-GRADED	MOD ACCEL	RAD ACCEL	AP COURSES	CONC ENROL
+	+								
+	+								
+	+	+				+	+		
+	+							+	
	+								
			+		+				
								+	
								+	
	+						+		
	+								
							+		
	+		−			−			−
−	−		+			+		−	
		+	−			−			
	+								

Note: The correlations shown are statistically significant at the .05 level. Due to missing data, the results are based on 986 rather than 1,172 districts.

Intercorrelations of Sixteen G/T Programs and Practices in 986 School Districts

Intercorrelations

Program/Practice	1	2	3	4	5	6
1. ENRICH	—			17		15
2. PT SP CL		—	11		24	12
3. FT SP CL		11	—	19	10	14
4. IND STUDY	17		19	—	17	30
5. ITINERANT		24	10	17	—	16
6. MENTORS	15	12	14	30	16	—
7. RESOURCE	12	18	12	26	27	23
8. SP SCHOOL			17			12
9. EARLY ENT	14			16		15
10. CONT PROG	23		14	23		16
11. NONGRADED						13
12. MOD ACCEL	16		10	25	15	24
13. RAD ACCEL	15		16	21	12	16
14. AP COURSES			24	13	11	20
15. FAST PACE				15		
16. CONC ENROL	11		17	22		22

Note: Each G/T option was scored 0 if not adopted, 1 for any offering, and 2 for a substantial offering; there were no scores of 2, however, for NONGRADED and FAST PACE. The only intercorrelations shown are those which reached or exceeded .10 in value; none were negative in value; decimal points omitted.

7	8	9	10	11	12	13	14	15	16
12		14	23		16	15			11
18									
12	17		14		10	16	24		17
26		16	23		25	21	13	15	22
27					15	12	11		
23	12	15	16	13	24	16	20		22
—	11	12	15		13	14			
11	—				11		14	10	12
12		—	25	13	25	18	16	14	23
15		25	—	14	30	20	19		22
		13	14	—	17	14			10
13	11	25	30	17	—	36	23	12	30
14		18	20	14	36	—	21	11	22
	14	16	19		23	21	—	15	26
	10	14			12	11	15	—	16
	12	23	22	10	30	22	26	16	—

References

Academic Preparation for College: What Students Need to Know and Be Able to Do. New York: College Entrance Examination Board, 1983.

Action for Excellence. Denver: Task Force on Education for Economic Growth, Education Commission of the States, 1983.

Adler, M. J. *The Paideia Proposal.* New York: Macmillan, 1982.

Baldwin, J. *Notes of a Native Son.* Boston: Beacon Press, 1955.

Bernal, E. "The Identification of Gifted Chicano Children." In *Educational Planning for the Gifted: Overcoming Cultural, Geographic, and Economic Barriers,* ed. A. Y. Baldwin, G. H. Gear, and L. J. Lucito. Reston, Va.: Council for Exceptional Children, 1978.

Boyer, E. L. *High School: A Report on Secondary Education in America by the Carnegie Foundation for the Advancement of Teaching.* New York: Harper & Row, 1983.

Brown, R. "Unique Science School Offers Hope," *State Educational Leader* (Winter, 1983) pp. 14–15.

Casserly, P. L. "What College Students Say about Advanced Placement," *College Board Review* (Fall, 1968), pp. 6–10, 28–34.

Colson, S. "The Evaluation of a Community-Based Career Education Program for Gifted and Talented Students as an Administrative Model for an Alternative Program," *Gifted Child Quarterly* 24 (1980): 101–106.

———, C. Borman, and W. R. Nash. "A Unique Learning Opportunity for Talented High School Seniors," *Phi Delta Kappan* 59 (1978): 542–543.

Cox, J. "Continuous Progress and Nongraded Schools," *G/C/T* no. 25 (Nov./Dec. 1982): 15–21.

Daniel, N., and R. A. Rayel. "International Education for Gifted Students," *Gifted International* 1, 1 (1982): 101–117.

Drews, E. M. "Leading Out and Letting Be," *Today's Education* 65, 1 (1976): 26–28.

Gardner, H. *Frames of Mind: The Theory of Multiple Intelligences.* New York: Basic Books, 1983.

Getzels, J. W., and J. T. Dillon. "The Nature of Giftedness and the Education of the Gifted." In *Second Handbook of Research in Teaching*, ed. R. M. W. Travers. Chicago: Rand McNally, 1973.

"Girl, 9, Going to College amid Maine Dispute," *New York Times*, September 9, 1984, p. 18.

Goodlad, J. I. *A Place Called School: Prospects for the Future.* New York: McGraw-Hill, 1984.

————, and R. H. Anderson. *The Nongraded Elementary School.* New York: Harcourt Brace, 1959.

Goodman, D. B., and G. Scott. "The International High School: A Challenge for Scholars." In *Action for the '8os: A Political, Professional, and Public Program for Foreign Language Education*, ed. J. K. Phillips. Skokie, Ill.: National Textbook Company, 1981.

Gray, W. A. "Mentor-Assisted Enrichment Projects for the Gifted and Talented," *Educational Leadership* 40, 2 (1982): 16–21.

Hirsch, S. P. *Young, Gifted, and Handicapped: Mainstreaming High-Potential Handicapped Students into the Executive High School Internship Program.* Washington, D.C.: U.S. Office of Education, 1979.

Karnes, M. B. *The Underserved: Our Young Gifted Children.* Reston, Va.: Council for Exceptional Children, 1983.

Maeroff, G. I. "North Carolina Opens Statewide High School for the Gifted in Math and Science," *New York Times*, October 12, 1980, p. 31.

————. *School and College: Partnership in Education.* Princeton, N.J.: Carnegie Foundation for the Advancement of Teaching, 1983.

Maker, C. J. *Curriculum Development for the Gifted.* Rockville, Md.: Aspen Systems Corporation, 1982.

Making the Grade. New York: Task Force on Federal Elementary and Secondary Education Policy, Twentieth-Century Fund, 1983.

Marland, S. P. *Education of the Gifted and Talented.* Report to the Congress of the United States by the Commissioner of Education. Washington, D.C.: U.S. Office of Education, 1972.

A Nation at Risk: The Imperative for Educational Reform. Washington, D.C.: U.S. Government Printing Office, 1983.

The Nation Responds: Recent Efforts to Improve Education. Washington, D.C.: U.S. Government Printing Office, 1984.

Renzulli, J. S. *The Enrichment Triad Model: A Guide for Developing Defensible Programs for the Gifted and Talented.* Wethersfield, Conn.: Creative Learning Press, 1977.

————. "What Makes Giftedness? Reexamining a Definition," *Phi Delta Kappan* 60 (1978): 180–184, 261.

Sanborn, M. "Career Development Problems of Gifted and Talented Students." In *Career Education for Gifted and Talented Students*, ed. K. B. Hoyt and J. R. Hebeler. Salt Lake City: Olympus, 1974.

Shwedel, A. M., and R. Stoneburner. "Identification." In *The Underserved: Our Young Gifted Children*, ed. M. B. Karnes. Reston, Va.: Council for Exceptional Children, 1983.

Sizer, T. R. *Horace's Compromise: The Dilemma of the American High School*. Boston: Houghton Mifflin, 1984.

Stanley, J. C. "On Educating the Gifted," *Educational Researcher* 9 (1980): 8–12.

Strassheim, L. A. "Broadening the Middle School Curriculum through Content: Globalizing Foreign Languages." In *Action for the '80s: A Political, Professional, and Public Program for Foreign Language Education*, ed. J. K. Phillips. Skokie, Ill.: National Textbook Company, 1981.

Strength through Wisdom: A Critique of U.S. Capabilities. A report to the President from the President's Commission on Foreign Language and International Studies. Washington, D.C.: U.S. Government Printing Office, 1979.

Teaching in America: The Common Ground. New Haven: Yale–New Haven Teachers Institute, 1983.

Torrance, E. P. *Mentor Relationships: How They Aid Creative Achievement, Endure, Change, and Die*. Buffalo, N.Y.: Bearly Limited, 1984.

Whitehead, A. N. "The Rhythm of Education." In *The Aims of Education and Other Essays*. New York: Macmillan, 1929.

Index